EMERGING CYBER THREATS AND COGNITIVE VULNERABILITIES

EMERGING CYBER THREATS AND COGNITIVE VULNERABILITIES

Edited by

VLADLENA BENSON
University of West London, London, United Kingdom

JOHN MCALANEY
Bournemouth University, Fern Barrow, Poole Dorset, United Kingdom

ACADEMIC PRESS
An imprint of Elsevier

Academic Press is an imprint of Elsevier
125 London Wall, London EC2Y 5AS, United Kingdom
525 B Street, Suite 1650, San Diego, CA 92101, United States
50 Hampshire Street, 5th Floor, Cambridge, MA 02139, United States
The Boulevard, Langford Lane, Kidlington, Oxford OX5 1GB, United Kingdom

Notices
Knowledge and best practice in this field are constantly changing. As new research and
experience broaden our understanding, changes in research methods, professional
practices, or medical treatment may become necessary.

Practitioners and researchers must always rely on their own experience and knowledge in
evaluating and using any information, methods, compounds, or experiments described
herein. In using such information or methods they should be mindful of their own safety
and the safety of others, including parties for whom they have a professional
responsibility.

To the fullest extent of the law, neither the Publisher nor the authors, contributors, or
editors, assume any liability for any injury and/or damage to persons or property as a
matter of products liability, negligence or otherwise, or from any use or operation of any
methods, products, instructions, or ideas contained in the material herein.

Library of Congress Cataloging-in-Publication Data
A catalog record for this book is available from the Library of Congress

British Library Cataloguing-in-Publication Data
A catalogue record for this book is available from the British Library

ISBN: 978-0-12-816203-3

For information on all Academic Press publications visit our website at
https://www.elsevier.com/books-and-journals

Publisher: Nikki Levy
Acquisition Editor: Joslyn Chaiprasert-Paguio
Editorial Project Manager: Barbara Makinster
Production Project Manager: Bharatwaj Varatharajan
Cover Designer: Mark Rogers

Working together
to grow libraries in
developing countries

www.elsevier.com • www.bookaid.org

Typeset by TNQ Technologies

Contents

6. Avoiding a cyber world war: rational motives for negative cooperation among the United States, China and Russia

Tomas Janeliūnas and Agnija Tumkevič

7. Standard operating procedures for cybercrime investigations: a systematic literature review

Stephen Jeffries and Edward Apeh

8. Information and communication technologies: a curse or blessing for SMEs?

Anne-Marie Mohammed, Bochra Idris, George Saridakis, and Vladlena Benson

9. Cyber personalities in adaptive target audiences

Miika Sartonen, Petteri Simola, Lauri Lovén, and Jussi Timonen

10. Privacy issues and critical infrastructure protection

Jussi Simola

Contributors

Edward Apeh   Department of Computing and Informatics, Bournemouth University, Poole, United Kingdom

Rami Baazeem   University of Jeddah, Jeddah, Saudi Arabia

Maria Bada   Cybercrime Centre, Computer Laboratory, University of Cambridge, Cambridge, United Kingdom

Vladlena Benson   Aston Business School, Aston University, Birmingham, United Kingdom

Lucy R. Betts   Nottingham Trent University, Nottingham, United Kingdom

Bochra Idris   Aston Business School, Aston University, Birmingham, United Kingdom

Tomas Janeliūnas   Institute of International Relations and Political Science, Vilnius University, Vilnius, Lithuania

Stephen Jeffries   Department of Computing and Informatics, Bournemouth University, Poole, United Kingdom

Juha Kukkola   Finnish National Defence University, Helsinki, Finland

Lauri Lovén   Center for Ubiquitous Computing, University of Oulu, Oulu, Finland

Peter J.R. Macaulay   Staffordshire University, Stoke-on-Trent, United Kingdom; Nottingham Trent University, Nottingham, United Kingdom

Anne-Marie Mohammed   Department of Economics, The University of the West Indies, St. Augustine, Trinidad and Tobago

Jason R.C. Nurse   School of Computing, University of Kent, Canterbury, United Kingdom

Alaa Qaffas   University of Jeddah, Jeddah, Saudi Arabia

Mari Ristolainen   Finnish Defence Research Agency, Riihimäki, Finland

George Saridakis   Kent Business School, University of Kent, Canterbury, United Kingdom

Miika Sartonen   Department of Leadership and Military Pedagogy, National Defence University, Helsinki, Finland

Jussi Simola   Department of Information Technology, University of Jyväskylä, Finland

Petteri Simola   Finnish Defence Research Agency, Tuusula, Finland

Oonagh L. Steer   Nottingham Trent University, Nottingham, United Kingdom

Jussi Timonen   National Defence University, Helsinki, Finland

Agnija Tumkevič Institute of International Relations and Political Science, Vilnius University, Vilnius, Lithuania

Namosha Veerasamy Council for Scientific and Industrial Research (CSIR), Pretoria, South Africa

Preface

Humans are adaptive creatures. Daily, we navigate a complex and changing social world. We have developed strategies to process information to allow us to identify what is important and what must be acted upon. This is not, however, something we do flawlessly. In the face of vast amounts of information, we often rely on cognitive shortcuts and biases to come to quick decisions. We do so to meet our desires and to achieve our personal goals, but as part of this must interact with others who have their own agendas and biases. Technology both enhances and potentially changes these interactions in ways that we still do not fully comprehend. It fundamentally alters the ways in which we establish trust with others and creates new ways in which this trust can be exploited by malicious actors. Yet it also provides new techniques that can be used to empower individuals and organizations to better protect themselves and their assets.

This book explores the opportunities for conflict and cooperation in human interactions that arise in the cybersecurity space. The discussions it contains range from individual factors that may predict cyber victimization to wider social determinants of cyber behaviour including religion, culture and nationality. It evaluates the challenges specific to investigating and altering behaviour and attitudes online, such as fluid and dynamic identities that individuals may present in cyber space. It further investigates the link between online actions and offline impacts, including the social and psychological consequences of cyber attack and how evidence can be collected to aid in the prosecution of cyber offenders.

Cybersecurity is a complex topic that requires interdisciplinary and transdisciplinary solutions, achieved through collaboration between stakeholders from different backgrounds. This publication contributes towards to this approach through the inclusion of chapters from academics and nonacademics from a range of disciplines and professional contexts.

Chapter 1. Factors leading to cyber victimization investigates the unique characteristics of online spaces that may increase the risk of victimization, including the individual and social factors that cyber aggressors focus on when selecting targets. Suggestions are made as to how to promote policy changes and best practice to protect individuals from this growing cyber threat.

Chapter 2. Cyberterrorism - the spectre that is the convergence of the physical and virtual worlds describes how technological advancements are being used by individuals and groups to commit acts of cyberterrorism. In doing so it discusses the varying definitions of cyberterrorism and how this can be differentiated from other acts including cybercrime and hacking.

Chapter 3. Closed, safe and secure — the Russian sense of information security provides an insight into the Russian sense of information security. Through use of examples it explores the use of historical, fear-based templates that promote the isolation rhetoric and celebrate the Russian approach to the Internet.

Chapter 4. The social and psychological impact of cyberattacks looks beyond the technological and financial consequences of cyberattack to the social and psychological impacts that these can have. It evaluates how cognitive processes relate to public reactions to malicious cyber events, focusing on incidents such as the WannaCry attack of 2017.

Chapter 5. The relationship between user religiosity and preserved privacy effect in the context of social media and cybersecurity outlines how user behaviour is influenced by religious belief, examined through the examples of online privacy and the use of social platforms. A proposed model is presented and evaluated, with the findings discussed in relation to policy and practice implications.

Chapter 6. Avoiding a cyber world war: rational motives for negative cooperation among the United States, China and Russia analyses cooperation and conflict in cyberspace between the three potential adversaries of the United States, China and Russia. It examines the motivations of states, its material and the information that the state has about the capabilities and intentions of other actors. A discussion is put forward on why cooperation between states is both possible and desirable.

Chapter 7. Standard operating procedures for cybercrime investigations: a systematic literature review provides a critical overview of the overt and covert collection of evidence in order to secure successful prosecution of cyber offenders. It explores the differences between cybercrime and more traditional forms of crime, before putting forward recommendations for new procedures that can be used to aid in the gathering of evidence in online and digital spaces.

Chapter 8. Information and communication technologies: a curse or blessing for SMEs? examines the risk and compliance challenges for small to medium-sized enterprises that arise from information and communication technologies. It explores how, in order to make business transactions quicker and more efficient, SMEs may be exposed to new and serious cybersecurity threats.

Chapter 9. Cyber personalities in adaptive target audiences discusses the role of target audience analysis in influence operations, and the challenges that are encountered when applying this approach to cyberspace. It suggests how through the use cyber personalities influence operations can be made more effective.

Chapter 10. Privacy issues and critical infrastructure protection examines how the development of smart technology is changing the nature of critical infrastructure. It addresses the debate around the use of information that is generated by consumer behaviour, and the conflict this creates between the need for security and the desire for privacy.

CHAPTER

1

Factors leading to cyber victimization

Peter J.R. Macaulay[1,2], Oonagh L. Steer[2], Lucy R. Betts[2]

[1]Staffordshire University, Stoke-on-Trent, United Kingdom; [2]Nottingham Trent University, Nottingham, United Kingdom

OUTLINE

Introduction

The emergence of digital technologies has seen the proliferation of new online communications, providing opportunities for increased social interaction in an accessible manner. This availability to communicate online is an embedded feature of society, particularly predominant amongst young people (Ofcom, 2016). While the Internet affords many social and recreational benefits, it also offers numerous positive implications across a variety of industry sectors (Finkelhor, 2014). Despite this, the increased access to online communication can increase vulnerability to a variety of online risks including harassment, cyberbullying and other cyberthreats on privacy or online data (Livingstone, Haddon, Görzig, & Ólafsson, 2011). Although experiences online including pornography, contact with strangers, sharing personal information, exchanging explicit personal photographs (i.e. sexting) and hacking may not lead to harm, their existence could increase the probability of harm. While experience with these cyberthreats can lead to negative experiences and adverse consequences, not all result in actual harm (Livingstone & Smith, 2014). Livingstone and Smith (2014) outlined different categories of online risks, including *content*, *contact* and *conduct* risks. *Content* risks involve the user being the recipient of age-inappropriate content, for example, young users accessing pornography. *Contact* risks are where the user is the recipient of an initiated online communication from another individual, where they intend to bully, groom or manipulate the targeted user. *Conduct* risks consider the digital footprint and the online behaviour of the user as part of a larger network of interactions (Livingstone & Smith, 2014; Smith & Livingstone, 2017). These risks and threats result in cyber victimization in the virtual community. 'Cyber victimization' has been used broadly (Law, Shapka, & Olson, 2010) to define other cyberattacks including cyber aggression, cyber bullying and cyber threats, while others use 'online harassment' to define online attacks (Hinduja & Patchin, 2010). This chapter will discuss cyber victimization across perspectives of cyber aggression, cyberbullying and cyber threats and crimes.

Aggression is defined as any behaviour that involves intent to cause harm to the targeted individual (Baron & Richardson, 1994). While aggression has predominantly been a concern in the offline environment, the development of digital technologies has seen the rise of aggressive acts in the virtual community. While there are many forms of cyber aggressive acts or threats, cyberbullying is more specifically refined through a set of recognized criteria. Cyberbullying is defined as 'an aggressive intentional act carried out by a group or individual, using electronic forms of contact, repeatedly and over time against a victim who cannot easily defend him or herself' (Smith et al., 2008, p. 376). Like bullying in the offline environment, cyberbullying consists of three distinct criteria: intent to cause harm, repetition and an imbalance of power, which makes the victim feel defenceless (Olweus, 1993; Smith et al., 2008; Vandebosch & Van Cleemput, 2008). Despite this, definitional issues arise with applying repetition and power imbalance in the online environment. While bullying in the *real* world can be identified as an ongoing incident, with the imbalance of power portrayed through physical strength or peer group status, the extent to which this is applicable in the *virtual* world is more ambiguous. For example, a single incident in the online setting can be repeated through the number of likes and shares on social networks, increasing the audience and consequences for the victim (Slonje, Smith, & FriséN, 2013; Smith et al., 2008). In terms of power imbalance, users with increased digital literacy and knowledge can perpetrate cyberattacks though sophisticated mediums, with the targeted victim unaware of the attack due to the anonymity the online environment offers (Smith et al., 2008). Findings from a recent review across 159 studies found the prevalence of cyberbullying ranged from 1.6% to 56.9%, with perpetration reports between 1.9% and 79.3% (Brochado, Soares, & Fraga, 2017). While some argue cyberbullying should be addressed as a standalone issue (Grigg, 2012), others propose the broader term of cyber aggression should be used due to difficulty identifying criteria in the online environment (Corcoran, Mc Guckin, & Prentice, 2015).

While cyberbullying is defined under set criteria, other acts of online abuse and cyberthreats can occur, defined under cyber aggression. Cyber aggression is the 'intentional harm delivered by the use of electronic means to a person or a group of people irrespective of their age, who perceive(s) such acts as offensive, derogatory, harmful or unwanted' (Grigg, 2010, p. 152). Cyber aggression involves a variety of aggressive acts in the online environment that do not constitute cyberbullying. Therefore, these cyberattacks can be one-off or repeated instances, with the intent to cause harm to the targeted recipient. Cyber aggressive acts are those that do not necessarily focus on power imbalance or repetition, rather the violent behaviour itself such as harassment, stalking or abuse (Smith, 2012).

Other forms of cyber victimization arise from more sophisticated attacks through cyberthreats and crimes. Cybercrime is an act of intentional violation using digital technologies and online communications to trespass, manipulate or sabotage stored information and knowledge on social networks and systems (Saini, Rao, & Panda, 2012). While the availability of online communications provides connectivity on a larger scale, an established feature in society (Hassan, 2008), it is this connectivity to online communications which has also seen the emergence of cybercrimes and threats. For example, some cybercrimes are centred in the financial or business sector with users seeking financial profit (Leukfeldt, Lavorgna, & Kleemans, 2017). Social Network Sites (SNS) store a large amount of personal information and data, and therefore users expect appropriate security safeguards to store and keep these data safe. However, the large amount of data stored in these sites are also vulnerable to cyberattacks through users with malicious intentions, and therefore it is important leading industry experts work to ensure this information is kept safe (Balduzzi et al., 2010). For example, social engineering has emerged as an escalating cyberthreat which attacks virtual communities and systems (Krombholz, Hobel, Huber, & Weippl, 2015). This involves a user manipulating a targeted individual, group or company to sharing private information or knowledge. This form of cyberthreat can create large vulnerabilities across a variety of social networks. The fact the attack can be performed with relative ease means these social engineers can attack on a larger scale, creating a larger impact for those involved (Krombholz et al., 2015).

Willard (2007) created a typology of cyber aggressive acts and cyberthreats, distinguishing across seven recognized forms including flaming; harassment; denigration; outing and trickery; impersonation; exclusion and cyberthreats. Other threats include hacking, data privacy and cyberstalking (Hasebrink, Görzig, Haddon, Kalmus, & Livingstone, 2011). These cyberthreats can be perpetrated through emails, mobile phones and the many online communications or networks the Internet offers (Rivers & Noret, 2010), which can lead to detrimental consequences to the target and/or industry. For example, these cyberthreats can lead to depression (Olenik-Shemesh, Heiman, & Eden, 2012), and in worst cases, suicide (Hinduja & Patchin, 2010). Users who are victimized online are more likely to experience suicidal thoughts compared to users who perpetrate these cyberattacks (Hinduja & Patchin, 2010). Implications of these research studies suggest online companies should work together to manage the negative repercussions for those who are victimized.

The development and accessibility of the Internet has evolved social communication. The nature of online communication and networks mean users can post private or sensitive information online that can be accessible to a wider audience (Krombholz et al., 2015). However, young people do show a desire to maintain privacy in the online environment, even if there is an expectation to be socially active in the online community (Betts & Spenser, 2017). This suggests social media companies need to implement strategies to make young people feel safer online. Online users who perceive they have a good awareness of controlling their information and privacy on SNS are less likely to be victims of cybercrime than those who do not (Saridakis, Benson, Ezingeard, & Tennakoon, 2016). This illustrates how digital literacy and knowledge of Information and Communication Technologies (ICTs) can influence vulnerability to some cyberthreats and attacks. While some responsibility is down to each user on the social network, providers can focus to ensure any information published public by the user is only visible to the intended audience through security settings.

The Internet is an evolving space so it is important governing bodies take a greater responsibility to put mechanisms and precautions in place to reduce online risks and cyberthreats for those who use it. For example, the education sector can encourage young people to use strategies to reduce vulnerability to these online risks. This digital awareness and training incorporated into leading industry platforms can help ensure those who use the Internet have the appropriate tools to stay safe online. Research has outlined several risk factors leading to vulnerability for online risks and dangers, for example, individual characteristics, peer relationships, time spent online and wider community factors, which will be discussed later in the chapter. This chapter will now explore the features of cyber victimization and the predictive factors that can lead to vulnerability to cyber aggressive attacks, cyberbullying and/or cyberthreats.

Features of cyber victimization

This section will explore specific features of cyber victimization, which can contribute to the vulnerability of cyberbullying, cyber aggression and cybercrimes or threats. In particular, topics such as efficiency of technology, roles of anonymity and bystanders, with a brief consideration of the bully–victim cycle will be discussed.

Efficiency of information and communication technologies

Since the mid-1990s, commercialization of the Internet has led to extraordinary global development and growth. ICTs provide platforms for education, businesses, finance, social communication and information sharing. Advancement in technology is a continuing evolution of efficiency, improvement and invention. The Internet has become more accessible via fourth generation (4G) smartphones and the worldwide distribution of broadband Internet infrastructure. More users can become connected, for infinite amounts of time and as such, larger volumes of data can be transmitted. Household Internet access in the United Kingdom has increased from 25% in the year 2000 to 90% in 2017 (Prescott, 2017). Global Internet usage has been reported to be 3.58 billion Internet users, which is approximately 47% of the world's population (Biggs & Lozanova, 2017). Inescapably, this number will continue to increase and those who have Internet access will eventually become the majority population. As the amount of users increase and ICT enhances, criminal activity can take place in the digital world which allows its existence to thrive.

Cybercrime can encompass various different sinister activities, all of which will utilize the opportunities and efficacy of ICTs. One of the most prominent elements to state is the global connection of ICTs, providing no restriction to physical locality. Digital offenders can pursue their victims from any position where there is connectivity to the Internet. It is important to note the difficulty this aspect presents itself to law enforce-ment and policy makers of different countries. Equally as prominent is the factor of time. ICTs and the Internet are constantly active 24/7, and so the constraints of time are non-existent and acts are instantaneous. While targeted users use simple strategies (i.e. power off on a computer or smartphone), this does not stop the asynchronous transmittal of messages and interactions. Together, global communication and non-existent time work alongside the amount of information that can be received, trans-mitted and gained using ICT. All perpetrated cyber activity exploits the advantages of ICT, increasing traditional crimes such as fraud or theft, or creating new crimes which are dependent on ICT, such as hacking or distributing viruses.

The efficiency of ICT can be clearly portrayed within the context of cyberbullying, from a victims' perspective. Acts of cyberbullying can occur both within and outside the school environment, illustrating its fluidity to occur at any time (24/7 notion). Furthermore, targets of cyberbullying can experience abusive online communication and humil-iation in front of an infinite audience via wide dissemination (Shariff & Hoff, 2007). The audience extends beyond close proximity of friends and peers, but can be accessible by wider social groups increasing the publicity of the incident, extending the impact on the victim. Removal of an online act, even if deemed regrettable by a perpetrator cannot easily be facili-tated. For instance, an original published photo online can be saved or shared a numerous amounts of time, by users beyond the intended audience. These factors are believed to possibly exacerbate the negative impact experienced by those who are cyberbullied (Bonanno & Hymel, 2013; Gualdo, Hunter, Durkin, Arnaiz, & Maquilon, 2015). Although the efficiency of ICTs can positively extend the boundaries of traditional social interaction, it can be easily exploited by those with negative intentions.

Anonymity

The digital world provides an opportunity for immunity and freedom to those who wish to communicate anonymously on a much greater scale than the physical world (Hinduja & Patchin, 2008). Between 9% and 69% of victims of cyber-aggressive attacks are targeted by anonymous online perpetrators (Kowalski & Limber, 2007; Wright & Li, 2013; Ybarra & Mitchell, 2004). Technology has provided a way of hiding 'true' identity. Mobile phone numbers are freely available and Internet users can create multiple email addresses or user accounts, making it difficult to ascertain the true identity of another individual. For example, a user could impersonate somebody else unknowingly to a targeted individual. In addition, a user is easily able to hide their true age and be vulnerable to content risks through age-restricted material, readily available online.

Although victimization in online and offline environments can occur anonymously, there are a number of unique characteristics which distinctly separate the concept of anonymous victimization in the cyber world. Firstly, personal information can efficiently be obtained from those users who are more vulnerable due to poor online security settings. Anonymous perpetrators are able to build relationships with their victims in order to gain further information for theft purposes or for those with malicious intent (Sodhi & Sharma, 2012). Secondly, the application of technology enables aggressive acts to be transmitted and received between a plethora of media (i.e. texting, smartphone apps, SNS, chat rooms and email) (Willard, 2011). The variety of media applications available highlight the extent to which perpetrators can choose to target other users. Thirdly, the cyber world is vastly populated and is not restricted by time or space (Sabella, Patchin, & Hinduja, 2013). In cyberspace, victims and offenders are united effortlessly and with little obstruction, allowing victimization prevalence to be much greater than the physical world (Reyns, Henson, & Fisher, 2011). Knowledgeable offenders are able to easily manipulate an infinite number of victims using their own personal information, various different methods and without divulging their own identity.

How a victim experiences an anonymous act also changes within the digital world. In terms of cyberbullying, Sticca and Perren (2013) found anonymous acts to be reported as the most severe form of bullying when compared to traditional forms, with distribution of photos/video clips seen as the strongest negative impact for the victim (Smith et al., 2008). Participants commented that victims are usually alone, helpless and with no support when experiencing the attack, which links with research indicating that a victim's experience of fear (Mishna, Saini, & Solomon, 2009), frustration, insecurity and powerlessness is augmented if a cyberattack is anonymous (Dooley, Pyzalski, & Cross, 2009; Nocentini et al., 2010).

The reasoning as to why perpetrators choose to remain anonymous is due to the reduced perception of being caught, which creates an imbalance of power (Smith, del Barrio, & Tokunaga, 2013; Olweus & Limber, 2018). A victim is blind to who is targeting them and therefore reporting an anonymous aggressor becomes troublesome (Vandebosch & Van Cleemput, 2008). Anonymity has been considered attributable to inducing abusive behaviour as it encourages and empowers those who in a face to face environment would usually refrain from behaving aggressively (Betts & Spenser, 2017; Lenhart, Purcell, Smith, & Zichuhr, 2010). Having anonymity and freedom in the digital world creates a space where social restrictions and inhibitions can be loosened (Herring, 2001). The sense of power and anonymity can work together enabling a skewed perception of our own behaviour.

The limitations of acceptability of our behaviour within the physical and cyber world are governed by our normative beliefs and social rules (Huesmann & Guerra, 1997). Empirical evidence provided by Barlett and Gentile (2012) suggest that positive perceptions of anonymity promote cyber aggressive behaviours. It has been argued that anonymity facilitates the perpetrator to dissociate from their own asocial behaviour and the impact it may be creating. Moreover, parameters differ when the fear of being judged or being caught are removed (Herring, 2001; Wright, 2014). Suler (2004) extensively focuses on anonymity being a primary factor of the Online Disinhibition Effect (ODE) and argues that users feel less vulnerable with a separate online and offline identity. It is widely acknowledged online disinhibition encourages asocial behaviour (Brown, Jackson, & Cassidy, 2006; Kowalski, Limber, & Agatston, 2008; Ritter, 2014). Anonymity can clearly be viewed as a contributing factor to phenomenon of cyber victimization and the impact it has on society.

Bystanders

In the digital world, bystanders observe acts of cyber aggression in situations where a perpetrator openly victimizes a target or group of people in sight of an audience. Therefore, bystanders are predominantly researched from a cyberbullying perspective. A bystander will witness a cyberbullying episode by viewing a shared message or piece of information. In a sample of 799 American 12–17 year olds, 67% report to have observed others participating in cyberbullying on SNS and 91% report they ignore the harassment they witnessed (Lenhart et al., 2011). Traditional bullying tends to be observed by a limited number of bystanders who play key roles (Craig & Pepler, 2007). In the cyber world, the potential number of bystanders of one episode of aggression is increased when shared or liked between individuals and peer groups, essentially repeating the act (Kowalski, Giumetti, Schroeder, & Lattanner, 2014; Slonje et al., 2013). With an audience so extensive in the cyber world, the role of a cyber bystander is not only meaningful for our understanding, but crucial for potential preventative measures (Holfeld, 2014).

DeSmet et al. (2014) divides bystander behaviour into active and passive practices, with active responses including negative and positive intentions. Negative examples of behaviour include reinforcing the act, participating or encouraging the aggressive behaviour by sharing the information. Positive behaviour includes directly defending or supporting the victim or reporting the incident to an adult. Passive bystander behaviours involve ignoring the incident, with no positive or negative response toward the perpetrator or victim. Passive bystanders attribute their behaviour to fear of being victims themselves (DeSmet et al., 2012), foreseeing the potential to further embarrass the victim (Thornberg, 2007), fear of not being able to achieve the desired result (Thornberg & Jungert, 2013) and also not feeling responsible (Olenik-Shemesh, Heiman, & Eden, 2015). Bystanders have previously been a research focus in terms of the bystander effect (Fischer et al., 2011; Latané & Darley, 1970) which states that a bystander is more likely not to help a victim due to a larger amount of bystanders present. It is therefore suggested the more bystanders who witness an act of cyberbullying, the more likely it will encourage passive responses (Machácková, Dedkova, & Mezulanikova, 2015; Olenik-Shemesh et al., 2015). The responsibility to positively behave becomes diluted amongst the audience, with bystanders believing that others will defend the victim, through diffusion of responsibility. This could be attributed to passive behaviour, which is the most common bystander behaviour to be reported across the literature (Brody & Vangelisti, 2016; Lenhart et al., 2011).

One method to tackle perceptions of the audience for a bystander is to be anonymous. Bystanders are able to hide their active or passive responses online and can choose to respond privately to the perpetrator or victim or both (Bastiaensens et al., 2014). Anonymity has been described as being empowering for bystanders, to reinforce perpetrators and to be fearless of accountability (Barlinska, Szuster, & Winiewski, 2013; Druck & Kaplowitz, 2005). If a bystander needs to decide on a particular response, perceptions of what an audience's response are important and may be suppressed (Ferwerda, Schedl, & Tkalcic, 2014). This is supported by research indicating that adolescents are more likely to respond negatively as a bystander when there are limited observers within more private settings (Barlińska et al., 2013).

Although more severe acts of aggression predict more supportive bystander behaviour (Bastiaensens et al., 2014), bystander perceptions would be adjusted with education and clarity around the realistic gravity of the cyberbullying perpetrations they witness. Furthermore, if bystanders could alter their view to perceive acquaintances as being worthy of a supportive response and not just their close friends (Bastiaensens et al., 2014; Brody & Vangelisti, 2016) the implication could be phenomenally meaningful. For instance, a rationale for this can be drawn from the results of a study by Beaman, Barnes, Klentz, and McQuirk (1978) who found participants who were educated in the bystander effect being more likely to intervene in an emergency. Empowering more bystanders to behave with morality needs to be at the forefront of any attempt to promote positive bystander behaviour.

The bully-victim role

The bully-victim role is considered within literature pertaining to cyberbullying victimization. The bully-victim role is important as it has unique characteristics which are generally under-researched yet in the digital world are unprecedented. In traditional and cyberbullying research, there are four categories of involvement; the victim, the perpetrator, the non-involved and the bully-victim (Kowalski, Limber, & Agatston, 2012; Olweus, 1993; Wong, Chan, & Cheng, 2014). The latter category entails a victim who also engages in perpetrator activity and is generally the minority group referred to in traditional bullying research with reported low prevalence rates (Lovegrove & Cornell, 2014; Nansel et al., 2001). However, in cyberbullying the prevalence rate for cyberbullies who are also victims of cyberbullying themselves is much higher (Mishna, Khoury-Kassabri, Gadalla, & Daciuk, 2012; Schultze-Krumbholz, Schultze, Zagorscak, Wölfer, & Scheithauer, 2016), with strong evidence to suggest the bully-victim role is the majority group in comparison to the perpetrator and victim groups (Brack & Caltabiano, 2014). Moreover, a meta-analysis of 131 studies by Kowalski et al. (2014) highly depicts cyberbullying perpetration as a leading factor for cyber victimization, clearly framing the impression that individuals who cyberbully others also are cyberbullied themselves. Unfortunately, despite the clear importance of the role, as yet there are few, empirically tested assumptions made around the cyberbully-victim role.

The high volume of reported bully-victims within cyberbullying has been attributed to the impulse to retaliate, as a form of defence (Jacobs, Goossens, Dehue, Vollink, & Lechner, 2015; Kowalski & Limber, 2007). By responding to an act of cyberbullying, a victim attempts to reduce the negative experiences created by the original perpetrator and regulate their own emotions (Frey, Pearson, & Cohen, 2015). Research also indicates that victims of traditional bullying are more likely to seek revenge within the online environment and become a cyberbully (Smith et al., 2008). Mishna et al. (2012) propose a combination of two characteristics which contribute to the ease of being a cyberbully-victim, the efficiencies and accessibility of ICTs and the manner in which communication via ICTs occurs, that is facial expressions, body language or tone heard in speech (Ang & Goh, 2010; Suler, 2004). It may be easier to retaliate online in comparison to face to face, more so if the perpetrator is physically bigger in size and strength. This explanation could be applicable for those cyberbully-victims who are not retaliating but are perpetrating for other, unknown reasons. However, what is known is that the online world can clearly influence individuals to behave in a manner that is different to their behaviour in the offline world (Suler, 2004).

The research area of cyber victimization in terms of the cyberbully-victim role has the potential to significantly enhance interventions for users of the ICTs. Evidence for this can be drawn from the high prevalence rate of the bully-victim role. For research to effectively contribute to society, consideration for the cyberbully-victim role will need to be considered more thoroughly. For instance, there are well-documented behavioural and psychological consequences associated with cyber victimization. Furthermore, reports of higher score of depression and alcohol abuse have been linked to not only victims of cyberbullying but also cyberbully-victims (Gamez-Gaudix, Gini, & Calvete, 2015). In order to effectively develop prevention strategies, future research will need to be addressed from a bully-victim standpoint, as well as perpetrator and victim.

Factors leading to cyber victimization

The purpose of this section is to consider what a victim of cybercrime or cyberthreat may look like in terms of susceptibility. By doing so, vital insight and understanding of cyber victimization can be developed whilst considering potential profiles of victims of cybercrime. The concept of cybercrime is vast and there are various different forms of cyber victimization. A crime data report by the City of London Police (2016) indicates that victims of cyber-dependent crimes such as spreading of viruses, malware or hacking have no gender bias but are more likely to occur to victims within the age bracket of 40−49 years. The data report also outlines the older age group of 60−69 years being more likely to be victims of cyber-enabled fraud, with no gender bias. Analysis of the British Crime Survey by Reyns (2013) upholds the older generations being more susceptible to online fraud, additionally finding males to be more vulnerable. Alternative findings between research results, authority reports and surveys conducted by ICT companies such as Norton or Microsoft are common. However inconsistencies have been attributed to lack of reporting unlawful crimes, disparate perceptions by the public of cybercrime and reports to alternative bodies such as Internet service providers or website administrators (McGuire & Dowling, 2013; van de Weijer, Leukfeldt, & Bernasco, 2018).

There is a great deal of literature concerning victims of online sexual harassment. Consistent research findings suggest women are far more likely to experience sexual harassment in chat rooms, and experience online sexual harassment, which includes receiving requests for intimate questions and receiving pornographic material (Henry & Powell, 2018). The approximate age group of 18−24-year-old females has been suggested to be the most likely to be sexually harassed online (Lindsay & Krysik, 2012; Pew Research Centre, 2014). An extensive qualitative and quantitative collaborative project across Hungary, Denmark and the UK found that females aged 11−17 years were more likely to experience sexualized online bullying and unwanted sexualization, thus increasing the probability of a negative outcome for young and older females (Project deShame, 2017).

Cyberbullying literature produces an inconsistent overview in terms of gender and age profiles. A number of studies concerning young people indicate females are disproportionately represented as victims of cyberbullying (Gorzig & Olafsson, 2013; Lasher & Baker, 2015) whilst some have found equal victimization prevalence rates for females and males (Hinduja & Patchin, 2008; Tokunaga, 2010). Fewer studies have considered cyberbullying in adulthood or the workplace; however, a meta-analysis of victimization literature concluded no substantial evidence for gender differentiation (Lund & Ross, 2017). A multi-national study of 3506 participants aged 15–30 years found no age bias yet respondents were statistically more likely to be male and the most experience to be defamation of one's character and threats of violence (Nasi, Oksanen, Keipi, & Räsänen, 2015). Cyber-victimization has been demonstrated by Kowaliski, Toth, and Morgan (2018) to continue after adolescence. Their compelling results indicate cyberbullying experiences are more likely to be reported than traditional acts of bullying in adulthood and in the workplace. From these findings, it is clearly paramount for future research to consider cyberbullying from the perspective of a wider field of age groups.

There is a scarce amount of literature available concerning cybercrime and minority groups with findings being inconsistent and contradictory. A narrative systematic review of cyberbullying and minority groups found varied findings for high involvement of victimization for minority and majority groups, with no difference found between the groups (Hamm et al., 2015). Despite these findings, analysis form Tynes, Reynolds, and Greenfield (2003) indicated that ethnic and racial slurs were significantly apparent in unmonitored chat rooms, suggesting that negative ethnic attitudes are prevalent within the online context which presents an environment without social controls. Moreover, in terms of cyber-dependent crimes, ethnic minority groups have been identified as being more vulnerable as they are less likely than white majority groups to have Internet security software and therefore are potentially more exposed to cyberattacks (Ipsos MORI, 2013). Scant research focus has been given to ethnic minority groups and specific cyber-dependent and enabled crimes as well as online sexual harassment, with literature still within the phase of considering homogenous groups. Future research must aim to answer research questions around heterogeneous groups for a full overview of the cybercrime prevalence rates (Hinduja & Patchin, 2010).

Yar (2005) considers the Internet to be a disorganized environment due to the efficiencies the digital world provides which themselves present potential enhanced risks. Leukfeld (2014) concludes that everyone is at risk in terms of cyber-dependent and enabled crimes. Despite this, specific research conclusions have identified some characteristics such as users with high trust scores (Wright, Chakraborty, Basoglu, & Marett, 2010), high submissiveness (Alseadoon, Chan, Foo, & Gonzales Nieto, 2012) who are more susceptible to phishing crimes. Research focussing on personality characteristics and cyberbullying has found a number of factors portray a profile of a potential victim. For instance, individuals who are impulsive or have low self-control (Holt, Bossler, Malinkski, & May, 2016), low emotional control (Hempehill & Heerde, 2014) and low self-esteem (Brewer & Kerslake, 2015; Mobin, Feng, & Neudorf, 2017) are more likely to be victimized online. Festl and Quandt (2013) reported personality factors such as conscientiousness and openness to experiences to be predictors of cyberbullying victimization. Identifying vulnerable individual characteristics enables early intervention to target areas of development. However, there is a need for more longitudinal research to consider direction of the association between individual characteristics of victims of cybercrime.

It is important to take into account additional risk factors beyond an individual's characteristics that can create vulnerabilities for targeted individuals, groups, companies and the wider community. In particular, how these risk factors impact across different settings including the home and school environment, and neighbouring community need to be acknowledged.

Peer relationships and group status has been recognized across an abundance of research as a strong risk factor for cyber victimization within cyberbullying, cyberthreats and cybercrimes. For example, individuals who experience dissatisfaction with existing friendships and/ or experiences difficulty creating new ones are likely to experience subsequent negative emotions. In particular, these individuals will experience loneliness and depressive symptoms associated with changes in mood levels, which can predict subsequent cyber victimization (Olenik-Shemesh et al., 2012). Those individuals who exhibit difficulties through social interaction may struggle to be satisfied with peer group relationships and as such experience a higher amount of peer rejection, associated with increased risk of cyber victimization. These group relationships can be an important interaction during adolescent development, and in particular can create challenges in the school environment as adolescents fight to retain and establish power in the peer group. Research has shown that adolescents associated with peer rejection from peer groups were more likely to show cyber aggressive and cyber victimization experience (Wright & Li, 2013). As cyber victimization can lead to unpleasant feelings and delinquent behaviour (Mitchell, Ybarra, & Finkelhor, 2007), educational practitioners should work to develop adolescents' cognitive and emotional empathy, to promote stronger peer-group support and friendships, a recognized protective factor for cyber victimization (Fridh, Lindström, & Rosvall, 2015; Williams & Guerra, 2007). Those who experience negative emotional reactions from peer rejection are likely to spend more time online and trigger increased social network use. For example, those who experience higher levels of depression and/or anxiety would show increased time spent online and online communications, acting as a risk factor for future cyber victimization (Oberst, Wegmann, Stodt, Brand, & Chamarro, 2017).

While young people can identify the benefits of digital technology, they also recognize the propensity to spend a lot of time online, creating a sense of attachment to the online domain (Betts & Spenser, 2017). The accessibility and scope to interact with others online can cause vulnerabilities to those who actively portray their real-world life in the online environment. For example, individuals can be vulnerable to cyber victimization as a result of prior actions online. In particular, individuals may regret certain comments or online actions in the future as they are unaware of the long-term wider ramifications (Betts & Spenser, 2017). While children, young people and adults use online communications on a daily basis, adolescence is a period of development that has been associated with increased online communication and interaction (Marcum, Higgins, & Ricketts, 2010; Ybarra & Mitchell, 2007). The time spent online interacting with others has been shown to be a significant risk factor for cyber victimization, as increased time online increases exposure as a potential victim. For example, adolescents who spent more time online for non-school-related work were more likely to engage in perpetration and/or victimization involvement (Álvarez-García, Núñez, García, & Barreiro-Collazo, 2018). In addition, online users who spend more time online in terms of hours per day are more likely to be vulnerable to cyber victimization and cyber aggressive attacks (Mishna et al., 2012; Rice et al., 2015). In terms of cyberbullying, individuals who exhibited a higher frequency of online communications through social networks were more likely to be involved in cyber victimization and perpetration (Sticca, Ruggieri, Alsaker, & Perren, 2013). The online domain consists of numerous SNS, increasing the opportunity for users to engage in risky online behaviour and vulnerability to cyberthreats and attacks. In particular, those users who had increased network groups were more likely to exhibit interactions that are not controllable (Buglass, Binder, Betts, & Underwood, 2016). Individuals who use SNS are at greater risk for having personal information exposed, and as such are more likely to experience cyber victimization (Mesch, 2009).

As such it is important to consider why people spend time online, increasing their vulnerability for cyberthreats and attacks. One such phenomena to explain this is the notion of Fear of Missing Out (FOMO). This account pertains to those individuals who perceive others are having rewarding experiences while they are absent. As such, FOMO could provide an explanation for cyber victimization. FOMO has been linked with lower levels of life satisfaction and higher levels of social media use and interaction (Przybylski, Murayama, DeHaan, & Gladwell, 2013). This suggests the notion of FOMO could be used to explain why individuals spend more time online, due to the fear of missing out from rewarding experiences. Those with increased negative emotional experiences are likely to experience greater FOMO (Przybylski et al., 2013), which can increase cyber victimization in the home and school environment (Alt, 2015). In relation to cybercrimes, research has found an association between time spent online in the home setting and increased risks of cyber-theft victimization (Song, Lynch, & Cochran, 2016). This was especially true for those users accessing the Internet when they were unemployed or engaged in increased online shopping, online banking, and in serious cases, sexting and exploitation (Song et al., 2016). For example, users who spent more time online, particularly through online shopping, were more likely to be subject to cyber fraud victimization (Pratt, Holtfreter, & Reisig, 2010). In addition, users who spent time online for Internet banking are 50% more likely to experience cyber victimization through identity theft (Reyns, 2013). This highlights the propensity for cyber victimization to those who spend more time in the online domain. Government and company organizations can ensure employees are aware of the online risks and dangers associated with increased online use, to promote increased awareness online and protection through additional security measures.

The school, home and family structure has also been explored as a risk factor for cyber victimization across cyberbullying, cyberthreats and crimes. For example, parents who exhibit high levels of control for technology use and mediation were less likely to be subject to cyber victimization in the home environment (Aoyama, Utsumi, & Hasegawa, 2012). Additionally, those parents who took a greater interest in their children's online activity through discussions and moderation of time spent online were less vulnerable to cyberthreats and attacks (Elsaesser, Russell, Ohannessian, & Patton, 2017; Taiariol, 2010). Floros, Siomos, Fisoun, Dafouli, and Geroukalis (2013) examined community and family protective factors for cyber victimization showing that adolescents who perceived a greater parental warmth, closeness and support from their family were less likely to experience cyber victimization. Considering the family structure, research has shown increased cyber victimization vulnerabilities in single-parent settings compared to other family structures. This suggests additional support should to be tailored toward single-parent families. Reflecting on the educational setting, consistent research has identified an increased positive school climate, quality and perceived safety act as protective factors for future cyber victimization (Bevilacqua et al., 2017; Kowalski et al., 2014; Williams & Guerra, 2007).

From a theoretical perspective, scholars have applied Routine Activity Theory (RAT) (Cohen & Felson, 1979) to explain cyber victimization in the online domain. Using components from RAT, for a cybercrime or attack to occur there needs to be a (a) suitable target, (b) motivated offender and (c) absence or lack of guardianship. In terms of the online setting, guardianship would portray an absence or lack of security settings/measures, and physical authority presence. The widespread nature of online communications has presented numerous opportunities for motivated offenders to target victims at any time and across different settings. Motivated offenders could be deterred by increasing online safety awareness for individuals and companies, providing additional security to the target (Reyns, 2013; Yar, 2005). While the application of the theory can be suitable to explain behaviours in the online domain, notable differences between the *real* world and *virtual* world exist, challenging the suitability of the theory to explain such behaviours.

One of the key threats across online communities, making people vulnerable to cyber victimization is the risk of social engineering attacks. The notion of social engineering is recognized as an escalating information security problem. More recently, these exploitations online are becoming more sophisticated, creating additional impact on the targeted victim(s) (Krombholz et al., 2015). In particular, the evolving nature of digital devices and new online mediums create new platforms for users to engage in social engineer attacks across virtual communities. These attacks manipulate a victim or multiple victims to exploit personal and/or private information (Conteh & Schmick, 2016; Heartfield & Loukas, 2016). These attacks can take a number of approaches, including physical, social and technical aspects, through different channels and can be perpetrated through software- or human-based operators (Krombholz et al., 2015). Such attacks include phishing, baiting, tailgating, file masquerading and web pop-ups through sophisticated systems to attack virtual communities for desired information (Conteh & Schmick, 2016; Heartfield & Loukas, 2016).

A coherent example of online social engineering is the fake anti-virus cyberattack (Sophos, 2011). A perpetrator of a fake anti-virus may use several avenues to reach their victim. A user may receive an email, a pop-up, unintentionally directed to a compromised website, or click on a link which has been planted within popular search results. From these different sources, a user is informed that they have an infected computer system, which does not really exist. Essentially, an individual is scared into believing something that is not true. The fake anti-virus will continually send alerts informing the user of the danger of the bogus threat until they install the software which then proceeds to administer a fake system scan where many non-existent threats are reported. Registration and payment of the software (malware) is then pushed onto the user in order to clean the reported threats. Personal and financial details are passed over by the user to be exploited by the cybercriminal. The whole scam can look professional and legitimate by clever design and illegal use of logos.

Research has considered profiles of victims of social engineering, focussing on what may be the reasoning behind their susceptibility to deception. An overview of literature points toward personality traits such as agreeableness and extroversion being linked to individuals who are more likely to be deceived by online social engineering (Weiner & Greene, 2008). Specifically, personality factors have been associated with age and gender, with females (Costa, Terracciano, & McCrae, 2001) and younger individuals (Srivastava, John, Gosling, & Potter, 2003) more likely to have higher scores of agreeableness, exhibit more trusting beliefs and avoid conflict. Interventions such as security awareness and anti-phishing training has been shown to be a beneficial way of providing protection against attacks by social engineers (Dodge, Rovira, Zachary, & Joseph, 2011; Kumaraguru, Sheng, Acquisti, Cranor, & Hong, 2010). Moreover, similar findings were reported by Saridakis et al. (2016) for those who perceived high levels of control to restrict access to personal information.

Conclusion

In summary, the chapter has provided an overview of immoral and unlawful behaviours that can be perpetrated through the use of ICTs. In particular, key features and factors have been reviewed that can lead to cyber victimization, across cyberbullying, cyber aggression and cyber-crimes. Whilst it is clear ICT can be exploited for various unethical gains, which can lead to detrimental consequences to the targeted user, the true extent of the issue has not yet been acknowledged. For example, due to inconsistencies in the measurement and definition of these cyberattacks, precautions should be taken when addressing intervention efforts and policy recommendations. Moreover, there is a lack of consensus concerning subjectivity regarding guidelines from the Crown Prosecution Service in the United Kingdom on cyber aggressive attacks, which creates continued opportunities for those who perpetrate online to target users (Bliss, 2017).

While there are many predictors of cyber victimization, the future of ICT security development needs to address some of the strongest pre-dictors outlined in this chapter. For example, while lifestyle and time spent online are becoming synonymous, future developments need to incorporate security measures to adequately keep users safe from cyberthreats and attacks. In addition, future research and policy considerations would highly benefit society by focussing on discouraging those who exploit the anonymous and transparent attributes of the cyber world. Overall, cyber victimization will continue to emerge across different populations and organizations as the proliferation of ICTs continue to evolve. However, the way in which cyber victimization is portrayed will continue to fluctuate as perpetrations online experiment with new opportunities to target vulnerable users.

References

Alseadoon, I. M. A., Chan, T., Foo, E., & Gonzales Nieto, J. (2012). Who is more susceptible to phishing emails? A Saudi Arabian study. In *ACIS 2012: Location, location, location: Proceedings of the 23rd Australasian conference on information systems 2012* (pp. 1–11). ACIS.

Alt, D. (2015). College students' academic motivation, media engagement and fear of missing out. *Computers in Human Behavior, 49*, 111–119.

Álvarez-García, D., Núñez, J. C., García, T., & Barreiro-Collazo, A. (2018). Individual, family, and community predictors of cyber-aggression among adolescents. *European Journal of Psychology Applied to Legal Context*, (2), 1–10.

Ang, R. P., & Goh, D. H. (2010). Cyberbullying among adolescents: The role of affective and cognitive empathy, and gender. *Child Psychiatry and Human Development, 41*, 387–397.

Aoyama, I., Utsumi, S., & Hasegawa, M. (2012). Cyberbullying in Japan: Cases, government reports, adolescent relational aggression, and parental monitoring roles. In Q. Li, D. Cross, & P. K. Smith (Eds.), *Cyberbullying in the global playground: Research from international perspectives* (pp. 183–201). Wiley-Blackwell.

Balduzzi, M., Platzer, C., Holz, T., Kirda, E., Balzarotti, D., & Kruegel, C. (2010). Abusing social networks for automated user profiling. In *International workshop on recent advances in intrusion detection* (pp. 422–441). Berlin, Heidelberg: Springer.

Barlett, C. P., & Gentile, D. A. (2012). Attacking others online: The formation of cyberbullying in late adolescence. *Psychology of Popular Media Culture, 1*, 123–135.

Barlinska, J., Szuster, A., & Winiewski, M. (2013). Cyberbullying among adolescent bystanders: Role of the communication medium, form of violence, and empathy. *Journal of Community and Applied Social Psychology, 23*, 37–51.

Baron, R. A., & Richardson, D. R. (1994). *Human aggression: Perspectives in social psychology*. Nova Iorque: Plenum Press.

Bastiaensens, S., Vandebosch, H., Poels, K., Van Cleemput, K., Desmet, A., & De Bourdeaudhuij, I. (2014). Cyberbullying on social network sites. An experimental study into bystanders' behavioural intentions to help the victim or reinforce the bully. *Computers in Human Behavior, 31*, 259–271.

Beaman, A. L., Barnes, P. J., Klentz, K., & McQuirk, B. (1978). Increasing helping rates through information dissemination: Teaching pays. *Personality and Social Psychology Bulletin, 4*, 406–411.

Betts, L. R., & Spenser, K. A. (2017). People think it'sa harmless joke": Young people's understanding of the impact of technology, digital vulnerability and cyberbullying in the United Kingdom. *Journal of Children and Media, 11*(1), 20–35.

Bevilacqua, L., Shackleton, N., Hale, D., Allen, E., Bond, L., Christie, D., et al. (2017). The role of family and school-level factors in bullying and cyberbullying: A cross-sectional study. *BMC Pediatrics, 17*(1), 160.

Biggs, P., & Lozanova, Y. (2017). *The State of broadband: Broadband catalysing sustainable development*. Retrieved May, 2018 https://www.itu.int/dms_pub/itu-s/opb/pol/S-POL-BROADBAND.18-2017-PDF-E.pdf.

Bliss, L. (2017). The crown prosecution guidelines and grossly offensive comments: An analysis. *Journal of Media Law, 9*(2), 173—188.

Bonanno, R. A., & Hymel, S. (2013). Cyber bullying and internalizing difficulties: Above and beyond the impact of traditional forms of bullying. *Journal of Youth and Adolescence, 42*(5), 685—697.

Brack, K., & Caltabiano, N. (2014). Cyberbullying and self-esteem in Australian adults. *Cyberpsychology: Journal of Psychosocial Research on Cyberspace, 8*(2), 12—22.

Brewer, G., & Kerslake, J. (2015). Cyberbullying, self-esteem, empathy and loneliness. *Computers in Human Behavior, 48*, 255—260.

Brochado, S., Soares, S., & Fraga, S. (2017). A scoping review on studies of cyberbullying prevalence among adolescents. *Trauma, Violence, & Abuse, 18*(5), 523—531.

Brody, N., & Vangelisti, A. L. (2016). Bystander intervention in cyberbullying. *Communication Monographs, 83*(1), 94—119.

Brown, K., Jackson, M., & Cassidy, W. (2006). Cyber-bullying: Developing policy to direct responses that are equitable and effective in addressing this special form of bullying. *Canadian Journal of Educational Administration and Policy, 57*, 1—36.

Buglass, S. L., Binder, J. F., Betts, L. R., & Underwood, J. D. (2016). When 'friends' collide: Social heterogeneity and user vulnerability on social network sites. *Computers in Human Behavior, 54*, 62—72.

City of London Police. (2016). *Cyber crime — victimology analysis*. Retrieved June, 2018, from https://www.cityoflondon.police.uk/news-and   appeals/Documents/Victimology%20Analysis-latest.pdf.

Cohen, L., & Felson, M. (1979). Social change and crime rate trends: A routine activity approach. *American Sociological Review, 44*(4), 588—608.

Conteh, N. Y., & Schmick, P. J. (2016). Cybersecurity: Risks, vulnerabilities and countermeasures to prevent social engineering attacks. *International Journal of Advanced Computer Research, 6*(23), 31.

Corcoran, L., Mc Guckin, C., & Prentice, G. (2015). Cyberbullying or cyber aggression?: A review of existing definitions of cyber-based peer-to-peer aggression. *Societies, 5*(2), 245—255.

Costa, P., Terracciano, A., & McCrae, R. (2001). Gender differences in personality traits across cultures: Robust and surprising findings. *Journal of Personality and Social Psychology, 18*, 322—331.

Craig, W. M., & Pepler, D. J. (2007). Understanding Bullying: From research to practise. *Canadian Psychology, 48*(2), 86—93.

DeSmet, A., Bastiaensens, S., Van Cleemput, K., Poels, K., Vandebosch, H., & De Bourdeaudhuij, I. (2012). Mobilizing bystanders of cyberbullying: An exploratory study into behavioural determinants of defending the victim. *Studies in Health Technology and Informatics, 181*, 58—63.

DeSmet, A., Veldeman, C., Poels, K., Bastiaensens, S., Van Cleemput, K., Vandebosch, H., et al. (2014). Determinants of self-reported bystander behaviour in cyberbullying incidents amongst adolescents. *Cyberpsychology, Behavior, and Social Networking, 17*(4), 207—215.

Dodge, R., Rovira, E., Zachary, R., & Joseph, S. (2011). Phishing awareness exercise. In *Proc. of the 15th colloquium for information systems security education, Fairborn, Ohio, June 13-15*.

Dooley, J. J., Pyzalski, J., & Cross, D. (2009). Cyberbullying versus face-to-face bullying: A theoretical and conceptual review. *Journal of Psychology, 217*, 182—188.

Druck, K., & Kaplowitz, M. (2005). Setting up a no-bully zone. *Virginia Journal of Education, 98*(4), 6—10.

Elsaesser, C., Russell, B., Ohannessian, C. M., & Patton, D. (2017). Parenting in a digital age: A review of parents' role in preventing adolescent cyberbullying. *Aggression and Violent Behavior, 35*, 62—72.

Ferwerda, B., Schedl, M., & Tkalcic, M. (2014). To post or not to post: The effects of persuasive cues and group targeting mechanisms on posting behaviour. In *Proceedings of the 6th ASE international conference on social computing, Stanford, USA* (pp. 1—12). May 27-31.

Festl, R., & Quandt, T. (2013). Social relations and cyberbullying: The influence of individual and structural attributes on victimization and perpetration via the internet. *Human Communication Research, 39*, 101—126.

Finkelhor, D. (2014). Commentary: Cause for alarm? Youth and internet risk research—a commentary on Livingstone and Smith (2014). *Journal of Child Psychology and Psychiatry, 55*(6), 655—658.

Fischer, P., Krueger, J. I., Greitemeyer, T., Vogrincic, C., Kastenmüller, A., & Frey, D. (2011). The bystander-effect: A meta-analytic review on bystander intervention in dangerous and non-dangerous emergencies. *Psychological Bulletin, 137*(4), 517.

Floros, G. D., Siomos, K. E., Fisoun, V., Dafouli, E., & Geroukalis, D. (2013). Adolescent online cyberbullying in Greece: The impact of parental online security practices, bonding, and online impulsiveness. *Journal of School Health, 83*(6), 445—453.

Frey, K., Pearson, C., & Cohen, D. (2015). Revenge is seductive, if not sweet: Why friends matter for prevention efforts. *Journal of Applied Developmental Psychology, 37*(1), 25—35.

Fridh, M., Lindström, M., & Rosvall, M. (2015). Subjective health complaints in adolescent victims of cyber harassment: Moderation through support from parents/friends-a Swedish population-based study. *BMC Public Health, 15*(1), 949.

Gamez-Gaudix, M., Gini, G., & Calvete, E. (2015). Stability of cyberbullying victimisation among adolescents: Prevalence and association with bully-victim status and psychosocial adjustment. *Computers in Human Behavior, 53*, 140—148.

Gorzig, A., & Olafsson, K. (2013). What makes a bully a cyberbully? Unravelling the characteristics of cyberbullies across twenty-five European countries. *Journal of Children and Media, 7*, 9—27.

Grigg, D. W. (2010). Cyber-aggression: Definition and concept of cyberbullying. *Journal of Psychologists and Counsellors in Schools, 20*(2), 143—156.

Grigg, D. W. (2012). Definitional constructs of cyber-bullying and cyber-aggression from a triangulatory overview: A preliminary study into elements of cyber-bullying. *Journal of Aggression, Conflict and Peace Research, 4*(4), 202—215.

Gualdo, A. G., Hunter, S. C., Durkin, K., Arnaiz, P., & Maquilon, J. J. (2015). The emotional impact of cyberbullying: Differences in perceptions and experiences as a function of role. *Computers and Education, 82*, 228—235.

Hamm, M. P., Newton, A. S., Chisholm, A., Shulhan, J., Milne, A., Sundar, P., et al. (2015). Prevalence and effect of cyber- bullying on children and young people: A scoping review of social media studies. *JAMA Pediatrics, 169*, 770—777.

Hasebrink, U., Görzig, A., Haddon, L., Kalmus, V., & Livingstone, S. (2011). *Patterns of risk and safety online: in-depth analyses from the EU kids online survey of 9- to 16-year-olds and their parents in 25 European countries.* EU Kids Online, London, UK.

Hassan, R. (2008). *The information society: Cyber dreams and digital nightmares.* Polity.

Heartfield, R., & Loukas, G. (2016). A taxonomy of attacks and a survey of defence mechanisms for semantic social engineering attacks. *ACM Computing Surveys (CSUR), 48*(3), 37.

Hempehill, S. A., & Heerde, J. A. (2014). Adolescent predictors of young adult cyberbullying perpetration and victimization among Australian youth. *Journal of Adolescent Health, 55*, 580—587.

Henry, N., & Powell, A. (2018). Technology-facilitated sexual violence: A literature review of empirical research. *Trauma, Violence & Abuse, 9*(2), 195—208.

Herring, S. C. (2001). Gender and power in online communication. In *Center for social informatics working papers.*

Hinduja, S., & Patchin, J. W. (2008). Cyberbullying: An exploratory analysis of factors related to offending and victimization. *Deviant Behavior, 29*, 129—156.

Hinduja, S., & Patchin, J. W. (2010). Bullying, cyberbullying, and suicide. *Archives of Suicide Research, 14*(3), 206–221.

Holfeld, R. (2014). Perceptions and attributions of bystanders to cyber bullying. *Computers in Human Behavior, 38,* 1–7.

Holt, T. J., Bossler, A. M., Malinkski, R., & May, D. C. (2016). Identifying predictors of unwanted online sexual conversations among youth using a low self-control and routine activity framework. *Journal of Contemporary Criminal Justice, 32*(2), 108–128.

Huesmann, L., & Guerra, N. (1997). Children's normative beliefs about aggression and aggressive behavior. *Journal of Personality and Social Psychology, 72*(2), 408–419.

Ipsos MORI. (2013). *A survey of public attitudes to Computer Security.* Home Office Research Report 75 (Annex B). London: Home Office.

Jacobs, N. C. L., Goossens, L., Dehue, F., Vollink, T., & Lechner, L. (2015). Dutch cyberbullying victims' experiences, perceptions, attitudes and motivations related to (coping with) cyberbullying: Focus group interviews. *Societies, 5,* 43–64.

Kowaliski, R. M., Toth, A., & Morgan, M. (2018). Bullying and cyberbullying in adulthood and the workplace. *The Journal of Social Psychology, 158*(1), 64–81.

Kowalski, R. M., Giumetti, G. W., Schroeder, A. N., & Lattanner, M. R. (2014). Bullying in the digital age: A critical review and meta-analysis of cyberbullying research among youth. *Psychological Bulletin, 140*(4), 1073.

Kowalski, R., & Limber, S. (2007). Electronic bullying among middle school students. *Journal of Adolescent Health, 41,* 22–30.

Kowalski, R. M., Limber, S. E., & Agatston, P. W. (2008). *Cyber bullying.* Malden MA: Blackwell Publishing.

Kowalski, R. M., Limber, S. E., & Agatston, P. W. (2012). *Cyberbullying: Bullying in the digital age* (2nd ed.). Malden, MA: Wiley-Blackwell.

Krombholz, K., Hobel, H., Huber, M., & Weippl, E. (2015). Advanced social engineering attacks. *Journal of Information Security and applications, 22,* 113–122.

Kumaraguru, P., Sheng, S., Acquisti, A., Cranor, L. F., & Hong, J. (2010). Teaching Johnny not to fall for phish. *Proc. of the ACM Transactions on Internet Technology, 10*(2), 1–31.

Lasher, S., & Baker, C. (2015). *Bullying: Evidence from the longitudinal study of young people in England 2, wave 2.* Retrieved on 2 June, 2018, from https://assets.publishing.service.gov.uk/government/uploads/system/uploads/attachment_data/file/570241/Bullying_evidence_from_the_longitudinal_study_of_young_people_in_England_2__wave_2_brief.pdf.

Latané, B., & Darley, J. M. (1970). *The unresponsive bystander: Why doesn't he help.* New York, NY: Appleton-Century Crofts.

Law, D. M., Shapka, J. D., & Olson, B. F. (2010). To control or not to control? Parenting behaviours and adolescent online aggression. *Computers in Human Behavior, 26*(6), 1651–1656.

Lenhart, A., Madden, M., Smith, A., Purcell, K., Zickuhr, K., & Rainie, L. (2011). *Teens, kindness and cruelty on social network sites: How American teens navigate the new world of "digital citizenship."* Washington, DC: Pew Research Center's Internet & American Life Project. Retrieved from http://www.pewinternet.org/2011/11/09/teens-kindness-and-cruelty-on-social-network-sites/.

Lenhart, A., Purcell, K., Smith, A., & Zichuhr, K. (2010). *Social media and mobile internet use among teens and young adults.* Washington, DC: Pew Research Center's Internet & American Life Project. Retrieved from http://www.pewinternet.org/2010/02/03/social-media-and-young-adults/.

Leukfeldt, E. (2014). Phishing for suitable targets in the Netherlands: Routine activity theory and phishing victimization. *Cyberpsychology, Behavior, and Social Networking, 17,* 551–555.

Leukfeldt, E. R., Lavorgna, A., & Kleemans, E. R. (2017). Organised cybercrime or cybercrime that is organised? An assessment of the conceptualisation of financial cybercrime as organised crime. *European Journal on Criminal Policy and Research, 23*(3), 287–300.

Lindsay, M., & Krysik, J. (2012). Online harassment among college students: A replication incorporating new internet trends. *Information, Communication & Society, 15*, 703–719.

Livingstone, S., Haddon, L., Görzig, A., & Ólafsson, K. (2011). *Risks and safety on the internet: The perspective of European children: Full findings and policy implications from the EU kids online survey of 9-16 year olds and their parents in 25 countries.*

Livingstone, S., & Smith, P. K. (2014). Annual research review: Harms experienced by child users of online and mobile technologies: The nature, prevalence and management of sexual and aggressive risks in the digital age. *Journal of Child Psychology and Psychiatry, 55*(6), 635–654.

Lovegrove, P., & Cornell, D. (2014). Patterns of bullying and victimization associated with other problem behaviors among high school students: A conditional latent class approach. *Journal of Crime and Justice, 37*(1), 5–22.

Lund, E. M., & Ross, S. W. (2017). Bullying perpetration, victimization, and demographic differences in college students: A review of the literature. *Trauma, Violence, & Abuse, 18*(3), 348–360.

Macháčková, H., Dedkova, L., & Mezulanikova, K. (2015). Brief report: The bystander effect in cyberbullying incidents. *Journal of Adolescents, 43*, 96–99.

Marcum, C. D., Higgins, G. E., & Ricketts, M. L. (2010). Potential factors of online victimization of youth: An examination of adolescent online behaviors utilizing routine activity theory. *Deviant Behavior, 31*(5), 381–410.

McGuire, M., & Dowling, S. (2013). *Cybercrime: A review of the evidence.* Retrieved June, 2018, from https://www.gov.uk/government/uploads/system/uploads/attachment_data/file/246749/horr75-summary.pdf.

Mesch, G. S. (2009). Parental mediation, online activities, and cyberbullying. *CyberPsychology and Behavior, 12*(4), 387–393.

Mishna, F., Khoury-Kassabri, M., Gadalla, T., & Daciuk, J. (2012). Risk factors for involvement in cyber bullying: Victims, bullies and bully–victims. *Children and Youth Services Review, 34*(1), 63–70.

Mishna, F., Saini, M., & Solomon, S. (2009). Ongoing and online: Children and youth's perceptions of cyberbullying. *Children and Youth Services Review, 31*, 1222–1228.

Mitchell, K. J., Ybarra, M., & Finkelhor, D. (2007). The relative importance of online victimization in understanding depression, delinquency, and substance use. *Child Maltreatment, 12*(4), 314–324.

Mobin, A., Feng, C. X., & Neudorf, C. (2017). Cybervictimization among preadolescents in a community-based sample in Canada: Prevalence and predictors. *Canadian Journal of Public Health, 108*, 475–481.

Nansel, T., Overpeck, M., Pilla, R. S., Ruan, W. J., Simmons-Morton, B., & Schmidt, P. (2001). Bullying behaviors among US youth. *Journal of the American Medical Association, 285*, 2094–2100.

Näsi, M., Oksanen, A., Keipi, T., & Räsänen, P. (2015). Cybercrime victimization among young people: A multi-nation study. *Journal of Scandinavian Studies in Criminology and Crime Prevention, 16*(2), 203–210.

Nocentini, A., Calmaestra, J. J., Schultze-Krumbholz, A., Scheithauer, H., Ortega, R., & Menesini, E. (2010). Cyberbullying: Labels, behaviors and definition in three European countries. *Australian Journal of Guidance and Counselling, 20*, 129–142.

Oberst, U., Wegmann, E., Stodt, B., Brand, M., & Chamarro, A. (2017). Negative consequences from heavy social networking in adolescents: The mediating role of fear of missing out. *Journal of Adolescence, 55*, 51–60.

Ofcom. (2016). *Children and parents: Media use and attitudes report.* London: Office of Communications.

Olenik-Shemesh, D., Heiman, T., & Eden, S. (2012). Cyberbullying victimisation in adolescence: Relationships with loneliness and depressive mood. *Emotional and Behavioural Difficulties, 17*(3–4), 361–374.

Olenik-Shemesh, D., Heiman, T., & Eden, S. (2015). Bystanders' behavior in cyberbullying episodes: Active and passive patterns in the context of personal–socio-emotional factors. *Journal of Interpersonal Violence, 32*(1), 23–48.

Olweus, D. (1993). *Bullying at school: What we know and what we can do.* Oxford, UK: Blackwell.

Olweus, D., & Limber, S. P. (2018). Some problems with cyberbullying research. *Current opinion in Psychology, 19,* 139–143.

Pew Research Center. (2014). *Online harassment.* Retrieved June, 2018, from http://www.pewinternet.org/2014/10/22/online-harassment/.

Pratt, T. C., Holtfreter, K., & Reisig, M. D. (2010). Routine online activity and internet fraud targeting: Extending the generality of routine activity theory. *Journal of Research in Crime and Delinquency, 47*(3), 267–296.

Prescott, C. (2017). *Internet access: Households and individuals 2017.* Retrieved May 2018 https://www.ons.gov.uk/peoplepopulationandcommunity/householdcharacteristics/homeinternetandsocialmediausage/bulletins/internetaccesshouseholdsandindividuals/2017.

Project deShame. (2017). *Young people's experiences of online sexual harassment.* Retrieved June, 2018, from https://www.childnet.com/ufiles/Project_deSHAME_Dec_2017_Report.pdf.

Przybylski, A. K., Murayama, K., DeHaan, C. R., & Gladwell, V. (2013). Motivational, emotional, and behavioral correlates of fear of missing out. *Computers in Human Behavior, 29*(4), 1841–1848.

Reyns, B. W. (2013). Online routines and identity theft victimization: Further expanding routine activity theory beyond direct-contact offenses. *Journal of Research in Crime and Delinquency, 50*(2), 216–238.

Reyns, B. W., Henson, B., & Fisher, B. S. (2011). Being pursued online: Applying cyberlifestyle- routine activities theory to cyberstalking victimisation. *Criminal Justice and Behavior, 38,* 1149–1169.

Rice, E., Petering, R., Rhoades, H., Winetrobe, H., Goldbach, J., Plant, A., et al. (2015). Cyberbullying perpetration and victimization among middle-school students. *American Journal of Public Health, 105*(3), e66–e72.

Ritter, B. A. (2014). Deviant behavior in computer-mediated Communication: Development and validation of a measure of cybersexual harassment. *Journal of Computer-Mediated Communication, 19*(2), 197–214.

Rivers, I., & Noret, N. (2010). 'I h8 u': Findings from a five-year study of text and email bullying. *British Educational Research Journal, 36*(4), 643–671.

Sabella, R. A., Patchin, J. W., & Hinduja, S. (2013). Cyberbullying myths and realities. *Computers in Human Behavior, 29,* 2703–2711.

Saini, H., Rao, Y. S., & Panda, T. C. (2012). Cyber-crimes and their impacts: A review. *International Journal of Engineering Research in Africa, 2*(2), 202–209.

Saridakis, G., Benson, V., Ezingeard, J. N., & Tennakoon, H. (2016). Individual information security, user behaviour and cyber victimisation: An empirical study of social networking users. *Technological Forecasting and Social Change, 102,* 320–330.

Schultze-Krumbholz, A., Schultze, M., Zagorscak, P., Wölfer, R., & Scheithauer, H. (2016). Feeling cybervictims' pain. *Aggressive Behavior, 42,* 147–156.

Shariff, S., & Hoff, D. L. (2007). Cyber bullying: Clarifying legal boundaries for school supervision in cyberspace. *International Journal of Cyber Criminology, 1,* 76–118.

Slonje, R., Smith, P. K., & FriséN, A. (2013). The nature of cyberbullying, and strategies for prevention. *Computers in Human Behavior, 29*(1), 26–32.

Smith, P. K. (2012). Cyberbullying and cyber aggression. In *Handbook of school violence and school safety* (pp. 111–121). Routledge.

Smith, P. K., del Barrio, C., & Tokunaga, R. (2013). Definitions of bullying and cyberbullying: How useful are the terms? In S. Bauman, J. Walker, & D. Cross (Eds.), *Principles of cyberbullying research: Definitions, measures, and methods* (pp. 26–40). New York: Routledge.

Smith, P. K., & Livingstone, S. (2017). Child users of online and mobile technologies—risks, harms and intervention. *Child Psychology and Psychiatry: Frameworks for Clinical Training and Practice*, 141—148.

Smith, P. K., Mahdavi, J., Carvalho, M., Fisher, S., Russell, S., & Tippett, N. (2008). Cyberbullying: Its nature and impact in secondary school pupils. *Journal of Child Psychology and Psychiatry*, 49(4), 376—385.

Sodhi, J. S., & Sharma, S. (2012). Conceptualizing of social networking sites. *International Journal of Computer Science*, 9(1), 422—428.

Song, H., Lynch, M. J., & Cochran, J. K. (2016). A macro-social exploratory analysis of the rate of interstate cyber-victimization. *American Journal of Criminal Justice*, 41(3), 583—601.

Sophos. (2011). *Stopping fake anti-virus*. Retrieved from Sophos, June 2018. Available at: https://www.sophos.com/en-us/medialibrary/Gated%20Assets/white%20papers/sophosstoppingfakeantiviruswpna.pdf.

Srivastava, S., John, O. P., Gosling, S. D., & Potter, J. (2003). Development of personality in early and middle adulthood: Set like plaster or persistent change? *Journal of Personality and Social Psychology*, 84, 1041—1053.

Sticca, F., & Perren, S. (2013). Is cyberbullying worse than traditional bullying? Examining the differential roles of medium, publicity and anonymity of the perceived severity of bullying. *Journal of Youth and Adolescence*, 42(5), 739—750.

Sticca, F., Ruggieri, S., Alsaker, F., & Perren, S. (2013). Longitudinal risk factors for cyberbullying in adolescence. *Journal of Community and Applied Social Psychology*, 23(1), 52—67.

Suler, J. (2004). The online disinhibition effect. *CyberPsychology and Behavior*, 7(3), 321—326.

Taiariol, J. (2010). *Cyberbullying: The role of family and school*. Wayne State University.

Thornberg, R. (2007). A classmate in distress: Schoolchildren as bystanders and their reasons for how they act. *Social Psychology of Education*, 10(1), 5—28.

Thornberg, R., & Jungert, T. (2013). Bystander behavior in bullying situations: Basic moral sensitivity, moral disengagement and defender self-efficacy. *Journal of Adolescence*, 36, 475—483.

Tokunaga, R. S. (2010). Following you home from school: A critical review and synthesis of research on cyberbullying victimization. *Computers in Human Behavior*, 26, 277—287.

Tynes, B., Reynolds, L., & Greenfield, P. M. (2003). Adolescence, race, and ethnicity on the internet: A comparison of discourse in monitored vs. unmonitored chat rooms. *Applied Developmental Psychology*, 25, 667—684.

Vandebosch, H., & Van Cleemput, K. (2008). Defining cyberbullying: A qualitative research into the perceptions of youngsters. *CyberPsychology and Behavior*, 11(4), 499—503.

van de Weijer, S. G. A., Leukfeldt, R., & Bernasco, W. (2018). Determinants of reporting cybercrimes: A comparison between identify theft, consumer fraud, and hacking. *European Journal of Criminology*, 0, 1—23.

Weiner, I., & Greene, R. (2008). *Handbook of personality assessment*. Hoboken, New Jersey: John Wiley & Sons.

Willard, N. E. (2007). *Cyberbullying and cyberthreats: Responding to the challenge of online social aggression, threats, and distress*. Research Press.

Willard, N. (2011). School response to cyberbullying and sexting: The legal challenges. *Brigham Young University Education and Law Journal*, 2011(1), 75—125.

Williams, K. R., & Guerra, N. G. (2007). Prevalence and predictors of internet bullying. *Journal of Adolescent Health*, 41(6), S14—S21.

Wong, D., Chan, H., & Cheng, C. (2014). Cyberbullying perpetration and victimization among adolescents in Hong Kong. *Children and Youth Services Review*, 36, 133—140.

Wright, M. F. (2014). Predictors of anonymous cyber aggression: The role of adolescents' beliefs about anonymity, aggression, and the permanency of digital content. *Cyberpsychology, Behavior, and Social Networking*, 17(7), 431—438.

Wright, R. T., Chakraborty, S., Basoglu, A., & Marett, K. (2010). Where did they go right? Understanding the deception in phishing communications. *Group Decision and Negotiation, 19,* 391–416.

Wright, M. F., & Li, Y. (2013). The association between cyber victimization and subsequent cyber aggression: The moderating effect of peer rejection. *Journal of Youth and Adolescence, 42*(5), 662–674.

Yar, M. (2005). The novelty of 'cybercrime' an assessment in light of routine activity theory. *European Journal of Criminology, 2*(4), 407–427.

Ybarra, M., & Mitchell, K. (2004). Online aggressor/targets, aggressors, and targets: A comparison of associated youth characteristics. *Journal of Child Psychology and Psychiatry, 45,* 308–316.

Ybarra, M. L., & Mitchell, K. J. (2007). Prevalence and frequency of Internet harassment instigation: Implications for adolescent health. *Journal of Adolescent Health, 41*(2), 189–195.

Cyberterrorism — the spectre that is the convergence of the physical and virtual worlds

Namosha Veerasamy

Council for Scientific and Industrial Research (CSIR), Pretoria, South Africa

OUTLINE

Emerging Cyber Threats and Cognitive Vulnerabilities
https://doi.org/10.1016/B978-0-12-816203-3.00002-2

27

Introduction

The concern over whether cyberterrorism could actually materialize has grown in recent years. Cyberterrorism refers to the convergence of cyberspace and acts of terrorism. This type of threat overlaps the physical and virtual domain with the risk of terrorists acting out in the digital world of cyberspace. 'Since terrorists can use cyber tools as a tactic to advance their agenda, then cyber terrorism can exist. Unfortunately some scoff at the notion that terrorists can use cyber techniques to accomplish violent aims (Paulose, 2013).' There is little to suggest that terrorist groups have the inclination, let alone the capability, to launch a major cyberattack (Hardy, 2017). While, the concept is not new, many debate whether cyberterrorism is a real threat and what the label of cyberterrorism actually refers to. This chapter aims to provide some background to where the term originates, what it denotes and its significance in this digital world we are living in.

The world of terrorism is expanding. New weapons are emerging with cyberattacks also having the ability to gain publicity, exposure and damage. As a spectre, cyberterrorism serves as a worrying threat about an imminent attack on a critical system, network or infrastructure that could cause wide-scale damage or affect numerous lives.

The term cyberterrorism was coined over 20 years ago but continues to be a debatable topic due to varying opinions about its likelihood and impact. One camp asserts that terrorists will not use cyber techniques to carry out violent acts. The other camp tries to show that critical information and communications technology (ICT) systems are vulnerable to attack which could have devastating consequences if targeted. Thus, the concept of cyberterrorism has mixed concerns.

The first definition stemmed from Barry C Collin in the late 1980s in reference to the confluence of cyberspace and terrorism (Samuel & Osman, 2014). Over the years, the terms has grown in response to the risk of cyberthreats and the increased use of the digital domain. There had been growing concern that terrorists may change their tactics, targets and weapons to the digital environment and this initiated the concept of cyberterrorism. 'Terrorist organisations have invaded cyberspace and made it a battleground. They no longer rely on military force such as weapons, armour and bombs only. Instead, they become more and more savvy, and their strategies and tactics have technological orientation (Zerzri, 2017).' The possibility that terrorists may use cyber tools as part of their arsenal has grown over the years. This chapter looks at clarifying the threat of cyberterrorism so as to analyze the underlying threat.

In order to understand the concept of cyberterrorism, it is important to place in context of terrorism in general. A discussion follows on the concept of terrorism.

Terrorism

Firstly, we look at unfolding the idea of terrorism to see how cyber-terrorism fits into it as a possible paradigm. Definitions of terrorism stem from the early 1970s and are still relevant and applicable today. In this section, various definitions of terrorism are discussed in order to place the concept of cyberterrorism in context.

The United States still utilizes the definition provided in the US Code Title 22 Section 2656f (d) since 1983 (United States Government, 1983). It states that terrorism refers to premeditated political violence carried out against non-combatant groups by sub-national or clandestine organizations or agents with the intention of creating an influence on their target. This definition emphasizes the use of pre-meditated violence stemming from political motivations that aims to influence a target group.

Furthermore, the term international terrorism has also surfaced. With international terrorism, it targets citizens or territorial regions in more than one country. Terrorist groups may operate in international terrorism when they have subgroups practicing across countries.

Moreover, the key statutory concepts defined in the United Kingdom Terrorism Act of 2000 (United Kingdom Government, 2000) state that:

(1) 'Terrorism' means the use or threat of action where:
   a. The action falls within subsection (2)
   b. The use or threat is designed to influence the government or to intimidate the public or a section of the public and

    c. The use or threat is made for the purpose of advancing a political, religious or ideological cause

(2) Action falls within this subsection if it:

    a. Involves serious violence against a person

    b. Involves serious damage to property

    c. Endangers a person's life, other than that of the person committing the action

    d. Creates a serious risk to the health or safety of the public or a section of the public or

    e. Is designed to seriously interfere with or seriously to disrupt an electronic system

(3) The use or threat of action falling within subsection (2) which involves the use of firearms or explosives is terrorism whether or not subsection (1) (b) is satisfied

Furthermore, Ruby (2002) has emphasized three critical aspects in the definition of terrorism and will be discussed next. Ruby looks at the motivation and the source of the attacks to indicate reasoning and operation of terrorists.

The first aspect that Ruby (2002) looks at is that terrorism must have a political motivation. In this way, violent acts like robbery, homicide or kidnapping that are carried out for personal or criminal goals do not constitute terrorism. The social and psychological reasoning behind such personal and criminal acts differ from terrorist goals.

Secondly, Ruby (2002) indicates that the focus of terrorist acts is non-combatants. Non-combatants denote civilians who do not belong to the military services or are involved in hostile military operations. However, a terrorist attack can be carried out on military members during peacetime. (For example, On June 116, the US Air Force housing complex in Khobar Towers in Dhahran, Saudi Arabia, was struck by a terrorist truck bomb.)

Thirdly, Ruby (2002) states that sub-national groups or clandestine agents execute terrorism. Therefore, political violence carried out by nation-states is not considered terrorism. Ruby expands this point by explaining that during declared war or announced conflict there is an expectation of attacks, which will most likely be on industrial or military complexes. However, violent attacks from clandestine groups are usually random and have a crippling effect on non-combatants.

In addition, terrorism results in fear in not only the victim but also the audience unrelated to the victim. Furthermore, terrorism can also occur through the threat of violence, with any actual act of violence as it creates fear of a possible attack. This generation of fear is a key aspect in the concept of terrorism.

In October 2004, the United Nations Security Council (UNSC) passed Resolution 1566 (2004), which defines terrorism and states that no terrorist acts will be condoned for political or ideological reasons:

Terrorist attacks justified by political, racial, ethnicity, religion, philosophy, ideologies reasoning may include:

• The targeting civilians to cause death or critical injury
• Taking of hostages in order to create a state of terror in a public area on a group of specific people
• Intimidation of the population of forcing of the government or international organization

In the Philippines and Australia, terrorism is seen to be related to the interference of electronic systems or critical infrastructure. Australia's Security Legislation Amendment (Terrorism) Act (Australian Governement, 2002) indicates that terrorism can consist of actions that:

1. Create a serious risk to the health or safety of the public or section of the public
2. Seriously interfere with, seriously disrupt, or destroy an electronic system including, but not limited to:
    a) An information system, or
    b) A financial system, or
    c) A system used for the delivery of essential government services, or
    d) A system used for, or by an essential public utility, or
    e) A system used for, or by a transport system

The Philippines' Anti-Terrorism Act (Phillipines Government, 2003) describes terrorism as acts that can cause serious interference with, or serious disruption of, essential service, vital facility, and critical infrastructure. This definition focusses on disruptions or interference with essential equipment or systems.

What we may find is that terrorism operates outside the rules of orderly society. In some instances, it may be difficult to clearly define an incident as terrorism. For example, if a nation's citizens are suffering and being brutalized by a corrupt government, were they to rebel against this regime, would this be considered terrorism? However, there are some key ideas that constitute terrorism and this will be summarized (Veerasamy, 2014).

Threats or actions that fall into and either sub-section (1) or (2) and sub-section (3).

1. Threats or actions to intimidate the government or the public, or
2. Threats or actions to promote a political or ideological issue
3. Threats or acts of serious violence

   a) Against people, or
   b) Causes major damage to property, or
   c) Harms a human life other than the person performing the act, or
   d) Causes a risk to health or safety of people or critical service, or
   e) Aims to cause interference with electronic systems, or
   f) Carried out by clandestine groups or sub-national groups
4. EXCEPTION: A threat or action that falls into condition 3 and
   involves firearms/explosives is terrorism even if condition 1 is not
   met.

Now that the concept of terrorism has been explained, the discussion
moves on to the clarification of cyberterrorism.

Cyberterrorism

Since 9/11 institutional fears of cyberattacks on financial institutions,
military installations, power grids, nuclear facilities, chemical plants,
dams, airports or telecommunications and navigation satellites have
grown exponentially (IT Web, 2018). Thus, there is increasing concern that
the threat of terrorism may move in the realm of cyberspace. With the
growing dependence on computers, networks and ICT infrastructure, a
major attack on a critical system could have a catastrophic result.

One of the most common definitions is from Dorothy Denning's testimony at the Special Oversight Panel on Terrorism in 2000. According to
Denning, cyberterrorism can be defined as (2000):

> The convergence of cyberspace and terrorism. It refers to unlawful attacks and
> threats of attacks against computers, networks and the information stored therein
> when done to intimidate or coerce a government or its people in furtherance of polit-
> ical or social objectives. Further, to qualify as cyberterrorism, an attack should result in
> violence against persons or property, or at least cause enough harm to generate fear.
> Attacks that lead to death or bodily injury, explosions, or severe economic loss would
> be examples.

Serious attacks against critical infrastructures could be acts of cyberterrorism, depending on their impact. Attacks that disrupt nonessential
services or that are mainly a costly nuisance would not necessarily
constitute cyberterrorism. Cybercrime is mainly carried out for economic
advantages and hacking is also often motivated by the thrill of the exploit
and to satisfy the hacker's ego. Cyberterrorism is typically driven by an
ideology with the goal of causing shock, alarm and panic.

Desouza and Hensgen (2003) define cyberterrorism as a purposeful act
motivated by personal or political reasons that aims to disrupt or destroy
stable organizations or nations using electronic devices targeted at ICT

systems like computers, programs and other methods of electronic communication, exchange and storage.

Furthermore, another popular definition stems from the Federal Bureau of Investigations (FBI, 2002). It says that cyberterrorism is the:

> Pre-meditated politically motivated attack against information, computer systems, computer programs and data which results in violence against non-combatant targets by sub-national groups or clandestine agents.

In summary cyberterrorism relates to the following issues:

- Political or ideological motivation (Ideological is an umbrella term referring to social, religious, activists, ethical and stand-alone issues driving terrorism)
- Threats or actions that aim to influence the government or public
- Causing harm through the infliction of fearful and shocking attacks on ICT systems
- May harm human lives, cause risks to the health and safety of people and critical systems
- Digital attacks on ICT infrastructure
- Performed by clandestine groups or sub-national groups

Thus, the combination of cyberattacks and terrorism has resulted in the concept of cyberterrorism that refers to exploits carried out against computer, networks, cyberspace and technological systems. In line with terrorism, cyberterrorism tries to sway or influence a sector of the population or the government in order to promote certain political, religious, social or ideological objectives. Typical examples of cyberterrorism would include:

- Breaching banking systems
- Breakdown of energy supply through attack on computer systems
- Disruption of governmental computer networks
- Sabotaging cell phone networks
- Interference of satellite-based systems
- Compromise of news services

A key component of whether an incident can be considered cyberterrorism is to look at the attacker's method of preparations, means, target and motive. For example, research can be done on the Internet on how to build a bomb, and then detonate it at a clothing warehouse. The preparation was digital and the attack was physical but whether it is considered as cyberterrorism will also depend on the motive. Since a physical storehouse of clothing is not directly related to critical ICT infrastructure, this would be considered more a terrorist act than cyberterrorism. However, if a terrorist group does research on the Internet, builds a bomb and then explodes it at a cell phone company and claims responsibility for interfering with the communications, then this would be an act of cyberterrorism. An attacker could also do research in a book on how a power plant functions; interfere with the electronic system and then cause an electrical explosion. This attack which is a combination of digital and physical interactions could also be considered cyberterrorism when motivated by some terrorist ideology.

Critical as to whether a cyberattack can be considered cyberterrorism will be the reasoning that motivates the attack in the first place. The next section looks at the motivation behind terrorism to place cyberterrorism in context.

Motivation

Various factors can influence the development of a cyberterrorist. The reasoning to carry out online onslaughts can occur as a result of a deeper motivation. In order to understand what drives cyberterrorism, it is important to look at the motivating factors of terrorist groups in general. Individuals who commit cybercrimes are personally motivated, but cyberterrorists have much deeper motivations, be it political, religious or social (Parker in Canter, 2009). The main types of terrorism are (Armistead, 2004; Flemming & Stohl, 2000; Nelson, Choi, Mitchell, & Gagnon, 1999; Weimann, 2004):

- Nationalist/Ethnic: aim to create a new political order, established based on view of ethnic dominance (e.g., Liberation Tigers of Tamil Eelam (LTTE), Provisional Wing of the Irish Republican Army (PIRA)
- Religious: belief in strong theological views and values (e.g., Aum Shinrikyo (AUM), ISIS)
- Political: left wing (revolutionary) and right wing (far-right extremists) intention to capture political power, sometimes based on belief of superiority (e.g. Japanese Red Army, German National Socialist Underground)
- Single issue (New Age) tend to promote a specific contentious issue (e.g. Earth Liberation Front, People for the Ethical Treatment of Animals (PETA))

One may find that terrorists mainly have an affiliation to specific group, organization or cause. Their malicious actions may aim to create a spectacle (theatrical and public incidents) so as to advance their groups' ideologies.

Overall, terrorist groups may choose the virtual domain in order to launch a digital attack in order to promote their ideological viewpoints.

With the growth and development of cyber arsenal, we could soon see technological weapons become the norm for terrorist groups. Cyberterrorism may present certain advantages over traditional terrorist tactics. The benefits of cyberterrorism over conventional terrorism approaches are discussed next.

Advantage

The execution of attacks on information technology instead of traditional methods on real-world physical targets offers certain benefits. Electronic attacks, hacking, viruses and digital threats can be favoured due to its affordability, remote accessibility and anonymity. According to Denning (2000), the advantage of cyberterrorism is that it can be conducted remotely, anonymously, as well less expensively as it does not require the purchase of explosives or sacrificing one's life in a suicide mission.

Gorge (2007) talks of the usefulness of cyberspace having no borders with physical control, the 'legal confusion' making it easier for attackers, great impact potential and ability for target identification in cyberspace. It is often very difficult to determine which laws apply when cyberattacks could span several jurisdictions. Furthermore, there is no singular controlling body that legislates activity in cyberspace which makes it quite difficult to monitor and enforce control. This makes the appeal of cyberspace hacking and exploits alluring to terrorists as their identity can be hidden and they have the ability to reach a wide audience remotely. Automation and the ability to reach a large number of targets are other advantages of using cyberspace as a platform to launch attacks. The dependence and widespread use of ICT has also become arsenal for adversaries to target and infiltrate.

Another critical aspect to consider in how terrorism differs from cybercrime is to look at the effects and outcomes of the attack. The next section addresses the main effects of cyberterrorism.

Effects

Another essential characteristic of cyberterrorism is the effect of the attack. Affecting crucial services may have a major impact on the civilian population. Disrupting core competencies like air travel, manufacturing, health care and emergency facilities could have a detrimental effect on the lives of the public. Terrorist organizations seek to create publicity and cause devastation with their attacks. Similarly, cyberterrorists will target critical infrastructure of vital community services in order to create the biggest effect. Disruption of sectors, data theft and disclosure, infiltration and destruction of systems and loss of availability are all effects that cyberterrorism would focus their efforts toward. Cyberterrorists want to expose weaknesses in the systems of their target in order to create disarray, outrage and disruption. A virus that opens up popup boxes would not be considered cyberterrorism as its effect is not as wide-scale as bringing down the water system in a community. The theft of a small amount of data does not compare to a full-blown attack that cripples the airport announcement system. Cyberterrorism has a far wider range of attack and effects than simple nuisance, annoyance or inconvenience.

A cyberterrorist could create a virus to start infiltrating a network at certain points in time, then mask itself for a short period and then reappear once more to cause more damage to computers and networks. Stuxnet operated on this approach whereby small changes were made to the centrifuges to degrade over time. A digital weapon, like a virus, can be programmed to operate to go off at a certain time or only if a certain condition is met (Matusitz, 2008). This differs with analog weapons which normally can only be activated once – a gas attack or a bomb that can only be triggered once and will unlikely be able to be reset or exploded again in the future. Conventional weapons thus operate in linearity whereby there is an attack that progresses from one stage to another. Cyberterrorist attacks may not necessarily have a linear sequential order. This also makes cyberattacks more difficult to detect as there may not have a defined start and end point. Cyberattacks may also become viral or propagate in a network and cause further damage. Thus, an attack could be targeted at a specific victim but eventually even reach a wider audience or affect other entities and parties.

Cyberterrorism sees a shift from 'spatialization' whereby space and time are challenged. There are no restrictive time constraints or spatial limitations for perpetrators. Time and space in the cyber world are indefinite, invisible and unclear. Budding terrorists can engage, delve and scour the virtual world for potential exploits without consideration of their physical location or boundaries at any time of day or night. Targets and weapons are accessible and can be acquired freely through research and information gathering in the digital world. In the underworld of the dark web, and even the open Internet, various tools are accessible that can be used to launch cyberattacks. Cyberterrorism as an attack vector may become more viable as the real and virtual worlds become more intertwined.

A further effect of cyberterrorism is the cascading failures that can occur as a result of a cyberattack on critical infrastructure. A cascading failure refers to a failure in a network or a system of interconnected parts (Matusitz, 2008). Once a vital node in a link is taken down, other key nodes can also be affected. The damage to a critical node can cause other key nodes to fail. Cyberterrorism has the potential to trigger serious system unavailability. This can further lead to widespread panic, alarm and confusion. Many crucial systems in emergency services, airports, banks and power plants now make use of computer control technology. A cascading failure in these environments would have significant effects and even unleash a wave of chaos or loss of life.

Practices

Cyberterrorism entails leveraging ICT infrastructure in order to create real-life damage or critical disruption with the goal of promoting the attackers' underlying political, religious or social issue. Terrorists may force their intentions into the digital space in order to advance their agendas. Typical practices of cyberterrorists may include:

- Denial of Service (Dos) attacks and Distributed Denial of Service attacks (DDos)
- Web defacement which may include negative or derogatory comments against the government, political parties or other religious organizations
- Misinformation campaigns
- Theft or corruption of critical data-unauthorized access to sensitive information with the goal of accessing, stealing or destroying data
- Exploitation of system vulnerabilities (to cause unavailability, loss of service, misrepresentation)
- Virus attacks which cause system failover, unavailability or disruption of services

Target

With the growing interconnectedness of critical infrastructures on ICT, the selection of a target that allows the maximum level of disruption would significantly influence terrorists (Ahmad & Yunos, 2012).

Cyberterrorists will typically focus their attack on core systems, networks and targets that serve a critical functionality. Systems that support daily operations and human life are prime targets for cyberterrorists. Efforts to interfere with critical systems would have a more detrimental effect and could cause more wide-scale disturbances, fear and hype. Examples of possible targets are shown in Fig. 2.1 (Collin, 1997; Desouza & Hensgen, 2003; Foltz, 2004; Lewis, 2002).

According to Desouza and Hensgen (2003) the inherent dependency of businesses on electronics will allow cyberterrorists to search for ways to reveal vulnerabilities in critical services like financial institutions (banks, brokers), e-commerce sectors, transportation services, fuel supplies, power and governmental systems. Folz (2004) also talks of the including interference or disruption of information and communications networks, emergency services, infrastructure systems, transportation systems, banking and finance systems and government services.

Other examples include cyberterrorist launching attacks against the emergency services department to prevent responses to emergency calls. This could result in injury and even death if patients cannot be reached. Cyberterrorists might attack a banking system such that funds are frozen. If people cannot access their money, this could cause wide-scale panic. Another example would be to interfere with the rail system and prevent trains from reaching their destinations. Militaries could also be targeted by attacks on their communication systems or ICT equipment. All these hypothetical scenarios show how detrimental an attack on a critical infrastructure could be.

Cyberterrorism can sometimes be blurred with cybercrime. However, there are some key differences that have been explained. The next section discusses a few queries about cyberterrorism.

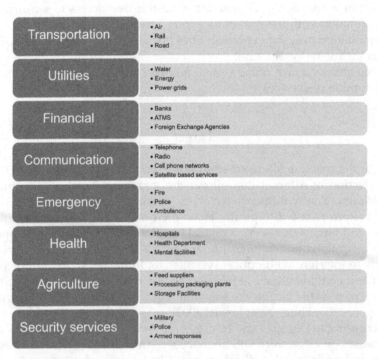

FIGURE 2.1 Potential cyberterrorist targets. *Credit: Own Compilation.*

In order to further explain the concept of cyberterrorism more effectively, five common queries surrounding cyberterrorism are briefly placed in context.

Query 1: If there is a cyberattack, should it be labelled as cyberterrorism?
Query 2: What is the difference between cyberterrorism and hacktivism?
Query 3: Can I become a victim of cyberterrorism? (Are cyberterrorists out to target me personally?)
Query 4: When terrorist groups use cyberspace to communicate, recruit or publicize their vision, mission and activities in a digital domain, can this be considered as cyberterrorism?
Query 5: Do cyberterrorists aim to steal money? When terrorists engage in the digital domain, this is cyberterrorism.

Query 1: If there is a cyberattack should it be labelled as cyberterrorism?

Any cyberattack should not be called cyberterrorism in the media. Cyberattacks occur on networks all the time and are typically carried out through weaknesses and exploits in the systems. Malicious hackers may want to prevent systems from being available, choose to destroy data or interfere with the proper operation of ICT infrastructure. In order to carry out a cyberterrorist attack, the perpetrator, motive, target, aim, and effect need to be evaluated. Attacks stemming from terrorist groups aiming to interfere/disrupt critical systems with the goal of promoting a philosophical ideal related to religion, political or socio-political uses may be termed cyberterrorism. However, an attacker trying to expose a company's password list may not be hacking to protest the government.

All acts of 'Internet anarchy' do not necessarily constitute cyberterrorism. Cybercriminals hack for different purposes than cyberterrorists. The goal in terrorism is to inflict pain, suffering and fear on its victims. Cybercriminals, however, hack for financial benefits, fraud, boosting their ego, challenging themselves or revenge. Cyberterrorists aim to destroy and damage critical infrastructure in order to promote their cause, gain publicity and overall to cause fear.

While cybercrime is often motivated by economic gain, and hacking, or Internet vandalism, often is done to satisfy the hacker's ego, cyberterror is fuelled by an ideology (Curran, 2016).

Query 2: What is the difference between cyberterrorism and hacktivism?

Various ideas surround the concept of cyberterrorism. In some instances, online directed action to protest a specific cause is being labelled cyberterrorism. Civil disobedience is now moving into the realm of cyberspace to become Electronic Civil Disobedience (ECD) to practice socio-political resistance within digital networks. One area to be debated is whether computer hacking for political activism should be considered cyberterrorism. Hacktivism and Internet vandalism may not directly threaten the lives and livelihoods of victims and so may incorrectly be labelled as cyberterrorism. The defacement of websites may be considered as a form on digital vandalism and initially was carried out to boost the ego of the attacker. Thus, the effect of the 'Internet anarchy' plays an influential role in whether a digital attack can be considered as an act of cyberterrorism. Cyberterrorism may incorrectly be confused with hacktivism and ECD and thus it would be good to consider the context of cyberterrorism.

Davis (2016) differentiates between hacking and cyberterrorism in the domain of health care as follows:

> Hacktivists are politically-motivated, targeting institutions with opposing political views to their agenda. They most commonly attack with a Dos method, overloading a server until it crashes. When it comes to healthcare, hacktivists are looking for specific patient data, intellectual property or they're trying to embarrass the institution.

> Cyberterrorists target systems to disrupt or destroy critical services and infrastructure of a specific nation, sector or organization. Attacks on the healthcare sector are designed to frame a lesser hacking group to cause turmoil or cause panic.

Hacktivists may hack to show support for a particular cause or issue and do so by interfering with services. Sites may be shut down or corporate information is disclosed. Thus, serious damage is not typically carried out. Cyberterrorists go a step further by targeting critical infrastructure and services and causing wide-scale damage and shock.

Hacktivism includes ECD and can consist of operations like virtual sit-ins and blockades, automated email bombs, web hacks and computer break-ins (Denning, 2001). Moreover, Denning describes each of these operations as follows:

- Virtual sit-in: Thousands of activists simultaneously visit a website and attempt to generate so much traffic against the site that other users cannot reach it.
- Email bombs: bombard with thousands of messages at once. It may be distributed with the aid of automated tools

- Web hacks and computer break-ins: A way in which hacktivists can alter what viewers see on a website by tampering with the Domain Name Service so that the site's domain name resolves to the Internet protocol address of some other site.

Query 3: Can I become a victim of cyberterrorism (Are cyberterrorists out to target me personally?)

A cyberterrorist would typically attack a critical national target or systems that support the government, state or core services. Cyberterrorism is the use of computer networks for the purpose of posing harm to human life or to destroy most of the important and national critical infrastructure in a way that will paralyze the nation and also its citizens (Ahmad, Yunos, & Sahib, 2012) Cyberterrorists are mainly driven by political, religious or philosophical reasoning and would seldom pick a random person to attack. The focus of their attack is to cause a wide-scale disaster and create publicity for their cause. Thus, it is very unlikely that single targeted civilian would be attacked by cyberterrorists. Cyberterrorists aim for destruction on a far bigger scale with more devastating consequences. Supervisory Control and Data Acquisition (SCADA) system may be especially vulnerable, and due to their importance for controlling infrastructure, they may become an attractive target for cyberterrorists (Wilson, 2005).

However, ordinary people can fall victim to other common hacks like phishing, identity theft and social engineering. Everyday criminals are on the prowl looking for victims that can be tricked into revealing sensitive passwords and credit card information. Therefore, while the risk of a cyberterrorist attack on an individual is very unlikely, there are still risks in falling victims to ordinary cybercriminals.

The effects of cyberterrorism could, however, affect individuals in a personal capacity. For example, if a bank system is taken offline by a political group protesting the government, an individual may not be able to access funds. Another example would be if a hospital system is hacked and tampered by a religious extremist; this could have a direct effect on a person. Cyberterrorists may not target a specific individual but the effects have far-reaching consequences as the goals are mainly to cause fear, panic and aggravate the wider population.

Query 4: When terrorists groups use cyberspace to communicate, recruit or publicize their vision, mission and activities in a digital domain, can this be considered cyberterrorism?

Talihärm (2010) states that the list of Internet-based terrorism actions includes propaganda, public relations, sharing information through instructions/manuals, fundraising, communication and recruitment. Such activities actually help terrorism in general and are not to be considered as acts of cyberterrorism. Cyberterrorism is the actual attack of information and communication infrastructure motivated by political, religious and philosophical objectives. Cyberterrorism entails a co-ordinated attack against a computer system or network to disrupt the equipment or operations in order to promote a political, religious or social cause.

Terrorist groups now use the Internet to communicate via websites, chat rooms and email to raise funds and to covertly gather intelligence on future targets (Wilson, 2005). Today, social media and the Internet are being used to radicalize, transform, misinform and recruit members into terrorist organizations. Such activities may support terrorism in general but do not constitute cyberterrorism. Use of the Internet to assist with terrorist activities is incorrectly being labelled as cyberterrorism instead of considering such activities as support functions to terrorism.

Query 5: Do cyberterrorists aim to steal money?

Terrorists may try to raise funds for their organization through auctions, fake drugs, casinos, donations and financial laundering through use of the digital world. However, this is not their primary goal. Driven by political, ideological or religious reasoning, cyberterrorists would pursue opportunities to cause disturbances to critical infrastructure. Terrorists groups may run phishing scams or commit crimes of credit card theft or online banking theft for financial support to their group. A terrorist who hacks into a personal bank account to steal credit card information is not a cyberterrorist, even if the funds are used to support terrorism — this is simply a case of hacking or cybercrime committed by a terrorist (Parker (in Canter 2009)).

The raising of funds can help assist terrorist groups in their operations but the primary practice of cyberterrorism is not merely to steal money. The purpose of interfering with a bank or foreign exchange facility would be to cause wide-scale panic and create publicity for their cause.

Terrorists mainly aim to look for ways to interfere in the way we live — the manner in which we eat, drink, communicate, move around and get help. Thus, while financial support is required to fund terrorist organizations, their primary goal is not to generate money. A genuine cyberterrorist will seek to identify ways to interfere with a critical infrastructure and thus cause discomfort, inaccessibility or inconvenience.

Overall, the differentiation between cyberterrorists, hackers and terrorists is explained with the use of examples in Fig. 2.2 to show the difference in their motivation and modus operandi.

In cyberterrorism, the lines between the physical and digital world become blurred. Terrorists may use the cyber world to engage in, facilitate communications and promote their causes. Cyberterrorists may target the ICT domain to cause destruction and devastation. Thus, cyberterrorism brings together these two worlds. In the next section, the merging of the physical and digital worlds will be elaborated on.

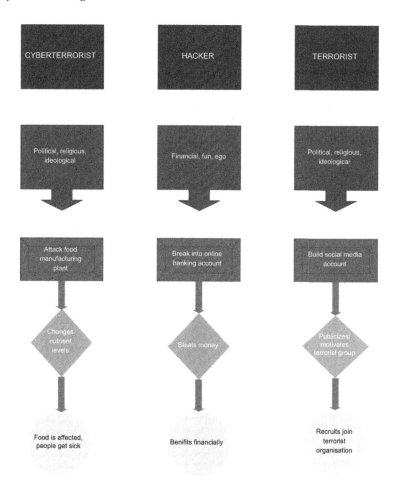

FIGURE 2.2 Differentiation between cyberterrorist, hacker and terrorist. *Credit: Own Compilation.*

Convergence of physical and digital worlds

The physical world and digital world have converged into devices and systems that now operate on the concept of being 'smart' (Fig. 2.3). The Internet of Things has opened up the possibility of using fridges that track grocery stocks, homes that have its lighting, heating and entertainment controlled by smartphones and garage doors that open based on the location of your car. Critical infrastructure like power plants and water systems use SCADA which is also the foundation of envisaged 'smart cities' and modern military equipment. Targeting these smart systems, terrorists could destroy and influence critical systems that affect the daily lives of society. Terrorists could cripple economic-, military- and civilian-dependent systems by attacking core ICT infrastructure. Due to the development of smart devices, systems and cities, this has opened up an avenue for digital exploitation.

In recent years, there has been an increase in the number of Advanced Persistent Attacks (APTs) that threaten governmental and civilian infrastructure (Fig. 2.3). A prime example is the Stuxnet virus that infected the nuclear facilities in Iran. It was nicknamed the 'world's first digital weapon' and showed the possibility of causing large-scale damage from computer equipment. Also, an energy provider in Ukraine was attacked resulting in large blackouts in 2015. A small dam in Rye Brook, New York, was reportedly attacked by an Iranian group in 2013. Hackers were able to access the core command and control system. In 2012, the Flame malware was able to render computers in the Iranian energy sector useless and was also considered as a huge cyber weapon. These are just a few of the many threatening attacks that have occurred on critical systems and demonstrate the negative outcomes from cyberattacks driven by terrorist objectives.

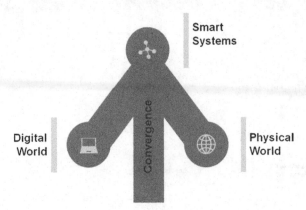

FIGURE 2.3 Spectre convergence of the physical and digital worlds. *Credit: Own Compilation.*

A cyberterrorist attack may not be restricted to industrial systems. A cyberterror attack vector could also include common hacking techniques like cross-site scripting, vulnerability exploitation and SQL injection to target a critical server or website. However, spear phishing, data theft, online casinos and gambling could also be used to fund and store monetary resources used to support real-world terrorism. These are more supportive functions that the digital domain plays in the world of terrorism.

The jihadist insurgents in Syria and Iraq use all manner of social media apps and file-sharing platforms, most prominently Ask.fm, Facebook, Instagram, WhatsApp, Paltalk, Viper, JustPaste.it and Tumblr (Klausen, 2015). Terrorist recruitment, fundraising, propaganda, and influence campaigns are also carried out in the digital domain. However, such support capabilities aid the activities of terrorist groups in general and are thus not cyberterrorist activities. Computer technology in this way can facilitate terrorism by providing ideal mediums through their organizational message, motive and activities are promoted. Digital technologies provide for mechanisms through which terrorists groups can communicate, co-ordinate and perform intelligence on their targets. Flemming and Stohl (2000) mentions that computer technology can help viable support structures to further terrorist tactical and strategic goals through the utilization of political propaganda (including disinformation programs), recruitment, financing, intra and inter-group communication, co-ordination and information/intelligence gathering. Thus, there exists a differentiation between how terrorists use the Internet for their benefit and actual cyberterrorism acts. Cyberterrorism should not be confused with terrorist organizations' radicalization campaigns on social media, websites, blogs and other interactive forums. Such practices serve as propaganda, publicity and recruitment into terrorist groups which eventually may lead to terrorism in general.

Overall, certain technological capabilities are also enhancing terrorism. Encryption software like TOR is used in communications with journalists to obscure locational information (Klausen, 2015). Encryption can hide terrorist group activities and conceal their true intentions. With the use of anonymizing technologies and even the use of the dark web, terrorist groups are finding ingenious ways to mask their actual communications and harmful plans. Thus, computer technologies are providing innovative methods that terrorists can use to their advantage. Such technological capabilities are aiding the terrorist groups in general in their operations but do not necessarily constitute cyberterrorism. Therefore, it is important to differentiate between cyberterrorism itself and support functions of ICT that aid terrorism.

Composition of an attack

Grant, Venter, and Eloff (2007) identified nine stages of an attack. They are: Footprinting, Reconnaissance, Vulnerability Identification, Penetration, Control, Embedding, Data extraction, Attack relay and Attack dissemination. Brummel (2010) classified the high-level stages as Footprint, Scanning, Enumeration and System Hacking. van Heerden, Irwin, and Burke (2012) proposed the stages of an attack as Target Identification, Reconnaissance, Attack Phase, Ramp-up, Damage, Residue and Post-attack reconnaissance. To simplify the most relevant phases will be expanded upon to show their application in a cyberterrorism attack.

- Target Identification – selection of the target and in this case motivated by religious, political or ideological standpoint. A specific device or entity (company, organization, state or governmental institution) is chosen as the target. For example, a terrorist organization could identify that it would like to infiltrate a critical service like the water sanitation system.
- Reconnaissance – information gathering and footprinting the target in order to identify potential weaknesses and how the system can be attacked. This would typically entail the terrorist organization gathering information about the water sanitation system and identifying a backdoor through which it will plant the exploit. Technical elements will be investigated in order to develop and ascertain how an exploit can be launched.
- Vulnerability Exploitation – the actual penetration of the system and execution of attack. A terrorist group may send in an operative into the organization posing as an employee and plant a virus using a USB device onto the systems. Once the device has been deployed onto the system the cyberattack will be executed. This may result in the water being tainted and contaminated water being distributed to the public. The perpetrators may want to create media coverage about their attack and claim responsibility. The attack may cause sickness and even death in the affected area due to the interference of the water checks.

The description of the attack composition indicates how a terrorist organization may go about pinpointing and executing a cyberattack with the goal of advancing their underlying objectives. A fundamental aspect of the attack is the creation of fear. Terrorist organizations operate on the basis of driving fear into the minds of the public. In the next section, the principle of fear generation by terrorists is discussed.

Fear

Ghosh, Prelas, Viswanath, and Loyalka (2010) state that cyberterrorism is the abuse of information technology to create violence, damage and fear. With terrorism, an underlying goal is the creation of fear in the minds of the victims. To extend this to the digital realm, for a cyberattack to be labelled as cyberterrorism, the incident should instill shock and panic due to the malfunction or unavailability of critical services. 'The term "cyberterrorism" unites two significant modern fears: fear of technology and fear of terrorism (Conway, 2008).' The potential for an airline system to be hacked with planes crashing or the water purification plant to be infected with a dangerous chemical are examples of fear-causing threats. A virus that pops up a drawing game does not elicit the same level of fear as does a threat against critical life-dependent systems like hospitals or emergency services. Attacks on ICT infrastructure of critical services would have a stronger impact than a small business in an obscure location. The act is intended to produce effects beyond the immediate physical damage (Embar-Seddon, 2002).

Stohl (2006) has defined cyberterrorism as a purposeful act or the threat of violence to create fear and/or compliant behaviour in a victim and/or audience of the act or threat. A critical aspect of this definition is the threat of violence with the intention of creating fear. In some cases, an attacker does not even have to cause a system malfunction. The mere insinuation that the airport system has been hacked or that the food manufacturing plant has been contaminated can cause wide-spread panic. Thus, cyberterrorists can utilize a digital platform to present the front of a potential attack without even executing any system damage. Due to the abstract nature of ICT, an attacker can heighten fear levels through public announcements and disinformation campaigns. Malicious parties could create extensive anxiety with warnings of disruptions or infections of critical systems. Through the generation of fear and publicity, the underlying goals of such perpetrators have been achieved. This is indicative of the movement of traditional terrorism into the Digital Age, whereby the principles of violence, fear and publicity still prevail.

In the postmodern era, cyberterrorism also brings with it the idea of hyperreal (the blurring of distinctions between the real in the unreal (Matusitz, 2008). Face-to-face interaction and engagement has been largely replaced with digital communication. Within this context, we are faced with simulated situations which are experienced as hyperreal encounters. With the hyperreal experience, physical dimensions and boundaries are no longer relevant. Occurrences that are not normally observable or controllable are now a reality. For example, previously, only a physical attack on a water plant would result in contamination. With the era of ICT and smart systems, attackers can now infiltrate a water treatment plant. Landlines were previously the only phone of telephone communication. However, with the advent of cell phone networks, mobile communication has proliferated and become a core dependency. Similarly, an attack on a cell phone network can result in mass disconnection from a service that is now considered critical.

Myth or reality?

A debate continues to rage that there has not been any actual catastrophic cyberterrorist attack. Denning (2012) states that for a politically motivated attack to be considered as cyberterrorism, it would have to be sufficiently serious to incite terror equal to that caused by violent physical attacks. Furthermore, Weimann (2004) asserts that the potential and the actual damage caused by cyberterrorism have been ignored. Various scenarios have been proposed that depict the potential chaos that could be caused if critical infrastructure were to be attacked (Squitieri, 2002)). Terrorism has metamorphosed from the traditional form to the cyber form of technology-aided terrorism known as cyberterrorism (Samuel & Osman, 2014).

Hacking tools are growing in sophistication and agitated terrorist groups may look for an innovative outlet for their political, religious or philosophical ideals. For cyberterrorists there is no shortage of new tools and new technologies that have allowed them to commit their criminal acts virtually anywhere and from anywhere in the world (Subrananian, Liu, & Winterdyk, 2016). Denning has stated that the next generation of terrorists are experiencing a digital world in which hacking tools provide for a much more powerful, simpler, easier and accessible environment (Elrom, 2007)). Terrorists could soon turn their focus of attack on critical infrastructure in order to have a far-reaching impact. Already, with the Stuxnet virus and malicious interruptions at power plants, the effects of tampering with core services can be felt.

Already in 2014, President Obama believed that cyberterrorism was one of the biggest threats to national security and expected cyberterrorism to only grow in the years ahead as 15 years ago cyberterrorism was not even on the radar screen but will be one of the biggest concerns for whoever is president after him (Gasparino, 2014). In the United States, cybersecurity has become a priority for the government. The Department of Homeland Security has recognized that sophisticated cyberattackers and nation-states could exploit vulnerabilities and go on to disrupt, destroy or threaten the delivery of essential services. Stemming from this, they have released a strategy to try and reduce vulnerabilities and build resilience in order to oppose cyberattacks and respond to incidents (Department of Homeland Security, 2018).

The terrorist attacks on 9 September 2011 in the United States took the world by shock due to its devastating and influential consequences. Terrorist strikes are in most instances random and elaborate. So too, an impending terrorist cyberattack on critical ICT infrastructure could also paralyze a state/organization and cause significant losses. Preparation, prevention and monitoring systems and networks can attempt to mitigate such a threat and provide a means through which organizations and countries can empower themselves to counteract becoming a victim. Cyber readiness, disaster recovery and risk strategy are all governance aspects that need to be developed in order to prepare, detect and react to large-scale cyberattacks. Security checks, code validation and testing all need to be implemented early on in the design process of applications and systems. Furthermore, cyberthreat intelligence can play a vital role in identifying possible attack vectors. Holistic security measures need to be implemented on infrastructure and systems to try and curb the incidents of cyberattacks that could potentially become cyberterrorist threats. Threat intelligence and cyber readiness are becoming increasingly important in the information society that we live in.

Conclusion

Many may downplay the potential for cyberterrorism but it has emerged as a potential influential threat in this digital age. While mainstream terrorists may still try to cause explosions, kidnappings or gas leaks to cause havoc, the new-age terrorist could move into the realm of cyberspace to inflict harm. Critical systems for transportation, emergency services, financial institutions, health sector, agriculture and even the military pose as ideal targets for terrorists. With the development of Advanced Persistent Threats (APTs) that attack core infrastructure, the new wave of cyberthreats may stem from terrorists trying to impose their ideological beliefs.

Cyberterrorism can be misconceived as cybercrime. However, critical to cyberterrorism is the underlying motive, target and effect. While cybercrime is mainly carried out for financial benefits, fun or egotistical reasons, cyberterrorism has an extremist stance. Terrorism stems from religious, political and ideological viewpoints. Similarly, a cyberterrorist would not attack a system just to profit monetarily or show a flaw in a system. Cyberterrorists, like terrorists, aim for the promotion of their cause largely through the generation of fear and panic. Simple ICT exploits would not cause a significant amount of public outrage, and a cyberterrorist is more likely to want to cause interference with a critical system.

Furthermore, ICT can also play a supportive role to terrorism in general. Communication, planning, co-ordination, recruitment, propaganda, fundraising and influence campaigns can all be carried out in the digital environment to back terrorism in general. Such activities cannot be considered as cyberterrorism but rather as terrorist support capabilities of ICT.

While cyberterrorism attacks have not been as frequent as traditional terrorist assaults, the threat should not be overlooked. With the increasing reliance on ICT, terrorists can easily direct their attention of critical systems that affect society. Technical flaws and hacks are being discovered at an increasing rate. Terrorists can now direct their interests into exploiting the digital domain and cause new forms of disorder and devastation.

References

Ahmad, R., & Yunos, Z. (2012). A dynamic cyber terrorism framework. *International Journal of Computer Science and Information Security, 10*(2), 149–158.

Ahmad, R., Yunos, Z., & Sahib, S. (2012). *Understanding cyber terrorism: The grounded theory method applied.* Cyber Security, Cyber Warfare and Digital Forensic (CyberSec) (pp. 323–328). IEEE. Retrieved from https://ijcsmc.com/docs/papers/May2014/V3I5201499b12.pdf.

Armistead, L. (2004). *Information operations: Warfare and the hard reality of soft power.* Dulles, VA, USA: Potomac Books Inc.

Australian Governement. (2002). *Australia Security Legislation Amendment (Terrorism) Act.* Comlaw.gov.au. Retrieved 12 14, 2013, from http://www.comlaw.gov.au/Details/C2004C01314.

Brummel, N. H., Tobias, S. M., & Cattaneo, F. (2010). Dynamo efficiency in compressible convective dynamos with and without penetration. *Geophysical and Astrophysical Fluid Dynamics, 104*(5–6), 565–576. https://doi.org/10.1080/03091929.2010.495067.

Canter, D. (2009). In D. Canter (Ed.), *The faces of terrorism multidisciplinary perspectives.* West Sussex, UK: Wiley-Blackwell.

Collin, B. (1997). The future of cyberterrorism: The physical and virtual worlds converge. *Crime and Justice International, 13*(2), 14–18.

Conway, M. (2008). *Media, fear and the hyperream: The construction of cyberterrorism as the ultimate threat to critical infrastructures.* Institutional Centre for Institutional Studies, Scholl of Law and Government. Dublin: Dublin City University. Retrieved from http://doras.dcu.ie/2142/1/2008-5.pdf.

Curran, P. (2016). *Cyber terrorism – How real is the threat?* Checkmarx. Retrieved 2018, from www.checkmarx.com/2016/05/04/cyber-terrorism-real-threat-2/.

Davis, J. (January 22, 2016). Hacktivist vs. cyberterrorist: Understanding the 5 enemies of healthcare IT security. *Healthy IT News.* Retrieved from https://www.healthcareitnews.com/news/hacktivist-vs-cyberterrorist-understanding-5-enemies-healthcare-it-security.

Denning, D. (2000). Cyberterrorism. In *Testimony before the special oversight panel on terrorism committee on armed services U.S. House of representatives* (Vol. 18)Georgetown University.

Denning, D. (2001). Activism, hacktivism, and cyberterrorism: The Internet as a tool for influencing foreign policy. In J. Arquilla, & D. Ronfeldt (Eds.), *Networks and netwars: The future of terror, crime* (pp. 239–288). RAND. Retrieved from https://www.rand.org/content/dam/rand/pubs/monograph_reports/MR1382/MR1382.ch8.pdf.

Denning, D. (2012). Stuxnet: What has changed? *Future Internet, 4*(3), 672–687.

Department of Homeland Security. (June 20, 2018). *Cybersecurity.* Retrieved from https://www.dhs.gov/topic/cybersecurity.

Desouza, K. C., & Hensgen, T. (2003). Semiotic emergent framework to address the reality of cyberterrorism. *Technological Forecasting and Social Change, 70*(4), 385–396.

Elrom, S. (December 2, 2007). *The dark web of cyber terror- the threat that got lost in traffic.* Global Politician. Retrieved April 16, 2011, from http://www.globalpolitician.com/default.asp?23820-cyberterror.

Embar-Seddon, A. (2002). Cyberterrorism: Are we under siege? *American Behavioral Scientist, 45*(6), 1033.

FBI. (2002). *Code of federal regulations,* 28 CFR.Section 0.85 on Judicial Administration.

Flemming, P., & Stohl, M. (2000). Myths and realities of cyberterrorism. In *22-24 September. Courmayeur, Italy: International conference on countering terrorism through enhanced international cooperation.*

Foltz, C. B. (2004). Cyberterrorism, computer crime, and reality. *Information Management and Computer Security, 12*(2), 154–166.

Gasparino, C. (2014). *Obama said to warn of crippling cyber attack potential.* Fox Business. Retrieved June 20, 2018, from https://www.foxbusiness.com/politics/obama-said-to-warn-of-crippling-cyber-attack-potential.

Ghosh, T., Prelas, M. A., Viswanath, D., & Loyalka, S. K. (2010). *Science and technology of terrorism and counterterrorism.* CRC Press.

Gorge, M. (2007). Cyberterrorism: Hype or reality? *Computer Fraud and Security,* (2), 9–12.

Grant, T. J., Venter, H. S., & Eloff, J. H. (2007). Simulating adversarial interactions between intruders and system administrators using OODA-RR. In *Proceedings of the 2007 Annual Research Conference of the South African Institute of Computer Scientists and Information Technologists on IT Research in Developing Countries* (pp. 46–55). South Africa: Port Elizabeth.

Hardy, K. (February 20, 2017). *Is cyberterrorism a threat?* Australian Institute of International Affairs. Retrieved Nov 28, 2018, from https://www.internationalaffairs.org.au/australianoutlook/is-cyberterrorism-a-threat/.

van Heerden, R. P., Irwin, B., & Burke, I. (2012). Classifying network attack scenarios using an ontology. In *Proceedings of the 7th International Conference on Information-Warfare & Security (ICIW 2012)* (pp. 311–324). Seattle, USA: Academic Publishing International.

IT Web. (April 19, 2018). *Cyber- terrorism: More hollywood fad than genuine fear.* IT Web. Retrieved November 27, 2018, from https://www.itweb.co.za/content/GxwQDq1ARgWqlPVo.

Klausen, J. (2015). Tweeting the Jihad: Social media networks of western foreign fighters in Syria and Iraq. *Studies in Conflict and Terrorism, 38*(1). Retrieved from https://doi.org/10.1080/1057610X.2014.974948.

Lewis, J. (2002). *Assessing the risks of cyber terrorism, cyber war and other cyber threats* (pp. 1–12). Center for Strategic and International Studies.

Matusitz, J. (2008). Cyberterrorism: Postmodern state of chaos. *Information Security Journal: A Global Perspective, 17*(4), 179–187.

Nelson, B., Choi, R., Mitchell, M., & Gagnon, F. (1999). *Cyberterror prospects and implications.* Centre for the Study of Terrorism and Irregular Warfare. Retrieved May 14, 2011, from http://www.nps.edu/Academics/Centers/CTIW/files/Cyberterror%20Prospects%20and%20Implications.pdf.

Paulose, R. (November 28, 2013). *Cyber terrorism: Fact or fiction.* A Contratio ICL. Retrieved December 4, 2012, from. https://acontrarioicl.com/2013/11/28/cyber-terrorism/

Phillipines Government. (2003). *Anti-terrorism act, S540* (p. 1353). Senate Bill.

Ruby, C. (2002). The definition of terrorism. *Analyses of Social Issues and Public Policy, 2*(1), 9–14.

Samuel, K. O., & Osman, W. R. (2014). cyber terrorism attack of the contemporary information technology age:issues, consequences and panacea. *International Journal of Computer Science and Mobile Computing, 3*(5), 1082–1090. Retrieved from https://ijcsmc.com/docs/papers/May2014/V3I5201499b12.pdf.

Squitieri, T. (May 5, 2002). Cyberspace full of terror targets. *USA Today.* Retrieved August 14, 2013, from http://www.usatoday.com/tech/news/2002/05/06/cyber-terror.htm.

Stohl, M. (2006). Cyber terrorism: A clear and present danger, the sum of all fears, breaking point or patriot games? *Crime, Law and Social Change, 46*(4–5), 223–238.

Subrananian, L., Liu, J., & Winterdyk, J. (2016). *Cyber- terrorism and cyber security: A global perspective.* In Justice Report.

Talihärm, A. (2010). Cyberterrorism: In theory or in practice? *Defence Against Terrorism Review, 3*(2), 59–74.

United Kingdom Government. (2000). *Terrorism act, Part 1, (1)-(3).* Legislation.gov.uk. Retrieved August 12, 2013, from http://www.legislation.gov.uk/ukpga/2000/11/contents.

United Nations Security Council (UNSC) 2004. (2004). *Resolution 1566.* Retrieved from http://daccess-dds-ny.un.org/doc/UNDOC/GEN/N04/542/82/PDF/N0454282.pdf?OpenElement.

United States Government. (1983). *US code title 22 section 2656f.* United States of America.

Veerasamy, N. (2014). *CLC-Cyberterrorism Life Cycle Model* (Thesis). Univeristy of Pretoria.

Weimann. (2004). *Cyberterrorism: How real is the threat?.* Report No 119. Washington, United States: United States Institute of Peace. Retrieved 25 July, 2011, from United States Institute of Peace http://www.usip.org/pubs/specialreports/sr119.pdf.

Wilson, C. (2005). *Computer attack and cyberterrorism vulnerabilities and policy issues for congress.* USA: Naval History and Heritage Command. Retrieved from https://www.history.navy.mil/research/library/online-reading-room/title-list-alphabetically/c/computer-attack-cyberterrorism-crs.html.

Zerzri, M. (2017). *The threat of cyber terrorism and recommendations for countermeasures.* Tunisia: Center for Applied Policy Research.

3

Closed, safe and secure — the Russian sense of information security

Mari Ristolainen[1], Juha Kukkola[2]

[1] Finnish Defence Research Agency, Riihimäki, Finland; [2] Finnish National Defence University, Helsinki, Finland

Emerging Cyber Threats and Cognitive Vulnerabilities
https://doi.org/10.1016/B978-0-12-816203-3.00003-4

53

Introduction

Security is a feeling that varies from culture to culture and it is sometimes specific to each individual society (cf. Gupta & Sharman 2009). Likewise, cybersecurity experienced within one state can radically differ from the cybersecurity experienced within another. In the Russian approach, cyber/information space is used by 'other countries' and hostile forces for the destabilization of Russia. The Internet is a by-product of the dominant American culture and, therefore, poses a threat to Russian cultural integrity and independence. (cf. Doktrina, 2000; Doktrina, 2016; Ristolainen, 2017.) 'RuNet' (from words 'Russian Internet') as an alternative and familiar Russian language platform has been gradually developing from the bottom up to challenge the English language-dominated Internet. Later, the Russian government began to plan top-to-bottom approach for technical disconnecting of the 'Russian segment of the Internet' from the global Internet. In 2014, a series of exercises was conducted to test 'national segment's' feasibility (Nikiforov, 2014; Demidov & Makhukova, 2016). During summer 2016, Russia declared that its 'national segment' would be disconnected from the global Internet by 2020 in order to protect the critical Russian Internet infrastructure (Minkomsviaz 2016; Programma, 2014). Furthermore, a 'road-map' tasking that Russia will be 'digitally sovereign'[1] by 2020 was presented in 2017 (Programma, 2017). During the past years, Russia has launched strategies (Strategiia 2015, 2017), doctrines (Doktrina, 2000, 2016), state programs (Programma, 2014, 2017) and action plans (Napravleniia, 2018) that demonstrate clearly how the Russian Federation is preparing the infrastructural basis for national control of the Internet (cf. Kukkola, 2018a, 2018b; Kukkola & Ristolainen, 2018; Kukkola, Ristolainen, & Nikkarila, 2017). It is clear that the Russian approach to cybersecurity differs fundamentally from the 'Western' understanding of cybersecurity that is based on global and the open Internet (Ristolainen, 2017, pp. 113−114).

The methodology of this chapter draws on an integrated approach. On the one hand, a dialectic method is applied to demonstrate the duality between 'RuNet' and 'the Russian segment of the Internet' and to investigate the synthesis of these two diverse approaches and how in this

---

[1] From the Russian perspective 'Digital Sovereignty' can be understood as the extension of the authority and control of a territorial state to the national segment of Internet which consists of Internet and other network-related ICT systems located on its territory or under its jurisdiction. A wider concept is 'information sovereignty' which additionally includes the information residing or flowing through those ICT systems and the interaction of its users (cf. Efremov, 2016; Streltsov & Pilyugin, 2016, pp. 26−27; Ashmanov, 2013).

process the Russian sense of security is developing, merging and fulfilling the people's and state's security needs. On the other hand, cross-cultural research and sociological perspectives are required to understand different national security solutions, human behaviour and decision-making in the field of cybersecurity. A sociocultural perspective is applied to describe the historical, social and cultural factors surrounding Russian cyber/information space and to show through examples how the Russian sense of information security is constructed. Cross-cultural research requires conceptual synchronization and understanding the cultural variation of the 'sense of security'. Thus, firstly, the key concepts are introduced and a dialectic method is used to explain their differences. Secondly, a sociocultural review and analysis as a theoretical framework and methodology is described. Thirdly, in the analytical part of this chapter it is shown how the sense of Russian information security is provided through historical fear-based template for the isolation rhetoric, awarding and celebrating the 'Russian way' of doing things and by cleaning together for a safer environment. Fourthly, the Russian under-standing of information security is examined through the state project to control of 'the national segment of Internet'. And finally, this chapter discusses how the Russian sense of information security is verified by the state.

Synthesis from 'RuNet' through the 'Russian segment of the Internet' to the 'unified information space'

Cyber concepts are constantly being developed and their definitions vary greatly in different languages. Thus, in this chapter, when speaking about Russia the concept of 'information security' is used instead of 'cybersecurity'. The Russian understanding of cyberspace is more comprehensive than in the West, which may explain why the Russian terms for cyberspace are 'information space' (*informatsionnaia sfera*) and 'information environment' (*informatsionnoe prostranstvo*). Russian infor-mation space includes all mass media, not only information and computer technology platforms. Information space emphasizes more the role of information flows, their content and value, and it stresses societal, psy-chological and cultural substances (Strategiia, 2008). Alternatively, framing cyber as information could be considered one of Russia's lines of effort when attempting to control the cyber domain (Kukkola et al., 2017, pp. 54–55). With its own peculiar concepts, Russia is, on the one hand, able to use cyber operations without sanctions and, on the other hand, able to legitimize a nationally governed network approach (Kukkola & Ristolainen, 2017). Additionally, an explanation for the Russian use of information instead of cyber could be related to the Soviet *kibernetik*[2] thinking (Gerovitch, 2002, 2008; Peters, 2016) and the historical associations that 'cyber' evokes in Russian (cf. Kukkola, 2018a).

In contradiction to the previous studies (e.g. Kukkola et al. 2017; Ristolainen, 2017), in this chapter the two entities 'RuNet' and 'the Russian segment of the Internet' are considered separately. In order to deepen the understanding of the Russian cyber/information security, it is argued that 'RuNet' represents the 'sociocultural basis' for 'the Russian segment of the Internet'. At the beginning, 'RuNet' developed largely free from state influence (Gorny, 2009), therefore 'the Russian segment of the Internet' is the materialization of the increased state control of 'RuNet', i.e. the state-controlled national segment represents an organization under control of a product of free spirit. Consequently, 'RuNet' as a concept has evolved from an alternative social universe to a state-controlled 'Russian segment of the Internet'.

Furthermore, in the spirit of dialectic method, it could be claimed that together 'RuNet' and 'the Russian segment of the Internet' create something that in Russian is called 'unified information space' (*edinoe informatsionnoe prostranstvo*). Here the Hegelian triadic idea 'thesis-antithesis-synthesis' could be used as a formula for explicating the change from 'RuNet' through the 'Russian segment of the Internet' to the 'Unified information space' and back. According to Kukkola (2018a), 'the unified information space' should be understood as a concept of control of information that encompasses information infrastructure (technical aspect) as well as information itself (psychological aspect). The originally Cold War concept of 'unified information space' is a collection of all resources, methods and control of consciousness, i.e. a horizontally integrated and centrally controlled national information network. In practice, this was known as the OGAS (the State-wide Automated Management System for Collection and Processing of Information for the Accounting, Planning, and Management of the National Economy) in Soviet times and it was meant to manage the whole Soviet economy — and as such the Soviet state and society according to *kibernetik* visions (cf. Gerovitch, 2008; Kukkola, 2018a; Peters, 2016).

'RuNet' is a relatively closed, online environment that is based on the Russian language. RuNet has been generally defined as 'a totality of information, communications and activities which occur on the internet, mostly in the Russian language, no matter where resources and users are physically located, and which are somehow linked to Russian culture and Russian cultural identity' (Gorny, 2009, p. 27). RuNet suggests the

---

[2] *Kibernetika* — cybernetics is a science studying the processes of control and information transfer in various systems (machines, living organisms, society etc.) (cf. Gerovitch, 2002, 2008; Peters, 2016).

existence of a distinct object or space and a collective 'we' (Schmidt, Teubener & Konradova, 2006, p. 14). Information is produced in Russian language and controlled within the 'RuNet community' that provides a certain sense of belonging and has a significant role in the Russian information security thinking.

'The Russian segment of the Internet' as a concept represents the national technical control of the information infrastructure. It is a multi-layered project and a 'system of systems' that aims to the state control of Russian national networks (cf. Kukkola, 2018c). Kukkola (2018a) has explained in detail the categories of infrastructure, services and authorities responsible for creating, monitoring and controlling this segment both from the civilian and military perspective. Whereas, the system of systems is a defence measure that could enable Russia to withstand cyberattacks against its critical national assets. The subsystems of this entity have different functions and are controlled by various actors but can be joined to a centrally controlled system (cf. Kukkola, 2018c).

Consequently, it could be argued that in the 'Unified information space' 'the Russian segment of the Internet' aims to protect the critical information infrastructure and 'RuNet' safeguards the 'spiritual–moral values' (*dukhovno-nravstvennye tsennosti*) from outside interference (cf. Kukkola, 2018a), i.e. the synthesis of control and free spirit forms a harmony that produces the essence of the Russian sense of information security. According to the Russian Information Security Doctrine (2016), 'increased information influence on the population of Russia, mainly on the young generation, aimed at erosion of traditional Russian spiritual and moral values' poses a serious threat to Russian information security. As noted earlier, the planning for the technical disconnecting of the 'Russian segment of the Internet' started at least in 2014. Nevertheless, the mental isolation and othering of 'RuNet' has started considerably earlier. In the following, the aim is to explain how to study the Russian sense of information security and how it is socioculturally, historically and institutionally situated.

Sociocultural approach to the Russian sense of information security

Sociocultural approaches emphasize the interdependence of social and cultural processes in the production of knowledge (John-Steiner & Mahn, 1996, pp. 191–192). In this chapter, the feeling of safety,[3] i.e. the sense of information security is understood as a sociocultural construct.

---

[3] Feeling of safety is understood in this chapter as the absence of threats, i.e. freedom from something; or in a positive sense, freedom to be or do something

'Sociocultural' refers to the Soviet roots of the social constructivist epistemology, e.g. Lev Vygotsky and the role of social context in the production of knowledge (John-Steiner & Mahn, 1996; Vygotsky 1962, 1978), i.e. all human mental functioning is socioculturally, historically and institutionally situated (cf. Daniels, 2017). Sociocultural approach gives an approximate theoretical framework for the analysis of the production of information security (cf. Sjösted, 2010; Wagoner, 2014) in the Russian 'unified information space'. In this case, the sociocultural approach is used to illustrate how a society influences and shapes peoples' experiences. This approach has been chosen as it emphasizes the role of the society and represents an original Soviet and Russian way of comprehending the production of knowledge.

In a sociocultural review and analysis are presented examples of the social, cultural and institutional features that can play a significant role in the production of knowledge (Cole, 1994; John-Steiner & Mahn, 1996). The aim is to show a relation between individuals and the society as well as culturally created artefacts in understanding the development of the sense of information security as a collective phenomenon. In this chapter we have identified four different examples of sociocultural production that provide a sense of security in the Russian 'information space'. These examples include the historical fear-based template for the isolation rhetoric, celebrating and awarding the 'Russian way' of doing things, cleaning together for safer information environment and the state project to control of 'the national segment of Internet'.

In the sociocultural approach language as a system of expressions plays a fundamental role in the production of knowledge (John-Steiner & Mahn, 1996, p. 192). Language is used as a tool for thinking collectively. This could be applied into cyberspace as well as one of the main reasons why RuNet started to develop was the language and the feeling of being left outside. Cyrillic script in a world of Latin alphabets creates significant obstacles, especially if the person does not know any other language than Russian.

According to Russian sources, Russian is the second most used language in the Internet and the amount of users of RuNet is considered the largest in Europe (Zinovieva, 2016, p. 22). For years Russians had been demanding ICANN (The Internet Corporation for Assigned Names and Numbers) to break the English language dominance of the Internet. The Cyrillic domain battle was aimed at raising the status of Russian as a global language, and it was hoped to expand Internet use among Russian speakers unfamiliar with Latin characters. Finally, using Cyrillic was approved by ICANN following a request by President Dmitry Medvedev in 2008 (Gorham, Lunde, & Paulsen, 2014, p. 190). The first Internet domains using the Cyrillic script were launched on May 13, 2010 after Russia was officially assigned the.pф (.rf, for 'Russian Federation') domain.

Currently Russia has three different domain types:.ru,.su, and.рф (.su stands for Soviet Union). In the Russian press, Cyrillic domain was celebrated as 'the end of the Latin script's domination of the internet' (Nocetti, 2015, pp. 121−122). Western commentators saw this leading towards segregated, hermetic Russian web that undermines the Internet's global spirit (Singer & Friedman, 2014, pp. 252−253; Vargas-Leon, 2016, pp. 175−177).

Consequently, the original meaning of RuNet is that the content of websites is available in Russian, i.e. it is the Russian language community on the Internet (Schmidt et al., 2006, p. 15). A sense of security is created by looking at what is common to the group, how one can find the best way to relate to others. The Russian sense of information security begins in the linguistic togetherness offered by RuNet, in sharing an understanding of the world with other Russian speakers.

Togetherness brings safety but it also offers a solid ground for self-attained isolation, especially if there is a shared historical experience that reinforces the 'withdrawnness'. In the following we present the historical contextualization of the Russian sense of information security.

Fear-based template for the isolation rhetoric

As noted earlier, in the Russian approach, information space is used by 'other countries' and hostile forces for the destabilization of Russia. This kind of 'besieged fortress' (*osazhdennaia krepost'*) mentality has characterized Russian thinking for decades (see, for example, Heller, 1988, pp. 108−109; Trenin, 2016, pp. 19, 36−39). It follows repeatedly the very same fear-based template − the enemy is plotting to encircle Russia, to invade and overthrow the Russian political system − on land, sea, air, space and now in the cyber/information space.

Fear cannot exist without a cause to be frightened of (cf. Heller, 1988, p. 99). After the Russian Revolution of 1917, the Soviet people were deliberately taught to think of themselves as being surrounded by enemies, 'the imperialists', who would crush them if they could. The perception of 'enemy' has been repeatedly deployed, both to mobilize against actual external danger, and also to justify the struggle against a supposed enemy on domestic ground (Fateev, 1999, pp. 102−104; Solomeshch, 2001; Gudkov, 2005, pp. 14−15).

Lev Gudkov (2005) has developed a so-called 'theory of an enemy' where the main function of enemy is that the enemy represents a threat to the very existence of the group, e.g. to a society or an organization, to any kind of group that identifies itself as a subject (Gudkov, 2005, p. 13). The group can either defend or hide itself from the enemy, escape or defeat the enemy. In any case, the enemy mobilizes all the members of the group, creates solidarity and unity inside the group that guarantees security and freedom and saves the group from destruction (Gudkov, 2005, p. 14). According to Gudkov (2005, p. 42), 'enemies' were one of the key factors in the formation of Soviet identity. The totalitarian propaganda focussed on producing two metaphors — 'the construction of a new society' and 'the formation of frontline' (Gudkov, 2005; p. 42).

In the contemporary Russian information security thinking can be seen reflections of the Soviet type 'enemy discourse' — 'the construction of a new society' and 'the formation of frontline'. As noted earlier, the Russian Information Security Doctrine implies that the traditional Russian spiritual and moral values are in danger (Doktrina, 2016). The content of websites is a threat to the Russian people and thus it must be tightly controlled for their own protection. Moreover, there exists a big concern of the Russian network's dependence on the global infrastructure and how the Internet 'can be switched off' from outside of Russia's borders. The Ministry of Digital Development, Communications and Mass Media[4] (*Minkomsvyaz*) has claimed that Russia needs its own reserve systems should its Internet segment be cut off from the rest of the world if, for instance, Russia were to face a national emergency, such as military action or serious protests (Golitsyna & Prokolenko, 2016; Minkomsvyaz, 2016, 2017; Vargas-Leon, 2016, p. 175). Furthermore, there is a persistent 'rumour' in the Russian 'information space' that if Russia would occupy, for instance, any European country, all Russian Internet connections would be disconnected in 24 h (Nazarov, 2016; Rozhkov, 2016.).

Here both the psychological and technical lack of control is represented as the origin of threat and a source of insecurity and disorder. The authorized rhetoric emphasis that the Russian 'unified information space' is controlled outside of Russia. Russia could end up in the state of not knowing, but Russia cannot be in the state of not knowing. As a result, this perceived lack of control leads to rhetoric where everything needs to be controlled, i.e. Russia does not manage to control the outcomes of future events without being able to control and, if needed, to close its own network. The response to the insecurity is solidarity and isolation of the 'unified information space' and the development of domestic technical solutions independent from the hostile world outside of Russia.

Celebrating and awarding the 'Russian way' of doing things

As noted earlier, RuNet is a relatively closed online environment that is based on the Russian language. Nevertheless, RuNet refers not only to the Russian language but also to the 'Russian way' of doing things. The

---

[4] NB: Unitill 2018 the name was the Ministry of Telecom and Mass Communications.

development of RuNet can be illuminated through the lens of 'RuNet award'. The 'RuNet award', i.e. 'a national award for the contribution to the development of the Russian segment of the Internet' is an annual award for the best initiatives, companies and applications issued by the Federal Agency on Press and Mass Communication (*Rospechat*) starting from 2004.

In 2004 RuNet celebrated its 10th anniversary as, in 1994, the domain.ru was registered and the official history of the Russian Internet had begun. (Schmidt et al., 2006, 51—52) have described the 10th anniversary celebrations as aims at integrating the Internet into an official cultural context and making the use of Internet as a national pride. In the final 'RuNet show' 15 companies and projects contributing to the development of 'the Russian segment of the Internet' were awarded. The show was featured by a prima ballerina of the Bolshoi Ballet and blessed by the Patriarch of Moscow Aleksii II (Schmidt et al., 2006).

The 'RuNet award' could be seen as one of the first events where state takes over the 'RuNet'-thinking. State-organized competitions are a Soviet phenomenon. Under Socialism everything was improving and different competitions supported the ideology. The guiding principle was to get better, to compete, to improve and then to compete again. Competitions, their calls and instructions and award categories indicate what is considered valuable and represent a top-down cultural production of meaning and influencing by familiarizing and personalizing. Issues that are excluded eliminate the 'not meaningful' issues from broad-based debate and contestation. In the RuNet case the award categories show what is needed for the development of Russian 'unified information space' and for ensuring safety.

In 2004 the first RuNet awards were given in three different categories: (1) RuNet Technologies (provider, equipment, software and developer); (2) Business RuNet (communication with RuNet consumers, e-Commerce in RuNet, business solutions in RuNet, and financial tool in RuNet) and (3) RuNet for users (search engine, e-mail, free service of the RuNet, content resource, entertainment project and community-resource).[5] Generally, the winners were companies and software providing services in Russian (Yandex, Rambler, mail.ru). Among others, a special nomination for contribution to the formation and development of the domain.ru was given to A. P. Platonov, Director of the Russian Research Institute for the development of public networks (RosNIIROS).

Next year, the award categories developed and increased from four to nine. New categories were Government and Society, Culture and Mass

---

[5] A complete list of the winners starting from 2004 till 2017 can be found at: https://ru. wikipedia.org/wiki/Премия_Рунета.

Communications, Science and Education, Economics and Business, Health and Leisure and Technology and Innovations, Personal prize, 'Gold medal of honour' and 'Folks' 10'. These new categories represent the 'holistic nature' of the RuNet. In 2006 one new category was added – RuNet outside of.RU. This category brought new and significant addition to RuNet. RuNet offers a 'sphere of influence' or 'near abroad' type of channel in digital form. Over the years, socially significant Internet projects and mobile applications have been added to the award categories. 'RuNet award' covers vertically all the fields of a modern society from state organizations to the people.

'Safe RuNet', i.e. the security aspect, was added in 2011 and the first winners were 'A guide on child safety on the Internet' (http://www. google.ru/familysafety/), 'Children Online' (a hotline for children to ask about Internet safety) and 'NetPolice.RU' (an online shopping filter). In 2012 the winners were the Kaspersky Lab, a mobile operator MTS's safety project and Directorate K18 – the Ministry of Internal affairs (MVD) component responsible for Internet crime. In 2013 the 'safety category' was awarded together with the Safe Internet League to the Group IB (a company dedicated to preventing and investigation of high-tech crimes and online fraud), letidor.ru (a family oriented website) and infowatch.ru (a company offering protection for corporate users against internal threats). In 2014 the safety category changed into 'Internet without extremism' category and it was awarded together with the MVD and the winner was MediaGuard. MediaGuard also won the popular vote. A category was added in 2014 'For contribution to the development of Russian Internet infrastructure' and it was awarded together with the RU/RF domain coordination centre to the MSK-IX computer network centre, Russian Institute of public networks (RosNIIROS), Rostelekom.

Today, the RuNet award is a nationwide award in the field of high technology and the Internet, which encourages outstanding achievements of leading companies in the field of information technology and electronic communications, government and public organizations, business structures, as well as individual figures who have made a significant contribution to the development of 'the Russian segment of the Internet'. In 2018 the goals and objectives of the RuNet award according to their website http://premiaruneta.ru/ are:

- To contribute to the development of information technologies, electronic media and electronic mass communications in Russia as an important sector of economic activity
- Consolidation and unification of the Internet community
- Promoting the creation of a 'unified information community' (*edinoe informatsionnoe obshchestvo*) in Russia (cf. *edinoe informatsionnoe prostransvo*, Kukkola, 2018a)

- Increasing the trust in the Internet environment, increasing the attractiveness of the Internet environment for advertisers and investors
- Assistance in the implementation of National projects of the Russian Federation in the field of Informatization
- Promotion of new information technologies in various sectors of the Russian economy
- Maintaining a high level of professional competence of Russian specialists in the field of information and communication technology (ICT) and high technologies
- Popularization of ICTs in Russia
- Presentation of the achievements of the Russian segment of the Internet at the state and international level

The factual 'Runet award' is a 43-centimetre statue made of bronze and completely covered with gold weighting about 5 kg. The statuette represents a column crowned with a three-dimensional letter designation of the Russian domain zone RU (cf. 'RuNet award' is sometimes called the 'Internet Oscar'). On the front side of the sculpture on a special plate is engraved 'Runet Award', year and the name of the winner.[6]

To win this nationwide award symbolized a patriotic/heroic act, i.e. it motivates individuals and companies to contribute their ideas and knowledge to a common project that further promotes the sense of nationalism and political legitimacy of 'unified information space'. Here the Russian sense of security is established by celebrating the 'Russian way' of doing things. Participation in the ritualistic events links people to the community's worldview and perception of its own history.

Cleaning together for safer information environment and creating a 'psychological firewall'

Online sources and social media played a central role in protests following the Russian parliamentary elections in December 2011. At that point, RuNet was still a somewhat loose and uncensored information space to obtain information and share ideas in the Russian language. In contrast, there was also a growing concern about piracy, pornography and violence and demand to control and moderate content among RuNet users. And as shown above, the 'safety features' of RuNet started to play a

---

[6] A picture of the 'RuNet award' can be found at https://en.wikipedia.org/wiki/Runet_Prize#/media/File:Premiya_runeta2006.jpg.

role in 2011 and a project called 'Clean internet' endorsed by *Minkomsvyaz* in 2012. The establishment of 'Clean Internet' is related to the law 'On the Protection of Children from Information Harmful to Their Health and Development', but more commonly known as the 'Blacklist Bill' that was passed in 2012 (Zakon, 2012). The 'blacklist' is instituted and maintained by Roskomnadzor[7] with the stated purpose of blocking the sites related to child pornography, materials on drug abuse or production and suicide. It includes measures that allow Roskomnadzor to censor individual URLs, domain names and IP addresses. Additionally, the law allows censoring websites that would encourage 'mass riots' or 'participation in unsanctioned events' (Soldatov & Borogan, 2015, pp. 263—264.).

According to their website[8] 'Clean Internet — Center for the protection of the rights and legitimate interests of citizens in the information sphere' (*Tsentr po zashchite prav i zakonnykh interesov grazhdan v niformatsionnoi sfere "Chistyi Internet"*) is a non-profit Russian organization established by the initiative of the Minkomsvyaz in December 2012. 'Clean Internet' aims to develop mechanisms for self-regulation of RuNet by controlling the distribution of illegal content and creating a positive Internet environment (*positivnaia internet-sreda*).

Within the 'Clean Internet' project a voluntary association 'Safe Internet League' was established (Soldatov & Boroganov, 2015, p. 298). According to its website, the Safe Internet League is the largest and most reputable Russian organization fighting dangerous web content. It is a voluntary association of citizens devoted to helping law enforcement organizations. Its volunteers monitor the Internet for violations on behalf of law enforcement. The site posts detailed information on the MVD Directorate K18 — the MVD component responsible for Internet crime — and provides a direct email link for reporting violations. In the league's view, violations include child pornography, pornography accessible to children, promotion of drug and alcohol abuse as well as violent or 'extremist' content. Despite the prominent role assigned to countering child pornography, the league's actual focus is social media. The league's website awards its members ranks based on the social networking sites they identify that contain malicious content. In many opinions, the league is actually law enforcement's monitoring attempt to match social media's expansion (Carr, 2011, pp. 240—241; Gorham et al., 2014, pp. 189—190; Soldatov & Boroganov, 2015, pp. 201—202.).

---

[7] In 2008, the Federal Service for Supervision of Communications, Information Technology, and Mass Media (*Roskomnadzor*) was established. *Roskomnadzor* is a Russian federal executive body responsible for overseeing the media, including the electronic media, and mass communications, information technology and telecommunications.

[8] http://clearrunet.ru/about.php.

Also in 2012, the United Russia party's youth wing launched a 'MediaGuard' project that will automatically block the maximum number of websites with 'illegal content'.[9] According to its website[10], 'Media-Guard' is a Federal project aimed at uniting the efforts of Internet users to jointly identify Internet sites, communities and groups in social networks specializing in the distribution of illegal content. MediaGuard's 'Register of banned sites' has been created to combat drugs, child pornography and suicide on the Internet. Their promotion speech includes the following: 'Thousands of sites are closed, but if you now score in the search engine any of these areas, you can find the necessary resources, not to mention those that are closed for indexing. We offer just a few clicks to make the Internet cleaner and safer. To do this, you must register on the site and send a request if you encounter on the Internet with prohibited information!' As noted earlier, 'MediaGuard' won the popular vote for 'the best Internet project' and was also awarded in the 'Internet without extremism' category in 2014.

All the joint cleaning projects reflect the Russian turn towards traditional values, creation of 'morally safe environment' and the isolation of the Russian 'unified information space'. The black and white lists maintained by the volunteers are used in several applications,[11] i.e. the cleaning together for safer information environment is considered productive. Both 'Safe Internet League' and 'MediaGuard' are presented as existing without government intervention. They resemble a Soviet *subbotnik* that means a free labour performed at leisure time for the benefit of society. Besides, 'MediaGuard' is openly a United Russia Party's project and it could be used for politically motivated censorship.

Furthermore, Nisbet, Kamenchuk, and Dal (2017) call the process developing in Russia as a creation of 'psychological firewall', i.e. people report they do not go to certain websites because the government says it is bad for them. 'Authoritarian regimes commonly justify Internet censorship by framing the Internet as a threat to their citizens that must be tightly controlled for their own protection. This threat rhetoric underpins government censorship and creates a "psychological firewall" driving public support for a censored Internet.' (Nisbet et al., 2017). 'The

---

[9] Over the past years, the Russian government has passed several laws that allow forming different types of blacklists, blocking and eventually aiming to at gaining a complete control over RuNet. Nevertheless, the aim of this chapter is not to list or analyze these laws comprehensively. The focus is more on the projects followed by the new legislation and the rhetoric implemented by the Russian authorities.

[10] http://mediagvardia.ru/.

[11] E.g. filter "home Alone" http://odindoma.org/and "Internet censor" http://icensor.ru/.

government has compared some websites it opposes to suicide bombers and tells citizens its response would be to use Internet control and censorship to create a "bulletproof vest for the Russian society".' (Nisbet et al., 2017)

'Cleaning together' calls for the responsibility of every citizen to take part in the creation of Russian information security. At the same time, these initiatives produce a feeling that everybody's input is important — the state listens to its citizens even though it knows what is best for them. Furthermore, self-censorship guarantees public safety and reduces the fear of 'crime' while the Russian sense of information security is created. The increasing 'closed, safe and secure' rhetoric encourages Russian Internet users to stay within the framework of the 'Russian segment of the Internet' and their synthesis in the 'unified information space' gives rise to a natural and self-attained isolation. Consequently, the Russian perception of information security is fundamentally related to territoriality and sovereignty that is offered to the people in the form of the independent 'Russian segment of the Internet'.

'Russian segment of the Internet' — a state-controlled project for protecting information security

The sociocultural production of security transforms the material or technological side of RuNet through the concept of the Russian or national segment of the Internet. If the three cases discussed above have been examples of the dialectics in psychological, informational or spiritual side of the Russian information space, here it is argued that by taking control of the free, borderless and open infrastructural base of RuNet the Russian state shapes it towards order, exclusion and control. This process, of course, feeds back to the psychological side so the ideational and material cannot be fully separated. They are two sides of the same coin in examining how the Russian understanding of information security is constructed.

The idea of creating 'a unified information space' on a technological level was already present when the Russian Federation emerged from the ashes of the Soviet Union. At the time, this space was still to be connected to the global information network and was seen as a way to enhance economic development (Kontseptsiia, 1995). This openness subsided at the end of the 1990s when the Russian government presented its first concept for the development of information society. This society was proposed to be achieved in a 'Russian way' (Kontseptsiia, 1999). Concurrently, in 1999 Russia adopted its first information security doctrine which clearly stated that the information threats emanating from the inside and outside necessitated the control of information space (Doktrina, 2000). Later, the strategy for development of information society (2008) connected information security to the military security and declared that the formation of 'unified information space' would help to solve issues of national security (Strategiia, 2008). So when the Russian state really began to take control of the RuNet after the 2012−13 demonstrations against President Putin (Svoboda internet, 2017), the idea of a secure state-controlled national segment of Internet was already formulated (Programma, 2014).

This idea is now being put into reality. If the current programs and plans of the Russian government materialize, the technological or material side of RuNet will become a vertically controlled and horizontally integrated information space (Doktrina 2000, 2016; Napravlenie, 2018; Programma 2014, 2017; Strategiia, 2015, 2017). In this vision, the Russian state can control the substance of Internet through censorship laws. Its security services are able to conduct targeted and mass surveillance. The information infrastructure of Russian Internet will be based on Russian hardware, software and cryptographic solutions. The state will own through state companies major parts of the infrastructure of the Russian Internet and control through laws the private sector operating critical information infrastructure. Moreover, the security services are able to monitor public and strategic industrial networks through national SIEM (Security Incident and Event Management) system. Ultimately, the whole national segment of Internet can be disconnected from the global Internet by state-controlled routing and addressing protocols (Kukkola, 2018c). This system of systems of security reflects sociocultural understanding of security and extinguishes the freedom and anarchy that were present in the early phases of RuNet's development.

Arguably, in a world of claimed unknown and unpredictable information (cyber) threats this state control of the 'national segment of Internet' provides security. If private citizens and corporations are unable to protect themselves or the information as a whole, the state has to intervene. But the way in which this intervention is conducted is based on the sociocultural understanding of security. The material basis of RuNet is changed through the national segment of Internet to something that belongs to the state and is protected from outside threats by technological means. It forms the material component of 'the unified information space' and produces a feeling of security that is particularly Russian. This is not to say that there is no resistance. There is always conflict in dialectics and synthesis is not about one side 'winning it all.' What is produced as the material component of 'the unified information space' is always situational and contextual − something evolving and undetermined.

Controlled digital harmony

This chapter has shown how 'RuNet' forms a 'sociocultural basis' of 'the Russian segment of the Internet' and how both of the concepts are situated culturally, historically and institutionally in the Russian 'unified information space'. The given examples demonstrate development of the Russian sense of information security and how it is produced in the historical fear-based template for the isolation rhetoric, by celebrating and awarding the 'Russian way' of doing things, by cleaning together for safer information environment and by the state project to control of 'the national segment of Internet'.

It can be argued that 'the unified information space' presents a kind of controlled digital harmony. It is the synthesis of freedom, and perhaps anarchy and fear, and security and control. It is a particular Russian sociocultural product where the spirit (psychology and information) and the land (technological infrastructure of Internet) are secured and brought under control under the benevolent will of the tsar (the state and it security services). It orders the people (private citizens and corporations) to take part in creating security by inviting them to create that security on the conditions that the state sets for them. This security through harmony is created by closing off the Russian digital society from malevolent outside influences.

References

Ashmanov, I. (April 24, 2013). *Doklad: Informatsionnyi suverenitet. Sovremennaia real'nost'.* http://rossiyanavsegda.ru/read/948/.

Carr, J. (2011). *Inside cyber warfare: Mapping the cyber underworld* (2nd ed.). Sebastopol: O'Reilly Media Inc.

Cole, M. (1994). *Cultural psychology.* Cambridge, MA: Harvard University Press.

Daniels, H. (Ed.). (2017). *Introduction to Vygotsky* (3rd ed.). London and New York: Routledge.

Demidov, O., & Makhukova, A. (2016). *Infrastruktura interneta v kontekste regulirovaia zhiznenno vazhnykh uslug i kriticheskikh informatsionnykh infrastruktur: obzor mezhdunarodnogo i rossiiskogo opyta.* http://www.eurasiancommission.org/ru/act/dmi/workgroup/Documents/07-09-2016/CIIP%20Research.pdf.

Doktrina. (September 9, 2000). *Doktrina informatsionnoi bezopasnosti Rossiiskoi Federatsii (information security doctrine of the Russian federation).* http://www.scrf.gov.ru/documents/6/5.html.

Doktrina. (December 5, 2016). *Doktrina informatsionnoi bezopasnosti Rossiiskoi Federatsii (information security doctrine of the Russian federation).* http://static.kremlin.ru/media/acts/files/0001201612060002.pdf.

Efremov, A. (2016). Problemy realizatsii gosudarstvennogo suvereniteta v informatsionnoe sfere. *Vestnik UrFO, 2*(20), 54—60.

Fateev, A. V. (1999). *Obraz vraga v sovetskoi propagande 1945—1954 gg.* Moskva: Institut rossiiskoi istorii RAN.

Gerovitch, S. (2002). *From newspeak to cyberspeak: A history of Soviet cybernetics.* Cambridge: The MIT Press.

Gerovitch, S. (2008). InterNyet: Why the Soviet union did not build a nationwide computer network. *History and Technology, 24*(4).

Golitsyna, A., & Prokolenko, A. (May 27, 2016). *Chnovniki khotiat podchinit' sebe ves' rossiiskii internet.* http://www.vedomosti.ru/technology/articles/2016/05/27/642739-chinovniki-hotyat-internetom.

Gorham, M., Lunde, I., & Paulsen, M. (Eds.). (2014). *Digital Russia: the language, culture and politics of new media communication.* London and New York: Routledge.

Gorny, E. (2009). *A creative history of the Russian internet.* Studies in Internet Creativity. Berlin: DVM Verlag Dr. Muller.

Gudkov, L. (2005). Ideologema "vraga": "Vragi" kak massovyi sindrom i mekhanizm sotsiokul'turnoi integratsii. In L. Gudkov (Ed.), *Obraz vraga* (pp. 7–79). Moskva: OGI.

Gupta, M., & Sharman, R. (Eds.). (2009). *Social and human elements of information security: Emerging trends and countermeasures.* New York: Information Science Reference.

Heller, M. (1988). *Cogs in the wheel: The formation of Soviet man.* London, UK: Collins Harvill.

John-Steiner, V., & Mahn, H. (1996). Sociocultural approaches to learning and development: A Vygotskian framework. *Educational Psychologist, 31*(3/4), 191–206.

Kontseptsiia. (November 23, 1995). *Kontseptsia formirovania i razvitiia edinogo informatsionnogo prostranstva Rossii i sootvetstvuuishchikh gosudarstvennykh informatsionnykh resursov.* Odobrena resheniem Presidenta Rossiiskoi Federatsii No. Pr-1694 http://lawru.info/dok/1995/11/23/n453820.htm.

Kontseptsiia. (May 28, 1999). *Kontseptsiia formirovaniia informatsionnogo obshchestva v Rossii.* Odobrena resheniem Gosudarstvennoi komissii po informatizatsii No. 32 http://www.iis.ru/library/riss/riss.ru.html.

Kukkola, J. (2018a). Civilian and military information infrastructure and the control of the Russian segment of internet. In *International conference on military communications and information systems (ICMCIS), 22-23 May 2018, Warsaw, Poland.*

Kukkola, J. (2018b). *New guidance for preparing Russian 'digital sovereignty' released.* Finnish Defence Research Agency. Research Bulletin 01 – 2018 https://puolustusvoimat.fi/documents/1951253/2815786/PVTUTKL+Tutkimuskatsaus+1-2018.pdf/64ed34db-e14a-4080-b5fa-d289d8472a43/PVTUTKL+Tutkimuskatsaus+1-2018.pdf.pdf.

Kukkola, J. (2018c). The Russian segment of internet as a resilient battlefield. In *ISMS annual conference 2018 "military sciences and future security challenges, 18-19 October, 2018, Warsaw, Poland.*

Kukkola, J., & Ristolainen, M. (2017). Russian conceptual control of the cyber domain: The five basic principles of war. In *Poster in the 16th European conference on cyber Warfare and security, 29-30 June 2017, Dublin, Ireland.*

Kukkola, J., & Ristolainen, M. (2018). Projected territoriality: A case study of the infrastructure of Russian 'digital borders'. *Journal on Information Warfare, 17*(2), 83–100.

Kukkola, J., Ristolainen, M., & Nikkarila, J.-P. (2017). *Game changer: Structural transformation of cyberspace.* Riihimäki: Finnish Defence Research Agency. http://puolustusvoimat.fi/web/tutkimus/tutkimuslaitoksen-julkaisut.

Minkomsvyaz. (October 11, 2016). *Federal'nyi zakon "O vnesenii izmenenii v Federal'nyi zakon "O sviazi" (Proekt).* http://regulation.gov.ru/projects#npa=58851.

Minkomsvyaz. (August 15, 2017). *Federal'nyi zakon "O vnesenii izmenenii v Federal'nyi zakon "O sviazi" (Proekt).* http://regulation.gov.ru/projects#npa=71277.

Napravlenie. (February 9, 2018). *O "dorzhnykh kartakh" po napravleniiam programmy "Tsifrovaia ekonomika Rossiiskoi Federatsii.* http://government.ru/orders/selection/401/30895/.

Nazarov, D. (2016). Rezervnaia kopiia: Mozhno li otkliuchit' rossiiskii internet ot global'noi seti? *FurFur.* http://www.furfur.me/furfur/freedom/freedom/218695-chto-takoe-rezervnaya-kopiya-interneta.

Nikiforov, N. (September 24, 2014). *Rabochaia vstrecha s Ministrom sviazi i massovykh kommunikatsii Nikolaem Nikiforovym (working visit with the Minister of mass communication nikolai nikiforov)*. http://www.kremlin.ru/events/president/news/copy/46668.

Nisbet, E. C., Kamenchuk, O., & Dal, A. (2017). A psychological firewall? Risk perceptions and public support for online censorship in Russia. *Social Science Quarterly, 98*(3), 958–975.

Nocetti, J. (2015). Contest and conquest: Russia and global internet governance. *International Affairs, 91*(1), 111–130.

Peters, B. (2016). *How not to network a nation: The uneasy history of the Soviet internet*. Cambridge: The MIT Press.

Programma. (August 27, 2014). *Gosudarstvennaia programma "Informatsionnoe obshchestvo" (2011-2020 gody)*. http://minsvyaz.ru/ru/activity/programs/1/.

Programma. (June 28, 2017). *Programma "tsifrovaia ekonomika Rossiiskoi Federatsii"*. http://static.government.ru/media/files/9gFM4FHj4PsB79I5v7yLVuPgu4bvR7M0.pdf.

Ristolainen, M. (2017). Should 'RuNet 2020' be taken seriously? Contradictory views about cybersecurity between Russia and the West. *Journal on Information Warfare, 16*(4), 113–131.

Rozhkov, R. (2016). Pervye litsa: Internet "liazhet" na sutki? Ia etogo voobshche ne ponimaiu" Gendirektor TTSI Aleksei Platonov ob osobennostiakh raboty interneta v Rossii. *Kommersant*.

Schmidt, H., Teubener, K., & Konradova, N. (Eds.). (2006). *Control + shift: Public and private usages of the Russian internet*. Nordersted: Books on Demand.

Singer, P. W., & Friedman, A. (2014). *Cybersecurity and cyberwar: What everyone needs to know*. Oxford: Oxford University Press.

Sjösted, R. (2010). *Talking threats: The social construction of national security in Russia and the United States*. Acta Universitatis Upsalaliensis. Report (p. 91). Department of Peace and Conflict Research.

Soldatov, A., & Borogan, I. (2015). *The Red Web: The struggle between Russia's digital dictators and the new online revolutionaries*. New York: Public Affairs.

Solomeshch, I. (2001). *Image of neighbour: The Karelian question in the 20th century Europe-an context*. Nordic Notes, 5/2001 http://diemperdidi.info/nordicnotes/vol05/articles/solomeshch.html.

Strategiia. (February 7, 2008). *Strategii razvitiia informatsionnogo obshchestva v Rossiiskoi Federatsii, No. Pr-212*. https://rg.ru/2008/02/16/informacia-strategia-dok.html.

Strategiia. (December 31, 2015). *Strategiia natsional'noi bezopasnosti Rossiiskoi Federatsii*. http://static.kremlin.ru/media/acts/files/0001201512310038.pdf.

Strategiia. (May 9, 2017). *Strategii razvitiia informatsionnogo obshchestva v Rossiiskoi Federatsii na 2017-2030 gody*. http://static.kremlin.ru/media/acts/files/0001201705100002.pdf.

Streltsov, A., & Pilyugin, P. (2016). K voprosu o tsifrovom suverenitete. *Informatizatsiia i sviaz'*, (2), 25–30.

Svoboda internet. (2017). *Svoboda interneta 2017: polzuchaiia kriminalizatsiia*. https://meduza.io/static/0001/Agora_Internet_Freedom_2017_RU.pdf.

Trenin, D. (2016). *Should we fear Russia?* Cambridge, UK: Polity Press.

Vargas-Leon, P. (2016). Tracking Internet shutdown practices: Democracies and hybrid regimes. In F. Musiani, D. Cogburn, L. DeNardis, & D. Levinson (Eds.), *The turn to infrastructure in internet governance. Information technology and global governance* (pp. 167–188). New York: Palgrave Macmillan.

Vygotsky, L. S. (1962). *Thought and language*. Cambridge MA: MIT Press.

Vygotsky, L. S. (1978). *Mind in society*. Cambridge MA: MIT Press.

Wagoner, B. (2014). A sociocultural approach to Peace and conflict. Peace and conflict. *Journal of Peace Psychology, 20*(2), 187–190.

Zakon. (2012). *Federalnyi zakon ot 28 iiulia 2012 g. No. 139-FZ. O vnesenii izmenenii v Federal'nyi zakon "O zashchite detei ot informatsii, prichiniaiushchei vred ikh zdorov'iu i razvitiiu.* https://rg.ru/2012/07/03/zakon-dok.html.

Zinovieva, E. (2016). Vozmoshnosti Rossii v global'nom informatsionnom obshchestve. *Vestnik MGIMO universiteta/MGIMO Review of International Relations, 3*(48), 17–29.

CHAPTER

4

The social and psychological impact of cyberattacks

Maria Bada[1], Jason R.C. Nurse[2]

[1] Cybercrime Centre, Computer Laboratory, University of Cambridge, Cambridge, United Kingdom; [2] School of Computing, University of Kent, Canterbury, United Kingdom

OUTLINE

Emerging Cyber Threats and Cognitive Vulnerabilities
https://doi.org/10.1016/B978-0-12-816203-3.00004-6

73

Introduction

The impact of cyberspace on society is undeniable. It has provided a platform for instantaneous communication, commerce and interaction between individuals and organizations across the globe. As cyberspace has grown in prominence, however, unfortunately so too have the number and variety of cyberattacks (Verizon, 2018). Cyberattacks are defined here as events which aim to compromise the integrity, confidentiality or availability of a system (technical or sociotechnical). These attacks range from hacking and denial-of-services (DoSs) to ransomware and spyware infections and can affect everyone from the public to the critical national infrastructure of a country (Nurse, 2018). In this article, we will examine this topic of cyberattacks from more of a social and behavioural science perspective, with the aim of exploring the social and psychological factors and impacts associated with these attacks.

Research has shown that members of the public are more likely to respond to the effects of a cyberattack rather than the attack itself (Gandhi et al., 2011; Minei & Matusitz, 2011). One example of this is a cyberattack where malware infects a national power station causing the hundreds of thousands of citizens to be without power. Here, the attack, that is, the malware infestation, may not worry individuals (the public); they will be much more considered about the effect, that is, being without power, thereby having no heating, ability to prepare food and so on. There are two key areas of impact that we aim to consider and provide an overview of the current research and thinking; these are the social and psychological (emotional and behavioural) impacts. The social impact of a cyberattack refers to aspects such as the social disruption caused to people's daily lives and widespread issues such as anxiety or loss of confidence in cyber or technology. Psychological impact can be informed by social impact and can include more personal aspects such as an individual's anxiety, worry, anger, outrage, depression and so on.

To inform our research, the chapter begins by first reflecting on some of the key issues relevant to understanding public reactions to malicious cyber events. We examine topics such as risk perception (Nurse, Creese, Goldsmith, & Lamberts, 2011; Rogers, Amlôt, Rubin, Wessely, & Krieger,

2007), locus of control (Ajzen, 2002), culture of fear (Stekel, 1930), the online disinhibition effect (Suler, 2004) and protection motivation (Blythe & Camp, 2012; Maddux & Rogers, 1983; Rogers, 1975), amongst others. Also, within scope of our assessment are the range of potential factors which can influence the public's level of perceived risk, such as the perpetrator's identity and the scale of the cyberattack.

Beliefs form an important component of our investigation. This is because a user's reaction to security generally and motivation to apply security mechanisms—if given the chance—depends on their beliefs about the perceived severity of an event, the susceptibility to the threat, the perceived self-efficacy and the cost and efficacy of preventative or mitigating behaviours (Blythe & Camp, 2012). These factors make it difficult to motivate protective cybersecurity practices (behaviours) as well as to predict public social and psychological responses to a cyberattack. This can be any form of attack ranging from existing threats to new concerns such as the cyber risks with Internet of Things or Artificial Intelligence (Nurse, Creese, & De Roure, 2017).

Another element of relevance is the general culture of fear related to crime and cyber events. Fear of crime can prompt people to change their behaviour. At the level of the individual, people generally respond to the fear of crime by adopting protective or avoidance behaviours (Reid, Roberts, & Hilliard, 1998). Phobophobia—the psychological fear of fears (Furedi, 2002)—can lead to stress, intense anxiety and unrealistic and persistent public fear of crime and danger, regardless of the actual presence of such fear factors. This phenomenon may also relate to the crime complex (Hale, 1996) and therefore cyberattacks and cybercrime.

Having discussed risk and attack perceptions, protection motivation theories and theories regarding public reactions to attacks and online crimes, we then critically reflect on two real-world cyberattack scenarios from 2017: the global WannaCry attack and the cyberattack on the Lloyds Banking Group. This seeks to understand the social and psychological impacts resulting from these attacks on an individual basis as well as to the wider society. These are all important topics for discussion and analysis as we aim to advance research into cyber threats from a cyberpsychology perspective.

Factors influencing perceptions of risk and reactions to risk

A user's motivation to react to perceived risk and apply security measures depends on their beliefs about the perceived severity of an event, the susceptibility to the threat, the perceived self-efficacy and the cost and efficacy of preventative or mitigating behaviours (Blythe &

Camp, 2012). Also, the general culture of fear related to crime and cyber events (Furedi, 2002) can prompt people to change their behaviour. In this section, the factors influencing perceptions of risk related to cyber events and reactions to risk are discussed. Moreover, different theories and theoretical models are presented as related to conduct online.

Perception of risk

Research in public perception of risk (Slovic, 1988, 2000; Sjöberg, 2000; Dickert, Västfjäll, Mauro, & Slovic, 2015) demonstrates that there are potential factors which can influence the public levels of perceived risk such as whether or not exposure to the risk is perceived to be: (1) voluntary (accepting increased risk through risky online activities or involuntary (as opposed to knowingly accepted), (2) familiar (due to the frequency of appearance in the media) or unfamiliar (i.e., lack of understanding of the causes and consequences), (3) controllable (due to safeguards that can be put in place) or uncontrollable (as opposed to feeling in control), (4) fair (i.e., random) or unfair (i.e., targeted) and (5) whether or not the risk causes 'dread'.

Also, it is suggested that attitude, risk sensitivity and specific fear can be used as explanatory variables for risk perception (Sjöberg, 2000). Nurse et al. (2011) further evidence this in considering that persons use four main dimensions in judging online risks, namely ability to control or avoid the risk, dread of consequences, unfamiliarity of risks and immediacy of consequences/impact. Members of the public acknowledge the threat of cyberattacks, but the steps that they take to address this threat vary. People react to risk in different ways based on dual information processing. Some react based on logic, analyzing risk, and others might react instinctual based on feelings about the risk (Dickert et al., 2015). Emotions can also serve as a spotlight for directing our attention but also motivating individuals to act. For example, people can decide on acting on risks related to technologies based on their feelings toward specific outcomes (Nurse, 2018).

Other authors propose that both experts and members of the public might confuse facts with their individual interpretation because perceptions of risk are often based on the interpretation of facts, which are fed by individual judgement, values, beliefs and attitudes (Beck, 1999). Blythe and Camp (2012) argued that overall, a user's motivation to apply security mechanisms depends on their beliefs about their susceptibility to exogenous security threats, their potential severity and the cost and efficacy of preventative or mitigating behaviours. This therefore fits with existing and prior literature.

Security decisions and behaviours are executed in a world of risk and uncertainty. Adams (2013) explains the notion of risk compensation by presenting a risk thermostat. He claims that individuals execute a balancing behaviour between their propensity to take risks (risk appetite) and perceived danger (risk perception), where risk propensity is determined by perceived rewards, whereas accidents (negative experiences) influence perceived danger.

Trust has been identified as a key issue impacting public perceptions of risk. The level of trust in an organizational body responsible for responding to the risk should be considered during both the policy-making and communication processes (Rogers et al., 2007). For example, a report by Symantec (2010) showed that nearly 9 in 10 adults are considering cybercrime and over a quarter actually expect to be scammed or defrauded online. Yet despite the universal threat and incidence of cybercrime, only half of adults in the study claim that they would change the way they behave online if they became a victim.

Therefore, policy makers need to understand how people think about and respond to risk and materialized attacks, given that without such insight policies or awareness, efforts might be unsuccessful.

Self-efficacy

Self-efficacy is considered not as skills themselves, but as the evaluation of what one can do with skills. It considers a person's belief in themselves and their abilities (Bandura, 1991). This concerns issues such as cyberattacks because it is important that individuals believe that they stand a chance of protecting themselves and responding successfully to an attack's occurrence.

Ajzen (2002) introduced a new concept about the relationship between self-efficacy and perceived behavioural control. He argued that "the central concept of perceived behavioural control consists of two factors: self-efficacy (about the ease/difficulty of performing a behavior) and the ability to control (the extent to which performance depends exclusively on the individual)". When individuals are able to determine or influence what is happening to them or what will happen to them, these individuals are considered to "be under control". Control is a central construction in psychology, and being under control is a worldwide desirable state of being for most people. The same reality holds in the online world, generally and in the face of a spate of emerging cyberattacks.

Protection motivation theory

According to Protection Motivation Theory (PMT) (Rogers, 1975; Rogers & Prentice-Dunn, 1997), environmental and personal factors are combined to pose a potential threat. The threat initiates two cognitive processes: threat appraisal and coping appraisal. The threat appraisal process evaluates the factors associated with the behaviour that potentially creates danger, including the intrinsic and extrinsic rewards accompanying the actions, the severity of the danger and one's vulnerability to the threat. The coping appraisal process evaluates one's ability to cope with, and avert, the threatened danger (self-efficacy and response efficacy), balanced with the costs (or efforts) associated with protective behaviour (response cost).

Threat appraisal refers to how susceptible one feels to a threat. For example, how vulnerable is an individual by the possibility of becoming a victim of a cyberattack such as phishing; naturally, susceptibility to phishing attacks is influenced by a range of other aspects (Iuga, Nurse, & Erola, 2016; Williams, Hinds, & Joinson, 2018). Coping appraisal evaluates the various factors that are likely to ensure that one engages in a recommended response that is preventive in nature. For instance, not opening emails being sent by an unknown sender, or untrustworthy or suspicious email address.

The theory therefore says that in order for an individual to adopt a safe behaviour, they need to believe that there is a severe threat that is likely to occur and that by adopting safe actions, they can effectively reduce the threat. The individual should also be convinced that they are capable of engaging in the behaviour and that it would cost only expected amounts in terms of effort expended. Measuring the 'intention' to engage in the recommended preventive activity is the most common indication of protection motivation.

Another key aspect of understanding the public response to malicious cyberattacks centres upon the fact that members of the public do not appear to perceive such attacks as a threat to themselves, and, if they do, they believe that there is very little that they can do to prevent such an attack. Instead, members of the public are more likely to respond to the event (e.g., loss of service), rather than the cyberattack, itself. We discuss this further in Case studies of cyberattacks section. Perceptions of what others expect or how others react to a threat are aspects of both types of appraisal. In general, increases in threat severity, threat vulnerability, response efficacy and self-efficacy facilitated adaptive intentions or behaviours. Conversely, decreases in maladaptive response rewards and adaptive response costs increased adaptive intentions or behaviours.

These factors make it difficult to infer social and psychological responses to a cyberattack. If we interpret malicious cyberattacks through the lens of PMT, the current state of the public understanding of the potential impact of such an event would possibly be described in high levels of threat appraisal, low levels of self-efficacy, confusion over response efficacy and high response costs due to the perceived difficulty of enacting security measures.

Locus of control

Another theory that can be utilized to describe emotional and behavioural responses to an online incident is that of locus of control (Ajzen, 2002). Locus of control aims to characterize whether people feel they have strong control over their life (internal locus of control) or whether they have to rely on external forces (external locus of control). The locus of control appears to affect learning, motivation and behaviour.

Persons with an internal locus of control feel that success or failure is due to their efforts or abilities. Alternately, individuals with an external locus of control are likely to believe that other factors such as luck or the difficulty of the target or the actions of other people are the cause of success or failure. For example, users with external locus of control might not often take protective measures against cyberattacks due to their beliefs that Internet providers or the government is responsible for ensuring a safer Internet.

Lack of control over a situation that is perceived as threatening or dangerous can give rise to feelings of emotional distress, fear and insecurity. Such strong emotions can on occasion lead to irrational behaviour (Sutherland, 2007) or other equally strong reactions. These are all aspects that can influence how members of the public (psychological) and society generally (social) are impacted by an attack.

Extended Parallel Process Model

Similar to PMT, the Extended Parallel Process Model (Witte, 1992a) suggests that when the perceived threat is low, independent from the level of perceived response efficacy, there may be no further processing of the message. Thus, there is no reaction to the invocation of fear because the threat is not subject to further processing (Witte, 1991). Also, the Model proposes that as the perceived threat grows while the counter-effect is high, the acceptance of a preventive advice will also increase. In such cases, individuals can realize that they are at risk of a serious threat and are motivated to protect themselves; consider that they can prevent the risk (high efficacy) and may deliberately and cognitively take action to address the risk. Fear invocations with high levels of threat and high levels of efficacy produce acceptance of a suggested behaviour (Kleinot & Rogers, 1982; Maddux & Rogers, 1983; Rogers & Mewborn, 1976; Witte, 1992a).

The cognitive processes that take place during risk control procedures trigger adjustment actions such as attitudes, intentions or behavioural changes that control the risk. However, as the perceived threat grows while the perceived efficacy is low, individuals will do the opposite of what is proposed. There is the argument that in order to control the unbearable fear of a state of low-perceived efficiency, a person will either consciously or unconsciously tend to deny the threat or react against the suggested preventive behaviour and perform even more risky behaviour to reduce fear or anxiety. This can relate to both the offline and the online environments. Overall, when the severity of the threat is high, combined with low efficacy, then people may tend to reject the suggested actions or are led to boomerang reactions (Kleinot & Rogers, 1982; Rippetoe & Rogers, 1987; Rogers & Mewborn, 1976; Witte, 1992a).

These points further evidence research around the effectiveness of cybersecurity awareness campaigns which often lead to failure of behaviour change (Bada, Sasse, & Nurse, 2015). In addition, when the perceived effectiveness is moderate, the critical point may not occur directly, but at a moderate level of the threat. For example, when perceived efficacy is moderate, people may initially think they can prevent a cyberattack. However, as the threat grows in intensity and relativity, individuals may begin to give up any hope of averting the threat or adequately addressing any subsequent impact.

Culture of fear

In the psychology of fear literature, Stekel (1930) makes the point that fear is in part hereditary, a legacy of centuries, that left its traces in our brain. Correspondingly, perceived efficacy consists of the individual's views on the severity of the threat, while perceived vulnerability consists of the person's attitudes about their chances of dealing with it.

The theory of self-efficacy (Bandura, 1977, 1986) presupposes that the perceived ineffectiveness of dealing with possible events is one that creates both fear expectations and avoidance behaviour. Individuals who judge themselves to be effective in managing potential threats, may feel neither fear nor avoid threats. On the contrary, if people judge themselves as ineffective in exercising control over potential threats, they react with stress and do not want to have any contact with them, therefore avoiding them. For example, in the occasion of a cyber-related incident such as a phishing scam, individuals might judge themselves as not having the necessary skills or knowledge in order to avoid such an incident, therefore avoiding to act or take any protective actions. If this is to occur on a large scale, it could have a notable social impact.

Fear expectations and avoidance behaviours are factors that can influence perceived inefficiency of managing situations. Acknowledging that human behaviour is largely regulated by personal efficacy beliefs, people can exercise their activities at the lowest levels of self-efficacy despite high fear invocation and can take preventive actions without having to wait for the feelings of fear and excitement to arise. Different theoretical approaches explain fear control procedures (Leventhal, 1970) or the way individuals cognitively recognize fear or threat, changing their attitudes, intentions or behaviours to avoid the threat (factors leading to acceptance of the message). Examining the causes of fear reveals some interesting realities. According to Witte (1994), the greater the threat, the greater fear is expressed. Also, the threat is related to the sense of fear and not to efficiency (Witte, 1994).

Witte (1992b) argued that perceived effectiveness only determines the nature of the reaction (control of fear or risk), while the perceived threat determines the intensity of the reaction (how much control of fear or risk is caused). Considering that the perceived threat and the fear-causing appear to be closely related, it is likely that the perceived threat and the emotion of fear cooperate to influence the intensity of a reaction to a call of fear. To place this in the context of online threats, when individuals are afraid of a major cyberattack and realize that a reaction could effectively prevent that threat, they are motivated to control the risk (protection incentive). This control process could begin with thinking about strategies to tackle that threat and reduce the impact of the corresponding risk on their lives. When risk control procedures dominate, people may arguably react to danger, not to fear.

Considering our case of cyberattacks, another example would be that victims of fraud and computer misuse who have been victimized before might take measures to avoid becoming a victim again in the future. The vast majority of victims of fraud and computer misuse have only been victimized once, with only a small proportion saying they have suffered two or more times. Statistics support this claim indicating that users can be quick to learn from their mistakes when they become victims of computer crime (Reeve, 2017).

Conversely, when perceived threat is high, but the perceived effectiveness is low, the fear control procedures are initiated. Fear is initially caused, and the threat becomes intense when individuals feel unable to prevent the threat. Thus, they are mobilized to manipulate their fear (defencive manipulation) by adopting reactions, such as denial. When fear control procedures dominate, individuals react to their fear, not to danger. Individuals might feel helpless and victimized while their lack of knowledge about cybercrime will lead them accepting the possibility of being victims or denying that possibility overall. Moreover, victims feel the usual set of emotions when they realize they have been scammed— from helplessness to rage.

According to Garland (2001), when it comes to fear of crime, *'our fears and resentments, but also our common-sense narratives and understandings, become settled cultural facts that are sustained and reproduced by cultural scripts'*. The idea of 'cultural scripts' can help to reveal much about emotions such as fear, arguably even in the cyberattack context. A cultural script communicates rules about feelings and also ideas about what those feelings mean. People interpret and internalize these rules according to their circumstances and temperament, while always remaining very much influenced by the rules. Consequently, the impact of fear is determined by the situation people find themselves in, but it is also, to some extent, the product of social construction (Altheide, 2002, p. 24). Fear is determined by the self, and the interaction of the self with others; it is also shaped by a cultural script that instructs people on how to respond to threats to their security.

The online disinhibition effect

Regarding the impact of cyberattacks on online behaviour, there are different aspects of cyberspace that need to be considered. One of these aspects surrounds the reality that individuals say and do things in cyberspace that they would not ordinarily say and do in the offline (face-to-face) world. For instance, they may loosen up, feel less restrained, and present themselves more openly. So pervasive is this phenomenon that a term has surfaced for it, namely the online disinhibition effect (Suler, 2004).

This disinhibition is empowered due to several factors. These consider the fact that people can form a different identity online and that they may feel less vulnerable in the way they express themselves or behave, in comparison to how they would act offline. Moreover, people can feel less visible online and therefore might engage in activities that they otherwise would not. This factor affects our discussions on impacts as the consequence of some online actions or activities may not be fully tangible to people in the offline world. This has also been discussed in other areas as it relates to cybercrime (Nurse, 2018).

Understanding public reactions to malicious cyber incidents

Emotional reactions to cybercrime

Research indicates that current forms of cyberattacks can cause psychological impact (Gandhi et al., 2011; Dallaway, 2016; Modic & Anderson, 2015). Depending on who the attackers and the victims are, the psychological effects of cyber threats may even rival those of traditional terrorism (Gross, Canetti, & Vashdi, 2016). Victims of online attacks and crime can suffer emotional trauma which can lead to depression. There is also some evidence of limited symptoms of acute stress disorder (ASD) in victims of crime in online virtual worlds, such as some anecdotal accounts of intrusive memories, emotional numbing and upset from victims of virtual sexual assault (Lynn, 2007).

As an example, the impact of identity theft on a victim at an emotional level can lead the person becoming distressed and be left feeling violated, betrayed, vulnerable, angry and powerless (Kirwan & Power, 2011). Often, victimization can lead victims to feelings of outrage, anxiety, a preference for security over liberty and little interest of adopting new technology due to loss of confidence in cyber. The victim can go into stages of grief, suffer from anger or rage. In some cases, victims may even blame themselves and develop a sense of shame; sextortion is a good example of this given how it initially starts (Nurse, 2018).

In other work, a Symantec (2010) study further showed that victims feel that they themselves are partly or wholly to blame; this in itself has consequences for the resulting psychological impact. The number of victims who act varies widely depending on location. For instance, 74% of those in Sweden contact the police, but this is significantly above the overall average of 44%. As a general rule, around half of victims will not contact anyone, although about a quarter might try taking some action themselves, even if it is only avoiding certain websites in the future. Other impacts can be isolation or even depression especially in the event of a financial loss.

According to Symantec, the top 10 emotional reactions to online attacks and cybercrime are the feelings of anger, annoyance and being cheated. Böhme and Moore (2012) found that directly experiencing cybercrime decreases the likelihood of shopping and banking online, while expressing concern about cybercrime has nearly twice as much negative impact on online behaviour than directly experiencing it. Modic and Anderson (2015) found that victims of financial fraud consistently reported emotional impact as more severe than financial impact across all fraud types.

Reflecting on the literature, we can see that it also demonstrates how even nonlethal forms of cyber terrorism have a considerable impact on the attitudes of victimized populations (Gross et al., 2016). Under attack, victims react with not only fear, as do victims of crime, but with demands for protection from the government, via surveillance and stronger regulations.

Estonia is frequently invoked in such discussions and a host of authors draw attention to the panic caused amongst the people of Estonia when parts of their cyber infrastructure were inaccessible due to DoS attacks in 2007 (Gandhi et al., 2011). However, the potential of large-scale malicious cyberattacks to change the public understanding and perception of cyber events could lead to an activation of the 'dread factors' of risk perception (i.e., catastrophic potential, fatal consequences, and high risks to future generations) which, in turn, can inform a multitude of spontaneous precautionary behaviours. This becomes of particular concern given the several predictions of possible future technology scenarios, and implications for security and privacy online (Williams, Axon, Nurse, & Creese, 2016).

Learnt helplessness

Findings show that less than 1 in 10 people (9%) claim that they feel 'very' safe online. Also, only half (51%) of adults asked, would change the way they behave online if they became a victim (Symantec, 2010). This provides an interesting comparison to our earlier discussions. People might accept a situation, even if it feels unpleasant just because they cannot understand it or do not know enough about it. Following this point, one might argue that persons may accept cyberattacks because of a sense of 'learnt helplessness'.

Due to a sense of learnt helplessness (for more on the term, see: Seligman, 1975; Hirtz, 1998) and a lack of knowledge about online attacks and ways to resolve an incident, users may simply accept the possibility of being victims. Indirectly, a key question therefore becomes, whether they also accept the reality of impacts and hope that the severity is low. The anonymous nature of cybercrime can lead to an acceptance that one (e.g., an individual, industry, government) will become a victim of cybercrime at some point. Moreover, the sense of learned helplessness can potentially also result in a low uptake of protective security behaviours.

Users are called upon to make many security-related decisions every day which can cause anxiety. These behaviours include: (a) not opening an email from a sender they do not recognize, (b) not accessing unknown attachments, (c) only downloading and running programs from trustworthy sources, (d) the use of antivirus software and security software (e.g., firewall) and (e) creating regular backups. Some of these decisions can also cause the user feelings of anxiety due to a lack of knowledge about the possible implications of making incorrect decisions.

Members of the public have often reported a lack of knowledge about a number of key areas within the cybersecurity domain. A few examples are lack of knowledge about how to use security packages, how to secure their technology devices and the threats online. Even when these individuals are aware of the threats, they may report that they do not understand them (Gross, Canetti, & Vashdi, 2017). These low levels of public understanding of cyber threats and security practices could lead to a lack of public engagement with security issues and a general loss of confidence in cyber and/or technology. This also has been seen in the domain of information privacy in the context of new forms of technology, where some users now consider privacy as 'the boring bit' (Williams, Nurse, & Creese, 2017). These issues characterize the broad social impacts.

Cyberattack-related variables

The public response to a cyberattack is informed by a number of cyber-specific variables such as the attacker identity, the target identity, the scale of the attack as well as the government communication of a cyberattack and the time of revelation of a malicious event.

Public reactions may differ according to the disclosed identity of a given attacker. The principal categories of an actor are terrorist, hacktivist and criminal—all of whom might be capable of launching attacks that could qualify as issues of serious public concern (Nurse & Bada, 2018). Criminals are, on average, less likely to publicly reveal their identity (assuming any identity, pseudonym or otherwise) because anonymity facilitates them better. Moreover, the target identity can impact the public response. For example, if a series of fraud incidents impact individuals at random, it may be expected that it will cause less panic or outrage as compared to a targeted attack towards a national financial, utility or health institution.

Additionally, the scale of an attack will influence its impact. The full extent of an attack might not become apparent immediately, particularly if second- and third-order systems fail. Finally, the way that the government will communicate a cyberattack and the time of revelation of a malicious event will impact the level of public response. This information can influence the direction and dynamics of public response. The ways in which members of the public are likely to find out about a cyberattack is also an important variable. Different levels of public response can be caused due to loss of service, public announcements from the attacker or from government announcements, as will be seen in the next section of this chapter.

Lawson (2013) draws upon the history of technology and failures of large sociotechnical systems, military history and—most pertinent here—disaster sociology to suggest that 'fear and panic' may not be the defining features of public reactions to future cyberattacks. As mentioned above, members of the public are more likely to respond to the event (e.g., loss of service), rather than the cyberattack itself.

Case studies of cyberattacks

Thus far in this chapter, we have reflected upon the literature pertinent to understanding the impact of cyberattacks at the psychological and social levels. We now extend this discussion to real-world cases of such threats that have occurred over recent years. In particular, this work focuses on two cyberattacks in 2017, namely the WannaCry attack and the cyberattack on the Lloyds Banking Group. Our aim is to examine these attacks and the impacts that they have had from a social and psychological perspective, while drawing on insights presented earlier in this chapter.

WannaCry ransomware attack in 2017

WannaCry was a computer worm responsible for one of the most devastating cyberattacks in recent history. In addition to spreading across computer networks using the Windows operating system, WannaCry (also known as WannaCrypt and WanaCrypt0r) encrypted files of the host computer and only allowed access to those files after a bitcoin ransom payment was made. While ransomware itself was not new, WannaCry was particularly successful because it targeted a computer vulnerability that many organizations and individuals did not yet install security patches (i.e., software updates) to address.

Reflecting on the social impact of the attack, WannaCry infected over 200,000 victims in at least 150 countries (Reuters, 2017). These included members of the public, but also healthcare organizations, car manufacturers, telecoms companies, delivery services and the education sector. Due to the nature of the attack, the disruption it caused at the social level was quite significant. Organizations closed (causing people to be sent home), production stopped (resulting in product backlogs), and many businesses were unaware of how best to restore services. Overall, people felt a loss of control (Ajzen, 2002) as the threat was so pervasive and the only option for recovery—assuming no recent backups were made—was to pay the ransom. In total, these disruptions led to an estimated $8 billion in economic costs globally (Barlyn, 2017).

In the United Kingdom, critical infrastructure such as the National Health Service (NHS) was also impacted. A total of 48 NHS trusts were infected in England and 13 in Scotland (BBC, 2017). This resulted in direct disruption to people's lives in the context of their health. Specifically, there were cancelled operations, certain scans and treatments were postponed and ambulances were diverted. This is a particularly worry situation given how long patients often have to wait for some treatments. WannaCry also prompted government responses—in the United Kingdom a Cobra meeting (i.e., an emergency response government committee meeting) was called, and in the United States, the homeland security adviser was ordered to coordinate the government's response and help to organize the search for the responsible parties (Sanger, Chan, & Scott, 2017). This level of response from governments further emphasized the impact of the threat in the eyes of the public.

An interesting point to note here is the government's comments on the attack. In particular, there was an emphasis on the fact that the attack had not targeted the NHS and that it was international. According to The Independent, the UK's Home Secretary stated: *"If you look at who's been impacted by this virus, it's a huge variety across different industries and across international governments. ... This is a virus that attacked Windows platforms. ... The fact is the NHS has fallen victim to this. ... I don't think it's to do with that preparedness"* (The Independent, 2017). This message was likely meant to remove the gloom and potential public despair associated with a targeted NHS attack, as well as to reassure people that the country is prepared for such events. This aims to support people's trust in the government and in technological systems.

The psychological impact of WannaCry was also significant. For many it resulted in worry, anguish, disbelief and a sense of helplessness—these are many of the issues discussed earlier in this chapter (Böhme & Moore, 2012; Nurse, 2018; Symantec, 2010). If we use the infection of NHS locations as an example, there are numerous cases to examine. Possibly one of the most well-reported in the set is that of a man who was preparing for a heart surgery and had it cancelled hours before it was due to take place (Fisher, Therrien, Hand, & McCague, 2017). This led to his frustration, inconvenience to family members who travelled to stay close by and bewilderment as to why anyone would wish to attack a hospital. Psychologically he was also impacted given that he had mentally prepared himself for the heart surgery being conducted on that date, and because it would now need to be rescheduled to some point in the future. These factors correlate with many of the emotional reactions to cybercrime discussed before (Symantec, 2010).

Psychologically, there was also the realisation by many that cyberattacks could now cause the loss of life. As reported by the BBC, a member of NHS staff noted: *"Absolute carnage in the NHS today. Two Hyperacute stroke centres (the field I work in) in London have closed as of this afternoon. Patients will almost certainly suffer and die because of this"* (Fisher et al., 2017). This view is also reported by another person—an IT specialist— interviewed in the article: *"This kind of attack usually causes some inconvenience or financial loss [to] its victims but in this case it may well cause loss of life"*. This is an important point as it relates to the severity of the threat (when considering PMT) but it can also cause further issues, given that individuals' behaviour will not necessarily prevent this type of attack.

Lloyds Banking Group Denial-of-Service attack in 2017

In January 2017, the Lloyds Banking Group and other banks in the United Kingdom fell victim to a DoS attack that persisted over a 2-day period. DoS describes an attack where systems are bombarded with illegitimate data or requests and therefore become unable to respond to legitimate requests (e.g., for a webpage or service access) in a timely manner (Nurse, 2018). In this instance, the financial institutions were attacked by a distributed DoS (DDoS) in which the illegitimate requests originated from multiple, dynamically changing locations. The Lloyds group were one of the most significantly targeted banks during this attack, and attack impacts included system unavailability and limited online service access for its customers.

At the broad social and societal levels, the attack affected millions of bank customers. According to reports, perpetrators attempted to block access to the bank's 20 million UK accounts (Collinson, 2017). The result was an impact on individuals and businesses, particularly their ability to login to online systems. As such, some customers would have been unable to view balances, make payments (e.g., for rent and bills), and conduct bank transfers (e.g., for necessary one-off transactions). Another pertinent factor here was that this type of DDoS attack targeting the banking sector had occurred in the past.

In 2015, a similar cyberattack occurred which compromised the services of UK banks, RBS and NatWest (Collinson, 2015). A particularly worrying reality of that attack was the time in which it occurred, that is, near to payday; this resulted in a maximum impact on some individuals and some widespread panic. One noteworthy difference and a key factor in the more recent attack was the number of days across which it took place. This extended period of 2 days (with some reports even suggesting it was longer for some customers) meant that not only was the reputation of the bank damaged, but also that customers' lives may have been seriously disrupted during that time.

To consider the response from government, one MP made the point that the cyberattack was worrying for society and that more needed to be done. According to The Guardian, the then-MP stated: *"The attack on Lloyds was deeply troubling. Thousands of customers were affected by this, the latest in a long list of failures and breaches of banking IT systems. … As I have already pointed out, it is time to consider whether a single point of responsible for cyber risk in the financial services sector is now required"* (Collinson, 2017). This demonstrates some high-level concern for the finance sector broadly as a result of these types of cyberattacks. There are also parallels for wider public confidence in technology. To consider the 2015 attack, one NatWest customer tweeted: *"Can't log in to #natwest yet again to check up on some transactions … and they want me to opt out of paper statements?! No chance"* (Collinson, 2015). This is poignant as it relates to how individuals perceive technology and risk, and how attacks can result in less trust in technology.

Analyzing the psychological impact of the Lloyds DDoS attack, it caused customers to be upset and frustrated—this was therefore mainly an emotional response. As reported by the BBC, one customer expressed: *"Haven't been able to access the site or app for over 36 h now—is anything being done about this?"* (Peachey, 2017). This was one of a series of complains made on social media about the ongoing issue. Here we see one of the prime uses of social media (e.g., Twitter, Facebook and blogging platforms) today—that is, allowing members of the public to directly reach out to companies (particularly for complains) and have their voice heard publicly.

While it is difficult to know the full extent of the psychological impact, we can assume that lack of access to bank accounts and potentially personal funds (e.g., if money had to be transferred from one account to the another to facilitate a withdrawal) would have significantly increased customer stress and anxiety. There could have been several crucial reasons for account access, and depending on those needs, the emotions of stress, anger, pain, depression or helplessness could have resulted. This means that many of the follow-up issues highlighted in Factors influencing perceptions of risk and reactions to risk and Understanding public reactions to malicious cyber incidents sections immediately become relevant here. As mentioned earlier, the length of the disruption was a core factor as it would have exacerbated any initial inconvenience. These are all important concerns because they could each incite a change in how the public views cyberattacks and whether they believe they have any control or skills to protect themselves or their families.

Conclusions

As online threats and cyberattacks continue to permeate the Internet, it is essential that we as a community develop a better understanding of these issues and how they can impact our lives. This chapter took a significant step towards that goal by exploring how members of the public perceive and engage with risk and how they can be impacted after a cyberattack has taken place. We focused on the social and psychological impacts of attacks as these are often overlooked in research and practice. These are, however, crucial factors in enhancing our understanding of the broader side of attack impacts. To ground our work, we examined two well-known cyberattacks and considered them in the context of the breadth of outcomes. It is expected that this research will motivate others to further investigate this area and the interaction between cybersecurity and cognitive factors.

References

Adams, J. (2013). Risk compensation in cities at risk. In H. Joffe, T. Rossetto, & J. Adams (Eds.), *Cities at risk. ANTHR* (pp. 25–44). Netherlands: Springer.

Ajzen, I. (2002). Perceived behavioral control, self-efficacy, locus of control, and the theory of planned behavior. *Journal of Applied Social Psychology, 32*, 665–683.

Altheide, D. L. (2002). *Creating fear; news and the construction of crisis.* New York: Aldine De Gruyter.

Bada, M., Sasse, A. M., & Nurse, J. R. C. (2015). Cyber Security Awareness Campaigns: Why do they fail to change behaviour?. In *Proceedings of the international conference on cyber security for sustainable society (CSSS) coventry, UK* (pp. 118–131). SSN+.

Bandura, A. (1977). Self-efficacy: Toward a unifying theory of behavioral change. *Psychological Re-view, 84*, 191–215.

Bandura, A. (1986). Fearful expectations and avoidant actions as coeffects of perceived self-inefficacy. *American Psychologist, 41*(12), 1389–1391.

Bandura, A. (1991). Social cognitive theory of self-regulation. *Organizational Behavior and Human Decision Processes, 50*, 248–287.

Barlyn, S. (2017). *Global cyber attack could spur $53 billion in losses - Lloyd's of London. Reuters.* Retrieved July 14 2018, from https://uk.reuters.com/article/uk-cyber-lloyds-report/global-cyber-attack-could-spur-53-billion-in-losses-lloyds-of-london-idUKKBN1A20AH.

BBC. (2017). *NHS 'robust' after cyber-attack.* Retrieved July 14 2018, from https://www.bbc.co.uk/news/uk-39909441.

Beck, U. (1999). *World risk society.* Cambridge: Polity Press.

Blythe, J., & Camp, J. L. (2012). Implementing mental models. In *IEEE symposium on security and privacy workshops, 24-25 May 2012, san Francisco, CA, 86-90.*

Böhme, R., & Moore, T. (2012). How do consumers react to cybercrime?. In *eCrime researchers summit* (pp. 1–12). Las Croabas.

Collinson, P. (2015). Cyber attack hits RBS and NatWest online customers on payday. *The Guardian.* Retrieved July 4 2018, from https://www.theguardian.com/business/2015/jul/31/rbs-and-natwest-customers-complain-of-online-problemss.

Collinson, P. (2017). Lloyds bank accounts targeted in huge cybercrime attack. *The Guardian.* Retrieved July 4 2018, from https://www.theguardian.com/business/2017/jan/23/lloyds-bank-accounts-targeted-cybercrime-attack.

Dallaway, E. (2016). #ISC2Congress: Cybercrime victims left depressed and traumatized. *Infosecurity Magazine.* Retrieved July 4 2018, from https://www.infosecurity-magazine.com/news/isc2congress-cybercrime-victims/.

Dickert, S., Västfjäll, D., Mauro, R., & Slovic, P. (2015). The feeling of risk: Implications for risk perception and communication. In H. Cho, T. Reimer, & K. A. McComas (Eds.), *The SAGE handbook of risk communication* (pp. 41–54). Thousand Oaks, CA: Sage Publications.

Fisher, M., Therrien, A., Hand, J., & McCague, B. (2017). *How cyber-attack is disrupting NHS.* BBC News. Retrieved July 4 2018, from https://www.bbc.com/news/live/39901370.

Furedi, F. (2002). *Culture of fear: Risk-taking and the morality of low expectation.* London: Continuum.

Gandhi, R., Sharma, A., Mahoney, W., Sousan, W., Zhu, Q., & Laplante, P. (2011). Dimensions of cyber attacks: Social, political, economic, and cultural. *IEEE Technology and Society Magazine, 30*(1), 28–38.

Garland, D. (2001). *The culture of control; crime and social order in contemporary society.* Oxford: OUP.

Gross, M. L., Canetti, D., & Vashdi, D. R. (2016). The psychological effects of cyber terrorism. *Bulletin of the Atomic Scientists, 72*(5), 284–291.

Gross, M. L., Canetti, D., & Vashdi, D. R. (2017). Cyberterrorism: Its effects on psychological well-being, public confidence and political attitudes. *Journal of Cybersecurity, 3*(1), 49–58.

Hale, C. (1996). Fear of crime: A review of the literature. *International Review of Victimology, 4,* 79–150.

Hirtz, R. (1998). Martin Seligman's journey from learned helplessness to learned happiness. *The Pennsylvania Gazette.* Retrieved August 4 2018, from http://www.upenn.edu/gazette/0199/hirtz.html.

Iuga, C., Nurse, J. R. C., & Erola, A. (2016). Baiting the hook: Factors impacting susceptibility to phishing attacks. *Human-centric Computing and Information Sciences, 6*(8). https://doi.org/10.1186/s13673-016-0065-2.

Kirwan, G., & Power, A. (2011). *The psychology of cyber crime: Concepts and principles.* IGI Global.

Kleinot, M. C., & Rogers, R. W. (1982). Identifying effective components of alcohol misuse prevention programs. *Journal of Studies on Alcohol, 43,* 802–811.

Lawson, S. (2013). Beyond cyber-doom: Assessing the limits of hypothetical scenarios in the framing of cyber-threats. *Journal of Information Technology and Politics, 10*(1), 86–103.

Leventhal, H. (1970). Findings and theory in the study of fear communications. In L. Berkowitz (Ed.), *Advances in experimental social psychology* (Vol. 5, pp. 119–186). New York: Academic Press.

Lynn, R. (2007). *Virtual rape is traumatic, but is it a crime?*. Retrieved August 4 2018, from http://www.wired.com/culture/lifestyle/commentary/sexdrive/2007/05/sexdrive_0504.

Maddux, J. E., & Rogers, R. W. (1983). Protection motivation and self-efficacy: A revised theory of fear appeals and attitude change. *Journal of Experimental Social Psychology, 19*, 469–479.

Minei, E., & Matusitz, J. (2011). Cyberterrorist messages and their effects on targets: A qualitative analysis. *Journal of Human Behavior in the Social Environment, 21*(8), 995–1019.

Modic, D., & Anderson, R. (2015). It's all over but the crying: The emotional and financial impact of internet fraud. *IEEE Security and Privacy, 13*(5), 99–103.

Nurse, J. R. C. (2018). Cybercrime and you: How criminals attack and the human factors that they seek to exploit. In A. Attrill-Smith, C. Fullwood, M. Keep, & D. J. Kuss (Eds.), *Oxford handbook of cyberpsychology* (2nd ed.). Oxford: OUP https://doi.org/10.1093/oxfordhb/9780198812746.013.35.

Nurse, J. R. C., & Bada, M. (2018). The group element of cybercrime: Types, dynamics, and criminal operations. In A. Attrill-Smith, C. Fullwood, M. Keep, & D. J. Kuss (Eds.), *Oxford handbook of cyberpsychology* (2nd ed.). Oxford: OUP https://doi.org/10.1093/oxfordhb/9780198812746.013.36.

Nurse, J. R. C., Creese, S., & De Roure, D. (2017). Security risk assessment in Internet of Things systems. *IT Professional, 19*(5), 20–26. IEEE https://doi.org/10.1109/MITP.2017.3680959.

Nurse, J. R. C., Creese, S., Goldsmith, M., & Lamberts, K. (2011). Trustworthy and effective communication of cybersecurity risks: A review. In *Proceedings of international workshop on socio-technical aspects in security and trust (STAST)* (pp. 60–68). IEEE. https://doi.org/10.1109/STAST.2011.6059257.

Peachey, K. (2017). Lloyds online banking problems enter second day. *BBC News*. Retrieved August 14 2018, from https://www.bbc.co.uk/news/business-38594058.

Reeve, T. (2017). Once bitten, twice shy: ONS stats reveal public response to cyber-crime. *Magazine*. Retrieved August 14 2018, from https://www.scmagazineuk.com/once-bitten-twice-shy-ons-stats-reveal-public-response-cyber-crime/article/1475468.

Reid, L. W., Roberts, J. T., & Hilliard, H. M. (1998). Fear of crime and collective action: An analysis of coping strategies. *Sociological Inquiry, 68*(3), 312–328.

Reuters. (2017). *Cyber attack hits 200,000 in at least 150 countries: Europol*. Retrieved August 14 2018, from https://www.reuters.com/article/us-cyber-attack-europol/cyber-attack-hits-200000-in-at-least-150-countries-europol-idUSKCN18A0FX.

Rippetoe, P. A., & Rogers, R. W. (1987). Effects of components of protection-motivation theory on adaptive and maladaptive coping with a health threat. *Journal of Personality and Social Psychology, 52*, 596–604.

Rogers, R. W. (1975). A protection motivation theory of fear appeals and attitude change. *Journal of Psychology, 91*, 93–114.

Rogers, M. B., Amlôt, R., Rubin, G., Wessely, S., & Krieger, K. (2007). Mediating the social and psychological impacts of terrorist attacks: The role of risk perception and risk communication. *International Review of Psychiatry, 19*, 279–288.

Rogers, R. W., & Mewborn, C. R. (1976). Fear appeals and attitude change: Effects of a threat's noxiousness, probability of occurrence, and the efficacy of the coping responses. *Journal of Personality and Social Psychology, 34*, 54–61.

Rogers, R. W., & Prentice-Dunn, S. (1997). Protection motivation theory. In D. S. Gochman (Ed.), *Handbook of health behavior research 1: Personal and social determinants* (pp. 113–132). New York, NY, US: Plenum Press.

Sanger, D. E., Chan, S., & Scott, M. (2017). Ransomware's aftershocks feared as U.S. Warns of complexity. *The New York Times*. Retrieved July 14 2018, from https://www.nytimes.com/2017/05/14/world/europe/cyberattacks-hack-computers-monday.html.

Seligman, M. E. P. (1975). *Helplessness: On depression, development, and death.* San Francisco: W.H. Freeman.

Sjöberg, L. (2000). Factors in risk perception. *Risk Analysis, 20*, 1–12.

Slovic, P. (1988). Risk perception. In C. C. Travis (Ed.), *Contemporary issues in risk analysis: Vol. 3: Carcinogen risk assessment* (pp. 171–181). New York: Plenum.

Slovic, P. (2000). *The perception of risk.* London: Earthscan.

Stekel, W. (1930). *Les etats d' angoisse nerveux.* Payot.

Suler, J. (2004). The online disinhibition effect. *Cyberpsychology and Behaviour, 7*(3), 321–324.

Sutherland, S. (2007). *Irrationality: The enemy within.* London: Pinter & Martin.

Symantec. (2010). *Norton cybercrime report: The human impact.* Retrieved June 14 2018, from https://www.symantec.com/content/en/us/home_homeoffice/media/pdf/cybercrime_report/Norton_USA-Human%20Impact-A4_Aug4-2.pdf.

The Independent. (2017). *NHS cyber attack: International manhunt to find criminals behind WannaCry ransomware that crippled hospital systems.* Retrieved July 14 2018, from https://www.independent.co.uk/news/uk/home-news/wannacry-wanna-detector-accident-and-emergency-patient-appointment-operation-a7734831.html.

Verizon. (2018). *2018 Data breach investigations report.* Retrieved August 4 2018, from https://www.verizonenterprise.com/verizon-insights-lab/dbir/.

Williams, M., Axon, L., Nurse, J. R. C., & Creese, S. (2016). Future scenarios and challenges for security and privacy. In *Research and technologies for society and industry leveraging a better tomorrow (RTSI), 2016 IEEE 2nd international forum on* (pp. 1–6). IEEE. https://doi.org/10.1109/RTSI.2016.7740625.

Williams, E. J., Hinds, J., & Joinson, A. N. (2018). Exploring susceptibility to phishing in the workplace. *International Journal of Human-Computer Studies, 120*, 1–13.

Williams, M., Nurse, J. R. C., & Creese, S. (2017). Privacy is the boring bit: User perceptions and behaviour in the internet-of-things. In *Proceedings of the 15th international conference on privacy, security and trust (PST).* https://doi.org/10.1109/PST.2017.00029.

Witte, K. (1991). *Preventing AIDS through persuasive communication: Fear appeals and preventive-action efficacy.* Doctoral dissertation. Irvine: University of California.

Witte, K. (1992a). The role of threat and efficacy in AIDS prevention. *International Quarterly of Community Health Education, 12*, 225–249.

Witte, K. (1992b). Putting the fear back in fear appeals: The extended parallel process model. *Communication Monographs, 59*, 329–349.

Witte, K. (1994). Fear control and danger control: A test of the extended parallel process model (EPPM). *Communication Monographs, 61*, 113–134.

Further reading

Bandura, A., & Adams, N.E. (1977). Analysis of self-efficacy theory of behavioral change. *Cognitive Therapy and Research, 1*(4), 287–310.

Betz, D. J., & Stevens, T. (2011). *Cyberspace and the state.* London: Routledge.

Blythe, J., Camp, J., & Garg, V. (2011). Targeted risk communication for computer security. In *15th international conference on intelligent user interfaces* (pp. 295–298).

Prochaska, J. O., Redding, C. A., & Evers, K. (2002). The transtheoretical model and stages of change. In K. Glanz, B. K. Rimer, & F. M. Lewis (Eds.), *Health behavior and health education: Theory, research, and practice* (3rd ed.). San Francisco, CA: Jossey-Bass, Inc.

Virtanen, S. (2017). Fear of cybercrime in Europe: Examining the effects of victimization and vulnerabilities. *Psychiatry, Psychology and Law, 24*(3), 323–338.

The relationship between user religiosity and preserved privacy in the context of social media and cybersecurity

Rami Baazeem, Alaa Qaffas

University of Jeddah, Jeddah, Saudi Arabia

OUTLINE

Emerging Cyber Threats and Cognitive Vulnerabilities
https://doi.org/10.1016/B978-0-12-816203-3.00005-8

93

Introduction

Humans always need to develop friendships, intimate relationships and the ability to argue or to engage in sexual activity in private (Rachels, 2017). If this information is leaked, it might affect the individual well-being, dignity or cost them more than that (Etzioni, 2017).

Online privacy is one of the major problems for internet users (LaRose & Rifon, 2006; Lwin & Williams, 2003). It has attracted much of research attention, particularly in the online and e-commerce settings. The past studies mainly focus on the technological aspects of privacy issues, with minimal light shed on the individual behaviours or views of privacy.

Although privacy is a right that all people should have, yet individual interpretation of the scope and extent of privacy made it difficult to investigate the issues. In addition, information and communication technologies (ICTs) change the nature of privacy. With the excessive use of search engines and the easy access to data, the individual privacy concerns have increased mainly in improper access, use and manipulation of personal information (Moor, 1997; Wilford, 2004).

Studies into information privacy have been conducted in corporate and commercial environments (Dinev & Hart, 2006; Smith, Milberg & Burke, 1996), while in recent years the focus has shifted to individual privacy levels (Saridakis et al., 2016). Surveys showed that online privacy concerns are the main reason for not using the internet or e-commerce (Metzger & Docter, 2003). In the information society, online privacy became an international human rights issue (Smith et al., 1996). This chapter will look at the literature of the online information privacy and its relation to five constructs, technical, behaviour, companies, social network and religion, which affect the cybersecurity. Also, it will explain how the individual religiosity affects the user privacy, which in return has an impact on the cybersecurity in general.

Cybersecurity

Cybersecurity entails the activities of protecting data and information systems such as applications, data centres, databases, computers and networks. Cybersecurity should be undertaken using the appropriate technological and procedural security measures. Organizations use technological solutions, antivirus software and firewalls to protect computer network systems and personal data (Wall, 2008). However, this is insufficient because cyberterrorists keep devising multiple ways to commit the crime that supersede the ability of these security measures. Besides implementing cybersecurity infrastructure, it is vital to educate the population on how to use it appropriately. There is a need to integrate cyber safety and cyber ethics in the educational process right from the start.

Most cyberattacks are indiscriminate and automated and tend to exploit the vulnerabilities instead of targeting certain organizations. In most cases, issues of cybersecurity lead to the disruption of operations, which can lead to considerable reputational and financial damage to an organization. According to Deibert (2012), an organization can lose clients, business, reputation and assets in case of a cyberattack. Additionally, it causes regulatory litigation and fines. Cybersecurity can be enhanced through the development of a solid foundation where the cybersecurity technology stack is grown.

The advancement of technology in today's evolving world means that people can store large volumes of information in cyberspace, which makes it easier for various individuals globally to access it. It has become more comfortable and fast to obtain information over the internet than it was decades ago. The sensitivity of data stored in the cyberspace requires the implementation of sound cybersecurity strategies to avoid unauthorized and malicious access to sensitive information relating to finances, government data and personal information. The following write-up presents a review of various literature materials dealing with the issue of cybersecurity.

The advancement of security has meant that every transaction or activity conducted on the online platform faces several risks from hackers, spyware and malware. According to Deibert (2012), organizations have been forced to employ reliable and effective cybersecurity strategies to deal with emerging cyber threats including warfare, espionage and cybercrime. The risks have led to the transformation of the domain into an issue of national security, which has become a critical force that has influenced global communication today. The threat has also led to policymakers developing strategies to deal with the ever-developing range of cyber threats due to the advancement of technology with innovations coming with new threats.

Bada and Sasse (2014) state that the increase in the application of technology has led to an increase in cybercrimes while also enhancing cybersecurity. The enhancement of cybersecurity is through the data protection methods such as the use of one-time password protection, detection of malicious attacks and user virtualisation. Cybersecurity is a complicated issue that cannot be reduced merely into an approach of individual security and network security. It relates to the broader point of the economy, the nation, the society and the state. Technology has become part of our everyday life, which further emphasizes the need for cybersecurity. Cybersecurity lies in the interlinkage between the threatened party, the threat itself and the source of the danger. The aspect of cybersecurity has become critical because of the increase in the integration of technology in different areas such as finance, banking, entertainment, national defence, communications, e-commerce and government departments (Deibert, 2011). The application of technology has made it possible to increase work efficiency, simplify work and solve problems. However, it has also exposed firms to the risk of losing their information due to cyber threats. Thus, protection of data becomes a critical aspect in the process of integrating technology in an organization.

Wall (2008) perceives that the lack of clear laws and regulations has led to an increase in cyber threats. Despite millions of people around the world receiving millions of cyber threats, the rate of prosecution is still low. As a result, it has led to a problem of uncertainty which impedes individuals from enjoying the full benefits of the internet through increased commerce, accessible and improved governance, online transactions and leisure benefits. The advancement of technology in recent decades has not been backed up by the progress of the criminal justice system. With the current two-century-old system designed to deal with the social effects of urban migration, it is unable to cope with globalized virtual threats.

de Lange and von Solms (2012) state that children are the most vulnerable group to online dangers. The advancement of technology means that children become acclimatised with from an early age. However, they do not possess the expertise and knowledge to protect themselves with most of the parents not understanding the online behaviours of their children. They also state that there is an apparent lack of education on the safe use of the internet, which leads to unconscious and unsafe online behaviour. On the other hand, parents are also unaware and ill-prepared of the cyber threats as they lack the relevant expertise, experience and education.

Social media has been used as an excellent reconnaissance tool where scammer engineers crime on their victims when they neglect their privacy settings or publicly put personal information, photos or posts (Kesan & Hayes, 2014). Phoney Facebook updates have been used to prey on users to click on a link purporting to offer free merchandise of participating in surveys. Users have placed much emphasis on the socialization bit and disregarding the risk part. The relaxed environment on social media has led to phishing being an easy expedition, which not only puts the user at risk but also the entire organization.

Lange and Solms (2012) state that the lack of awareness and know-how about the cyber risks that social media pose leads to the risky practises that expose them to cybercrime. Some of the risky behaviours that children engage in include posting of personal information and whereabouts on the social media and public websites. Halevi, Lewis and Memon (2013) add that the advancement of the internet has led to the increased popularity of social media platforms such as Twitter, Email and Facebook. The demand has led to security concerns because of the rise in phishing attacks targeting the user's personal information. Scammers have used social media to extract monetary gain or personal information. The lack of cybersecurity measures such as privacy settings that limit the possibility of sharing personal information to unintended parties facilitates this activity on social media.

According to Bada and Sasse (2014), the creation of awareness and training of employees is critical in the modern-day world. It is because it allows for the dissemination of information to employees and users on the need to be secure and enhance cybersecurity. Education on phishing threats reduces the likelihood of individuals clicking or replying to phishing information that is meant to extract personal information from them. Training also helps in communicating pertinent security information that may expose private information about an individual or organization to malicious individuals through social media. For the training and awareness creation information to be useful, it must be current, relevant, quickly understood and easily recalled. Additionally, this training serves to implement a security-aware culture where individuals understand the risks posed by social media. Users should be aware of the security threats that social media poses and therefore limit the amount of information shared online.

According to James et al. (2017), users do not only share their information but also other individual information which leads to privacy breaches and trust issues. It is the role of the providers to ensure that sound cybersecurity strategies are employed to reduce negative user experiences and increase effectiveness as well as earn the trust of the users. Cybercriminals use social media to spread phishing applications and malware that access information using the social engineering methods. Kesan et al. (2014) state that in addition to education and awareness creation, online behaviour is an essential cybersecurity strategy for users. Individuals should be aware of clickable links by having a service that detects malicious content. Verification of the source of the links is as necessary as regularly changing the social media passwords. The author also argues that the use of different passwords for different accounts also limits the impact of cybercrimes. Cybersecurity measures have emphasized passwords with a mix of numbers and characters with at least one upper and one lower aspect.

Information privacy

With the rapid growth of ICT, accessing information became easy and available to almost everyone. Thus, protecting the individual data became a hard task especially with every security incident that happens in any part of the world; new regulation or governmental demands on accessing private information occur now and then.

According to Westin (1968), information privacy is the ability to control the individual private information in which they have the full power on their information, to share it or not. It is considered one of the top ethical, legal, social and political issues of the information era (Cho and Hichang, 2010). Laufer and Wolfe (1977) stated that to understand privacy we must understand the concept of privacy from the individual view and also consider the social historical perspective. Four dimensions of information privacy have been identified by Smith et al. (1996), which are a collection, unauthorized secondary use, improper access and errors. On the other hand, Solove (2005) found different dimensions which are information collection, information processing, information dissemination and invasion. On the other hand, Mekovec and Hutinski (2012) stated that online privacy perception referred to online shopping and e-banking service users' anxiety about how an online company or bank (which is providing the e-service) will handle information that they collect about users during their online interaction.

Some researchers have done metaanalyses on the information privacy to locate what other researchers focused on or miss (e.g., Bélanger & Crossler, 2011; Smith, Dinev & Xu, 2011). In 2011, Smith, Dinev and Xu undertook a metadata analysis of 320 articles and 128 books on information privacy. They classify the literature in two ways, using an ethical-based nomenclature and based on their level of analyses. As a result of this classification, they identify three main areas that former researcher contribution locates: the first one is the conceptualization of information privacy; second, the relationship between information privacy and other constructs; and, third, contextual nature of this relationship. They found that there are many theoretical developments in the body of normative and purely descriptive studies that have not been addressed in empirical research on privacy. They also found that some analyses receive less attention and researchers should focus on antecedents to privacy concern and its outcomes.

Similarly, Belangar and Crossler (2011) performed metadata analyses on 142 journals and 102 conference papers. They assert that information privacy is a multilevel concept, but rarely studied as such. The researchers mainly focus on explaining and predicting theoretical contributions with less attention to the action contributions. The paper also finds that information privacy research has been heavily reliant on student-based and USA-centric samples, which results in findings of limited generalizability. Finally, information privacy can be studied at multilevel analyses.

Information system researchers have studied information privacy from different perspectives and found different approaches to protect information privacy. They studied it under the e-commerce, organization, behaviour and technical among other perspectives. Furthermore, researchers have tried to secure and protect information privacy through different approaches and methods. Some of them used technical solutions (e.g., Sutanto, Palme & Tan, 2013), while others tried to change the user's behaviour (e.g., Boss et al., 2015; Gross & Acquisti, 2005, pp. 71—81; Johnston & Warkentin, 2010; Johnston, Warkentin & Siponen, 2015; Siponen & Vance, 2010; Wang, Gupta & Rao, 2015). Furthermore, some researchers argued that companies could be saved and secure users' private information (e.g., Lee, Ahn & Bang, 2011; Smith, 2010).

Corporate information privacy policy

The information system researchers also focus on the companies' policies and strategies to improve their privacy such as Lee et al. (2011) and Smith Winchester, Bunker and Jaimeson (2010).

Lee et al. (2011) found that firms can improve social welfare privacy at the expense of personal welfare. They also found that regulation enforcing the implementation of fair information practises can be efficient from the social welfare perspective. They conducted a strategic analysis and privacy perceptions to find a solution to the consumer privacy invasion which happened by firms. However, they considered the impact of the consumer information disclosure, which will affect the company's income. To do so, they used a game theoretic approach to explore the firm's motivation for privacy protection and its influence on competition and social welfare.

A strategy based on organization subunit size is helpful in motivating and assisting the organization to move towards accreditation (Smith, Winchester, Bunker and Jaimeson, 2010). They came up with this finding by conducting a survey, interviews, observations and focus groups on 89 users. However, they only focused on government organization where this strategy proved to be good. It needs a further study on a private organization, considering the massive types of private organization, and on the effect of the cultural, social, gender and context on using the strategy.

Personal information privacy on the social network

Online users and e-commerce consumers become the main information provider to the social media, blogs and websites, which make their personal information vulnerable. Online social network (OSN) is the online environment where people can introduce themselves on a profile, connect with others and communicate with them (Gross & Acquisti, 2005, pp. 71–81). This social network may benefit various parties by using the user's private information, where the users show and update it voluntarily, in data mining, online advertising or even psychological evaluation for job candidates. The OSNs themselves are evaluated according to active user participation instead of financial performance (Krasnova et al., 2009).

Furthermore, the personalized web services and business intelligence software are using the users' personal information (Li & Sarkar, 2006), where the data can be collected without individual awareness. Hence, it is a high risk to disclose private information to the OSN, but people still do it. Krasnova et al. (2010) stated that users are motivated to disclose their information because it is easy to access, maintain and develop relations and platform enjoyment. However, their perception of risk can be reduced by their trust in the network provider and the availability of control options.

Siponen and Vance (2010) used the neutralization theory, a criminology theory, in the information security context. The neutralization theory claims that both law-abiding citizens and rule breakers believe in the same norms and the value of the society (Sykes & Matza, 1957). Sykes and Matza (1957) proposed five techniques of neutralization were appealing to higher loyalties is one of them. This technique is used by people who feel that they are in a predicament that must be solved by breaking the law or policy. This variable will be used to rationalize the behaviour of the religious belief users if they considered religion as a higher loyalty, and if so, it will affect the preserved online privacy.

Technical

Protecting the information resources of the firm is the main goal in managing firms. Information security specialists and managers used to be responsible for protecting the privacy and confidentiality of the organization information (Dhillon & Backhouse, 2001). However, recently, the individuals with access to sensitive organizational information share the same roles and responsibilities (Stanton et al., 2005). Old IT security effort concentrates mostly on technical methods to achieve protection, but the new researches consider the individual, social and organizational influences as an attribute to achieve information security (Choobineh et al., 2007; Dhillon & Backhouse, 2001). Sutanto et al. (2013) proposed a solution aimed to reduce user's perception and led to an increase in the process and content gratification. Their IT solution was a personalized, privacy-safe application. This application delivered personalized services without giving any private information to a third party. They also found that the users saved the personalized messages more frequently only when it was privacy safe one.

Behaviour

Some researchers have looked at the online privacy through the behaviour lens. They applied many theories and approaches to figure the relation between behaviour and privacy. Posey, Roberts and Lowry (2013) argued that using a systematic approach is the best way to understand protection motivation behaviours (PMBs). However, they pointed out that future researchers should consider the changes in the information security threats and technology might need new PMBs. They focused on the organization insider's behaviour without considering their culture, gender or religion.

Privacy protection, generally, means managing the release of personal information while diverting unwanted intrusions (Goodwin, 1991). Self-protection behaviour concerning privacy was found to be multidimensional when it's looked at with other attitudinal variables. Two separate factors underpinning the action people may take to protect their online privacy have been identified by Joinson et al. (2010), which are a general concern and technical protection of privacy. General concern is the logical steps that people use to protect their online privacy, whereas technical protection is the use of software and hardware as tools to protect their online privacy.

Three defensive measures (fabrication, protect and withhold), which can be used by individuals, have been identified by other studies (e.g., Lwin,

Wirtz & Williams, 2007). Fabrication is when the user is trying to disguise his/her identity by using false information; protect is when the user uses technology to protect his/her privacy and withhold is when the user refuses to provide information or to patronize websites. Another three privacy protection rules have been prescribed by Metzger (2007), which are withholding information, falsifying information and information seeking. Furthermore, a simpler classification consists of two dimensions: passive protection and active protection introduced by Dolnicar and Jordaan (2006) and Yao, Rice and Wallis (2007), respectively. Passive protection is depending on others such as government law to protect privacy, whereas active protection is when users take action to protect their privacy.

Fear appeal manipulation theory has been used to change the user's behaviours by enhancing and protecting information privacy by some information system researchers (e.g., Boss et al., 2015; Johnston & Warkentin, 2010; Johnston et al., 2015; Siponen & Vance, 2010). They argued that by enforcing the fear appeal factor, the online users would be more careful and comply with the privacy policy and countermeasures. Siponen and Vance (2010) showed that fear appeal does impact end users' behavioural intention to comply with recommended individual acts of security. However, the impact is not uniform across all end users. Boss et al. (2015) gave a comprehensive review of 125 users and a field experiment on 327 users using the protection motivation theory (PMT) and fear appeal manipulation to motivate individuals to use a more secure behaviour. They found that in the information systems (IS), PMT research should use PMT and fear appeal manipulation before adding non-PMT constructs. They also state that IS researcher should perfectly use fear appeal manipulation and measure fear.

Furthermore, they said that ISec PMT research should model and measure users' behaviour. PMT, which is protection motivation theory, is the use of convincing message which warns the user of a personal threat and describes balance measures which subsist of protective behaviour (Floyd, Prentice-Dunn and Rogers, 2000). On the other hand, fear appeals are 'persuasive messages designed to scare people by describing the terrible things that will happen to them if they don't do what the message recommends' (Witte, 1992, p. 329). Boss et al. (2015) study was a long-term study which used the main base of PMT and added fear appeal, and the experience of fear to the situation of data bucked up. The second study used the full nomology of PMT to a malware situation in a short-term cross-sectional experiment survey. It also has the fear appeal manipulation, but with adding a measurement to maladaptive responses.

Johnston and Warkentin (2010) conducted an experiment and a survey on 780 participants using fear appeal to investigate its influence of the end user compliance. The result of the study was that the intention of end user behaviour to comply with recommended individual acts of security is affected by the fear appeal. However, the impact is not uniform across all end users. They used a fear appeal model which is an extension of the danger control process as described by PMT. In the model, the concepts of threat severity and susceptibility are located as direct antecedents of response efficacy and self-efficacy and not immediately influence behavioural intent. Behavioural intent is directly influenced by perceptions of response efficacy.

Johnston et al. (2015) also used fear appeal theory and made an enhanced fear appeal rhetorical framework to motivate people compliance with information security policy and procedures. They argued that fear appeal and PMT have two major problems when applied to information security. First, the fear appeal has been used to grasp the individuals an existing threat without concern for behaviour change mechanism. Second, PMT assumes that all threats are personally related to the recipient. Thus, they made an enhanced fear appeal rhetorical framework where they add the elements of fear appeal to elements of formal and informal forms of sanction severity, certainty and clarity. They conducted a survey and interviews on 559 employees of Finnish city government, and they found that using the enhanced fear appeal rhetorical framework will provide a significant positive influence on compliance intention. In another word, these studies have limited their focus primarily to the construct of PMT, thereby ignoring other determinants of behaviour that may be important such as religious beliefs. They mostly focused on employees who mostly have rules and policies to follow. Finally, they suggested a technical solution to change the behaviour without considering the variety of the context.

Siponen and Vance (2010) reviewed 174 ethical decision-making and surveyed 790 employees using neutralization theory. Their results suggested that practitioners should work to counteract employees' use of neutralization techniques. The neutralization theory, according to Sykes and Matza (1957), stated that law-abiding citizens and criminals or rule breakers believe in the norms and values of society. Sykes and Matza (1975) suggested five techniques of neutralization: denial of responsibility, denial of injury, denial of the victim, condemnation of the condemners and appeal to higher loyalties. This study applied only to a specific context and culture where it cannot be generalized. It also failed to show the cause of the noncompliance to the policy.

Wang et al. (2015) observed the behaviour of 14,680 online users and argued that the result of their study supports the empirical application of routine activity theory in comprehending insider threats and providing a vision of how various applications have a different level of exposure to threats. Gross and Acquisti (2005, pp. 71–81) analyzed the online behaviour of 4000 Carnegie Mellon University students. They found out that the majority of the students are willing to provide and share private information, and they do not change the privacy preferences. Although this study proves that college-aged users mostly are willing to disclose as much private information as possible to many people, it cannot be generalized. There are other variables that could change the outcome such as different age, religion, culture, context or marital status.

Researchers applied many theories trying to understand what affects the user behaviour such as PMBs, self-protection behaviour, fear appeal manipulation theory, etc. By reviewing the literature, we identified a gap that religious beliefs are commonly not considered in the study of the user behaviour in the social media context.

Religiosity

Religion is a system of symbols which creates strong, extensive and permanent attitudes and motivation in people (Geertz, 1973). The attitudes and motivation lead to a diverse level of commitment to follow any religious teachings, which are called religiosity. Religion has no equal impact on individuals and results in a different effect on them. Accordingly, religion cannot be used as a measure by itself, but religiosity, which is the degree of commitment, practise, belief and acceptance, can be used as a measurement tool (Mukhtar & Butt, 2012). Khraim (2010) argued that religiosity is one of the powerful tools which can predicate consumer behaviour.

By looking at the literature, the focus shifts from religion to religiosity because of the ability of religiosity to measure individual's commitment to a religion, which converges with behaviour (McDaniel & Burnett, 1990; Schneider, Krieger & Bayraktar, 2011; Swimberghe, Flurry & Parker, 2011; Vitell, 2009; Wilkes, Burnett & Howell, 1986).

McDaniel and Burnett (1990, p. 103) define religiosity as a belief in a God with a commitment to follow the set of principles for that religion. Alongside, Worthington et al. (2003, p. 85) claimed that religiosity is the degree of individual commitment and compliance to a certain religion value, practise and belief. These two definitions clarify the difference between religiosity and spirituality because spirituality engages in an exploration of 'meaning, unity, connectedness to nature, humanity and the transcendent' (Vitell, 2009, p. 156). Religiosity, on the other hand, grants faith, focussing on beliefs, attitudes and behaviours (Emmons, 2005; Vitell, 2009). Any person may carry a certain degree of religiosity, which makes it unique. However, it cannot be easily considered as a measurable variable (Abou-Youssef et al., 2011; Wilkes et al., 1986). Being a highly practised person for a certain religion does not mean being a highly religious one because the practise sometimes gets mixed with the daily routine (Khraim, 2010). Researchers develop or adopt measures that fit their context to measure religiosity because there is no standardized scale to measure religiosity (Khraim, 2010).

Vitell and Paolillo (2003) stated that one of the main determinants of values and human convictions is religiosity. The individual level of religiosity has a clear effect on attitudes and behaviours (McDaniel & Burnett, 1990; Weaver, 2002). An extensive attempt to explain the relationships between personal religiosity and personal characteristics with the decision-making process is being done by researchers since the mid-1970s (Barton & Vaughan, 1976; Choi, 2010; Clark & Dawson, 1996; Donahue, 1985; Miller & Hoffmann, 1995; Smith, Weigert & Thomas, 1979; Swimberghe et al., 2011; Tate & Miller, 1971; Welch, 1981; Wiebe & Fleck, 1980; Wilkes et al., 1986). Nevertheless, these studies have produced divergent results (McDaniel & Burnett, 1990).

Some studies (e.g., Barton & Vaughan, 1976; Kahoe, 1974; Slater, 1947) have shown that there is a link between religiosity and emotions, where the more religious the person is, the more emotional he/she becomes, and vice versa. Other studies linked religiosity with self-esteem. Ranck (1961) stated that the more religious the person is, the lower self-esteem he/she has. To the contrary, Smith et al. (1979) found that it's a positive relationship, where the more religious the person is, the more self-esteem he/she has. According to Kohlberg (1981), morality and religiosity are not linked. He argued that the revelations of religious authorities is based on religious reasoning, while morality is based on rational opinions and influenced by cognitive development. Regardless of prior evidence, some studies showed a strong link between religion and morality and considered personal religiosity to be a representative for the ethical nature of behaviour (Geyer & Baumeister, 2005; Magill, 1992).

Despite the external influence, the diverse finding imposes that religiosity is a subjective characteristic, due to the individuals and its dimensions of expression which are not smellier in different disciplines and contexts (Donahue, 1985; McDaniel & Burnett, 1990; Vitell, 2009; Wilkes et al., 1986).

According to Baazeem (2018), religiosity has an effect on the individual's perceived privacy, which in turn affects the individual use of technology. He suggested a model where the effect of religiosity on perceived privacy and the use of technology can be measured. Allport and Ross (1967) used religious orientation scale (ROS) to determine the level of commitment the individual has to follow for a religion.

The study

In this section, we will present a small study that applies the model proposed by Baazeem (2018). The model claims that individual religiosity has an effect on the preserved privacy, which in turn affects the cybersecurity. Allport and Ross (1967) used ROS to measure the intrinsic religiosity of the individual to know their level of dedication.

Method

This study took place in Saudi Arabia and used the privacy concern model by Xu, Dinev, Smith & Hart (2011) and ROS by Essoo and Dibb (2010). Privacy concerns have been found to have an impact on behavioural intentions of users. Furthermore, other risk dimensions play a role in determining usage intentions shown by Xu et al. (2011). They used communication privacy management (CPM) to explain individual privacy concerns formation through a cognitive process involving perceived privacy risk, privacy control and their disposition to value privacy. Individuals' perceptions of institutional privacy assurances affect the risk control assessment from information disclosure, thus being an essential component of privacy concerns. There is a dearth of studies linking privacy concerns and religious beliefs to self-disclosure, system adoption and use. To explore whether religiosity affects privacy perceptions, impacts privacy concerns and links to self-disclosure, we put forward the model as you can see in Fig. 5.1 and came with 13 hypotheses (Table 5.1).

The initial questionnaire section with the check for eligibility was followed by the measurement scale of the two mean constructs, which are intrinsic ROS and CPM. The questionnaire scales have been adopted from previous studies to fit the research context. CPM was adopted from Xu et al. (2011), and intrinsic ROS was adopted from Essoo and Dibb (2010). The scales used seven-point Likert scale where 1 is 'strongly disagree' and 7 is 'strongly agree'. The participant age ranged from 18 years to over 60 years old. From the 509 participants, there were 279 males (54.6%) and 232 females (45.4), all belonging to Muslim Sunni and being active social media users.

To reach out to a large number of participants, the data collected from questionnaires electronically distributed to active users in Saudi Arabia. The questionnaire was constructed following two focus groups with Islamic religion experts and consisted of some questions on participants' use of social networks and their beliefs. For the purposes of this study, the whole sample was used, covering a wide range of participants totalling

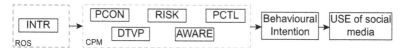

FIGURE 5.1 Religiosity and privacy concerns proposed model. *DTVP,* disposition to value privacy; *PCON,* privacy concerns; *PCTL,* perceived privacy control; *ROS,* religious orientation scale.

TABLE 5.1   Proposed hypotheses.

Hypotheses

H1: Intrinsic religiosity, affects disposition to value privacy (DTVP).

H2: Intrinsic religiosity, affects privacy risk (RISK).

H3: Intrinsic religiosity, affects privacy concerns (PCON)

H5: Intrinsic religiosity, affects privacy control (PCTL).

H6: Intrinsic religiosity, affects privacy awareness (AWARE).

H7: Disposition to value privacy (DTVP), negatively affects perceived privacy control (PCTL).

H8: Disposition to value privacy (DTVP), positively affects perceived privacy risk (RISK).

H9: Disposition to value privacy (DTVP), positively affects privacy concerns (PCON).

H10: Perceived privacy control (PCTL), negatively affects privacy concern (PCON).

H11: Perceived privacy risk (RISK), positively affects privacy concerns (PCON).

H12: Privacy awareness (AWARE), positively affects privacy concern (PCON).

H13: Privacy concerns (PCON), negatively affects behaviour intentions.

509 adult Muslim Sunni Saudi nationals. Similar to previous studies, our sample exceeds the required minimum of 400 participants for the population of over 100,000 (Isaac & Michael, 1995; Krejcie & Morgan, 1970).

Using SurveyGizmo to distribute the questioner on social media websites such as Facebook, Twitter, WhatsApp, etc., increased the response rate of the survey. Only over 18 Saudi Muslims who are active on social media can access the survey. Total of 1020 individuals participates in the survey, with 509 useable responses.

Results

The model in Fig. 5.2 was estimated using partial least squares (PLS), a composite-based approach to structural equation modelling (Lohmöller, 2013). To estimate the model, the SmartPLS (Ringle, Wende & Becker, 2017) was employed. After an initial examination of the loadings onto each construct, one item was omitted because of low loadings from intrinsic religiosity scales. After this, the reliability and validity of the measures used were reassessed. We employ two measures of construct reliability: Cronbach's alpha and composite reliability. As shown in Table 5.2, both reliability measures exceed the benchmark 0.70. Alongside the measures of reliability, Table 5.2 also reports a measure of convergent validity: average variance extracted (AVE).

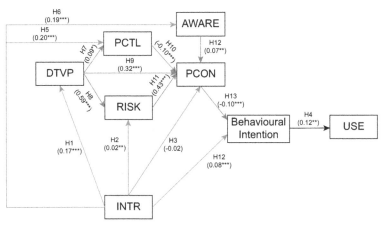

FIGURE 5.2 The research model. *DTVP*, disposition to value privacy; *PCON*, privacy concerns; *PCTL*, perceived privacy control.

As Table 5.2 shows, the AVE values for the constructs range between 0.51 and 0.68 and are generally considered acceptable as it shows that the construct explains more than half of the variance of its indicators (e.g., Hair et al., 2016).

We also test for the discriminant validity of the constructs (i.e., the extent to which the constructs are distinct from each other). First, we apply the Fornell and Larcker criterion that the square root of the AVE of a construct should be greater than that construct's correlations with other constructs. This is shown in Table 5.3 where the square root of the AVE values are shown in the top right to bottom left diagonal, and correlations

TABLE 5.2 Reliability and validity.

	Cronbach's alpha	Composite reliability	Average variance extracted
Aware	0.75	0.86	0.66
Disposition to value privacy	0.77	0.86	0.68
Intrinsic	0.84	0.88	0.51
Privacy concerns	0.84	0.89	0.68
Perceived privacy control	0.81	0.88	0.64
Risk	0.81	0.88	0.64
Self-Disc	0.85	0.87	0.54

TABLE 5.3   Fornell and Larcker criterion.

	Aware	Disposition to value privacy (DTVP)	Intrinsic	Privacy concerns (PCON)	Perceived privacy control (PCTL)	Risk
Aware	**0.81**					
DTVP	0.62	**0.82**				
Intrinsic	0.19	0.17	**0.72**			
PCON	0.48	0.61	0.10	**0.82**		
PCTL	0.16	0.12	0.22	−0.03	**0.80**	
Risk	0.51	0.60	0.17	0.65	0.06	**0.80**

between constructs are shown in the other cells in the table. In all cases, the Fornell–Larcker criterion is met as you can see in Table 5.3.

In addition to the Fornell and Larcker criterion, we report the heterotrait-monotrait (HTMT) Ratio proposed by Henseler et al. (2015), which compares between-construct and within-construct correlations. Values above 0.85 (0.9 if the model contains constructs which are conceptually similar) suggest a lack of discriminant validity. The HTMT ratios are shown in Table 5.4; all of them fall below the 0.85 benchmarks as you can see in Table 5.4.

Structural model path coefficients

Chin (2010) argued that PLS structural equation modelling (SEM) is a soft modelling approach. Thus, PLS-SEM does not assume that the data are normally distributed. Accordingly, parametric significance tests are not useable to inspect the significance of the loading and the structural path (Hair et al., 2014). Instead, a nonparametric bootstrap test is conducted (Chin, 1998). Hair et al. (2014) suggested that when conducting a bootstrap, *'a large number of subsamples (i.e., bootstrap samples) are drawn from the original sample with replacement'* (p. 130). Furthermore, they illustrate that in bootstrap the number of the samples is higher than the number of observation and ranged between 500 and 5000.

The significance of the structural path was tested by applying the bootstrap procedure (in SmartPLS) using 1000 subsamples and at a significant level of 10%. In agreement with Hair et al. (2014), the P-value, 'the probability of erroneously rejecting a true null hypothesis' (p. 196), is used to assess the significant level. As reported in Table 5.5, all individual paths were directed as hypothesized. Out of 37 paths, only 25 paths were

TABLE 5.4 Heterotrait-monotrait ratio.

	Aware	Disposition to value privacy (DTVP)	Intrinsic	Privacy concerns (PCON)	Perceived privacy control (PCTL)	Risk	Self-disc
Aware							
DTVP	0.79						
Intrinsic	0.21	0.20					
PCON	0.56	0.73	0.11				
PCTL	0.20	0.17	0.25	0.09			
Risk	0.62	0.75	0.19	0.74	0.13		
Self-disc	0.11	0.27	0.10	0.18	0.07	0.28	

TABLE 5.5 Path coefficients.

Paths	Original sample	T statistics	P-values
Behaviour intentions			
Behaviour intention > use	0.17	2.53	0.01**
Communication privacy management			
DTVP > PCON	0.36	7.63	0.00***
DTVP > PCTL	0.10	1.39	0.85
DTVP > risk	0.59	17.20	0.00***
PCON > behaviour intention	−0.05	1.55	0.06*
PCTL > PCON	−0.09	2.41	0.01**
Risk > PCON	0.45	9.96	0.00***
AWARE > PCON	0.07	1.74	0.04**
Religious orientation scale			
Intrinsic > behaviour intention	0.06	1.80	0.07*
Intrinsic > aware	0.18	3.37	0.00***
Intrinsic > PCTL	0.19	3.38	0.00***
Intrinsic > risk	0.08	2.30	0.02**
Intrinsic > DTVP	0.16	3.09	0.00***
Intrinsic > PCON	−0.03	0.71	0.48

*$P < 0.10$; **p, 0.05; ***p, 0.01; underlined numbers are results of two-tailed tests. *DTVP*, disposition to value privacy; *PCON*, privacy concerns; *PCTL*, perceived privacy control.

significant ($P < 0.10$) and the remaining 12 were not significant. In the paths from INTR to CPM, all the paths were significant with the exception of the path between intrinsic religiosity and privacy concerns (PCON). Intrinsic religiosity and PCON has a nonsignificant negative relationship where the *P*-value is 0.48, which is not $P < .10$.

The paths between intrinsic religiosity and privacy were significant, which support the hypotheses, except the path between intrinsic religiosity and privacy concerns (PCON) as shown in Table 5.5. Intrinsic religiosity has a significant 0% positive relationship with privacy awareness (AWARE), privacy control (PCTL) and disposition to value privacy (DTVP), which support H1/H5 and H6. Intrinsic religiosity has a significant 5% positive relationship with privacy risks (RISK), which support

H2. On the other hand, intrinsic religiosity has no significant relationship with privacy concern which rejects H3.

All paths within the privacy concerns, as shown in Fig. 2, were significant except one (see Table 5.5). DTVP has a high-coefficient significant 0% positive relationship with perceived privacy risk (RISK) and privacy concerns (PCON), which support the hypotheses H8 and H9. Perceived privacy risk (RISK) has a high-coefficient 0% significant positive relationship with privacy concerns (PCON), which support H11. Perceived privacy control (PCTL) has a negative coefficient with 5% significant relationship with privacy concerns (PCON), which support the hypotheses H10. Privacy awareness (AWARE) has a 5%, small coefficients, significant relationship with privacy concerns (PCON) which support the hypotheses H12. Privacy concerns (PCON) has a 10%, negative coefficients, significant relationship with behaviour intentions which support the hypotheses H13. In contrast, DTVP relationship with perceived privacy control (PCTL) is not significant, which rejects the hypotheses H7. In another word, valuing personal privacy does not affect the individual concerns on how to control his/her privacy. Behaviour intentions have a positive coefficient 5% significant relationship with the use of social media to disclose information (Use).

Conclusion

In conclusion, the results show that religiosity has an indirect impact on the use of social media through privacy concerns; the more religious the person is, the less information he/she will disclose using social media, which in turn will affect the cybersecurity. As a result, policymakers and social media companies should consider religion as one of the main factors that affect users on how they use social media and fully reveal their private information. Amending the terms of service and use to accommodate privacy concerns raised by the user's religion would be a potential solution to the issue raised here.

References

Abou-Youssef, M., et al. (2011). Measuring islamic-driven buyer behavioral implications: A proposed market-minded religiosity scale. *Journal of American Science, 7*(8), 788–801. https://doi.org/10.1017/CBO9781107415324.004.

Allport, G. W., & Ross, J. M. (1967). Personal religious orientation and prejudice. *Journal of Personality and Social Psychology, 5*(4), 432–443. https://doi.org/10.1037/h0021212.

Baazeem, R. M. (2018). The role of religiosity in technology acceptance: The case of privacy in Saudi Arabia. In *Psychological and behavioral examinations in cyber security* (pp. 172–193). IGI Global.

Bada, M., & Sasse, A. (2014). Cyber Security Awareness Campaigns: Why do they fail to change behaviour?. In *Global cyber security capacity centre*. University of Oxford.

Barton, K., & Vaughan, G. M. (1976). Church membership and personality: A longitudinal study. *Social Behavior and Personality: An International Journal. Scientific Journal Publishers*, 4(1), 11–16.

Bélanger, F., & Crossler, R. (2011). Privacy in the digital age: A review of information privacy research in information systems. *MIS Quarterly, 35*(4), 1–36. https://doi.org/10.1159/000360196.

Boss, S. R., et al. (2015). Research article what do systems users have to fear? Using fear appeals to engender threats and fear that motivate protective security behaviors 1. *MIS Quarterly, 39*(4), 837–864.

Chin, W. W. (1998). The partial least squares approach to structural equation modeling. *Modern Methods for Business Research. London, 295*(2), 295–336.

Chin, W. W. (2010). How to write up and report PLS analyses. In *Handbook of partial least squares* (pp. 655–690). Springer.

Cho and Hichang. (2010). Determinants of behavioral responses to online privacy: The effects. *Journal of Information Privacy and Security, 6*(1).

Choi, Y. (2010). Religion, religiosity, and South Korean consumer switching behaviors. *Journal of Consumer Behaviour, 9*(3), 157–171. https://doi.org/10.1002/cb.292.

Choobineh, J., et al. (2007). Management of information security: Challenges and research directions. *Communications of the Association for Information Systems, 20*(1), 57.

Clark, J. W., & Dawson, L. E. (1996). Personal religiousness and ethical judgements: An empirical analysis. *Journal of Business Ethics, 15*(3), 359–372. https://doi.org/10.1007/BF00382959.

Deibert, R. (2012). Cybersecurity: The new frontier. *Foreign Policy Topic, 4*, 45–58.

Dhillon, G., & Backhouse, J. (2001). Current directions in IS security research: Towards socio-organizational perspectives. *Information Systems Journal, 11*(2), 127–153. Wiley Online Library.

Dinev, T., & Hart, P. (2006). Privacy concerns and levels of information exchange: An empirical investigation of intended e-services use. *e-Service Journal, 4*(3), 25–60. https://doi.org/10.2979/ESJ.2006.4.3.25.

Dolnicar, S., & Jordaan, Y. (2006). *Protecting consumer privacy in the company's best interest*.

Donahue, M. J. (1985). Intrinsic and extrinsic religiousness: The empirical research. *Journal for the Scientific Study of Religion*, 418–423. https://doi.org/10.2307/1385995.

Emmons, R. A. (2005). Striving for the sacred: Personal goals, life meaning, and religion. *Journal of Social Issues, 61*(4), 731–745. https://doi.org/10.1111/j.1540-4560.2005.00429.x.

Essoo, N., & Dibb, S. (2010). Religious influences on shopping behaviour: An exploratory study. *Journal of Marketing Management, 20*(7–8), 683–712. https://doi.org/10.1362/0267257041838728.

Etzioni, A. (2017). *The new normal: Finding a balance between individual rights and the common good*. Routledge.

Floyd, D. L., Prentice-Dunn, S., & Rogers, R. W. (2000). A meta-analysis of research on protection motivation theory. *Journal of Applied Social Psychology, 30*(2), 407–429. Wiley Online Library.

Geertz, C. (1973). *The interpretation of cultures: Selected essays*. Basic books.

Geyer, A. L., & Baumeister, R. F. (2005). *Religion, morality, and self-control: values, virtues, and vices*. Guilford Press.

Goodwin, C. (1991). Privacy: Recognition of a consumer right. *Journal of Public Policy & Marketing. JSTOR*, 149–166.

Gross, R., & Acquisti, A. (2005). *Information revelation and privacy in online social networks*. Wpes'05. https://doi.org/10.1145/1102199.1102214.

Hair, J. F. J., et al. (2014). *A primer on partial least squares structural equation modeling (PLS-SEM), long range planning.* https://doi.org/10.1016/j.lrp.2013.01.002.

Hair Jr, J. F., Hult, G. T. M., Ringle, C., & Sarstedt, M. (2016). *A Primer on Partial Least Squares Structural Equation Modeling (PLS-SEM).* Sage publications.

Halevi, T., Lewis, J., & Memon, N. (2013). A pilot study of cyber security and privacy related behavior and personality traits. In *WWW 2013 companion - Proceedings of the 22nd international conference on world wide web* (pp. 737–744). https://doi.org/10.1145/2487788.2488034.

Henseler, J., Ringle, C. M., & Sarstedt, M. (2015). A new criterion for assessing discriminant validity in variance-based structural equation modeling. *Journal of the Academy of Marketing Science, 43*(1), 115–135.

Isaac, S., & Michael, W. B. (1995). *Handbook in research and evaluation: A collection of principles, methods, and strategies useful in the planning, design, and evaluation of studies in education and the behavioral sciences.* Edits publishers.

James, T. L., et al. (2017). Exposing others' information on online social networks (OSNs): Perceived shared risk, its determinants, and its influence on OSN privacy control use. *Information and Management, 54*(7), 851–865. https://doi.org/10.1016/j.im.2017.01.001. Elsevier B.V.

Johnston, A. C., & Warkentin, M. (2010). Fear appeals and information security behaviors: An empirical study. *MIS Quarterly, 34*(3). pp. 549-A4. doi: Article.

Johnston, A. C., Warkentin, M., & Siponen, M. (2015). An enhanced fear appeal rhetorical framework: Leveraging threats to the human asset through sanctioning rhetoric 1. *MIS Quarterly, 39*(1), 113–134.

Joinson, A., et al. (2010). Privacy, trust, and self-disclosure online. *Human-Computer Interaction, 25*(1), 1–24. https://doi.org/10.1080/07370020903586662.

Kahoe, R. D. (1974). 'Personality and achievement correlates of intrinsic and extrinsic religious orientations. *Journal of Personality and Social Psychology. American Psychological Association, 29*(6), 812.

Kesan, J. P., & Hayes, C. M. (2014). Creating a circle of trust to further digital privacy and cybersecurity goals. *Mich. St. L. Rev. HeinOnline,* 1475.

Khraim, H. (2010). Measuring religiosity in consumer research from an Islamic perspective. *Journal of Economic & Administrative Sciences, 26*(1), 52–79.

Kohlberg, L. (1981). *The meaning and measurement of moral development.* Clark Univ Heinz Werner Inst.

Krasnova, H., et al. (2009). "It won't happen to me!": Self-disclosure in online social networks'. *Amcis 2009 Proceedings,* 343. Available at http://aisel.aisnet.org/amcis2009%5Cn http://aisel.aisnet.org/amcis2009/343.

Krasnova, H., Spiekermann, S., Koroleva, K., & Hildebrand, T. (2010). Online social networks: Why we disclose. *Journal of information technology, 25*(2), 109–125.

Krejcie, R. V., & Morgan, D. W. (1970). Determining sample size for research activities', Educational and psychological measurement. *Sage Publications Sage CA: Los Angeles, CA, 30*(3), 607–610.

de Lange, M., & von Solms, R. (2012). An e-safety educational framework in South Africa. In *Proceedings of the Southern Africa Telecommunication networks and applications conference (SATNAC)* (p. 497).

LaRose, R., & Rifon, N. (2006). Your privacy is assured - of being disturbed: Websites with and without privacy seals. *New Media & Society, 8*(6), 1009–1029. https://doi.org/10.1177/1461444806069652.

Laufer, R. S., & Wolfe, M. (1977). Privacy as a concept and a social issue: A multidimensional developmental theory. *Journal of Social Issues, 33*(3), 22–42. Wiley Online Library.

Lee, D.-J., Ahn, J.-H., & Bang, Y. (2011). Managing consumer privacy concerns in Personalisation: A strategic analysis of privacy protection. *MIS Quarterly, 35*(2). pp. 423-a8.

Li, X.-B., & Sarkar, S. (2006). Privacy protection in data mining: A perturbation approach for categorical data. *Information Systems Research. INFORMS, 17*(3), 254–270.

Lohmöller, J. (2013). *Latent variable path modeling with partial least squares.* Springer Science & Business Media.

Lwin, M. O., & Williams, J. D. (2003). A model integrating the multidimensional developmental theory of privacy and theory of planned behavior to examine fabrication of information online. *Marketing Letters, 14*(4), 257–272. Springer.

Lwin, M., Wirtz, J., & Williams, J. D. (2007). Consumer online privacy concerns and responses: A power–responsibility equilibrium perspective. *Journal of the Academy of Marketing Science, 35*(4), 572–585. Springer.

Magill, G. (1992). Theology in business ethics: Appealing to the religious imagination. *Journal of business ethics, 11*(2), 129–135. Springer.

McDaniel, S. W., & Burnett, J. J. (1990). Consumer religiosity and retail store evaluative criteria. *Journal of the Academy of Marketing Science, 18*(2), 101–112. https://doi.org/10.1007/BF02726426.

Mekovec, R., & Hutinski, Ž. (2012). The role of perceived privacy and perceived security in online market. In *MIPRO, 2012 Proceedings of the 35th international convention* (pp. 1883–1888).

Metzger, M. J. (2007). Communication privacy management in electronic commerce. *Journal of Computer-Mediated Communication, 12*(2), 335–361. Wiley Online Library.

Metzger, M. J., & Docter, S. (2003). Public opinion and policy initiatives for online privacy protection. *Journal of Broadcasting & Electronic Media, 47*(3), 350–374. Taylor & Francis.

Miller, A. S., & Hoffmann, J. P. (1995). Risk and religion: An explanation of gender differences in religiosity. *Journal for the Scientific Study of Religion, 63.* https://doi.org/10.2307/1386523.

Moor, J. H. (1997). Towards a theory of privacy in the information age. *ACM SIGCAS Computers and Society. ACM, 27*(3), 27–32.

Mukhtar, A., & Butt, M. M. (2012). Intention to choose halal products: The role of religiosity. *Journal of Islamic Marketing, 3*(2), 108–120.

Posey, C., Roberts, T., & Lowry, P. (2013). Insiders' protection of organizational information assets: Development of a systematics-based taxonomy and theory of diversity. *MIS Quarterly, 37*(4), 1189–1210. Available at https://www.researchgate.net/publication/254934954_Insiders'_Protection_of_Organizational_Information_Assets_Development_of_a_Systematics-Based_Taxonomy_and_Theory_of_Diversity_for_Protection-Motivated_Behaviors.

Rachels, J. (2017). Why privacy is important. In *Privacy* (pp. 11–21). Routledge.

Ranck, J. G. (1961). Religious conservatism-liberalism and mental health. *Pastoral Psychology, 12*(2), 34–40. Springer.

Ringle, C. M., Wende, S., & Becker, J. M. (2017). *Product | SmartPLS.* Available at https://www.smartpls.com/.

Saridakis, G., et al. (2016). Individual information security, user behaviour and cyber victimisation: An empirical study of social networking users. *Technological Forecasting and Social Change, 102,* 320–330. https://doi.org/10.1016/j.techfore.2015.08.012.

Schneider, H., Krieger, J., & Bayraktar, A. (2011). The impact of intrinsic religiosity on consumers' ethical beliefs: Does it depend on the type of religion? A comparison of christian and moslem consumers in Germany and Turkey. *Journal of Business Ethics, 102*(2), 319–332. https://doi.org/10.1007/s10551-011-0816-y.

Siponen, M., & Vance, A. (2010). Neutralization: New insights into the problem of employee information systems security. *MIS Quarterly, 34*(3), 487–502 (Article).

Slater, E. (1947). Neurosis and religious affiliation. *The British Journal of Psychiatry, 93*(391), 392–396. RCP.

Smith, C. B., Weigert, A. J., & Thomas, D. L. (1979). Self-esteem and religiosity: An analysis of Catholic adolescents from five cultures. *Journal for the Scientific Study of Religion, 51–60.* JSTOR.

Smith, H. J., Dinev, T., & Xu, H. (2011). Theory and review information privacy research: An interdisciplinary review 1. *MIS QuarterlyInformation Privacy Research, 35*(4), 989–1015. https://doi.org/10.1126/science.1103618.

Smith, H. J., Milberg, S. J., & Burke, S. J. (1996). Information privacy: Measuring individuals' concerns about organizational practices. *MIS Quarterly, 20*(2), 167–196. Available at http://search.ebscohost.com/login.aspx?direct=true&db=buh&AN=9610124512&site=ehost-live.

Smith, S., et al. (2010). Circuits of power: A study of mandated compliance to an information systems security" de jure" standard in a government organization. *MIS Quarterly. JSTOR, 34*(3), 463–486.

Solove, D. J. (2005). A taxonomy of privacy. *University of Pennsylvania Law Review, 154*, 477. HeinOnline.

Stanton, J. M., et al. (2005). Analysis of end user security behaviors. *Computers & Security, 24*(2), 124–133. Elsevier.

Sutanto, J., Palme, E., & Tan, C. (2013). Research article addressing the personalization – privacy paradox: An empirical assessment from a field experiment on smartphone users 1. *37*(4), 1141–1164.

Swimberghe, K., Flurry, L. A., & Parker, J. M. (2011). Consumer religiosity: Consequences for consumer activism in the United States. *Journal of Business Ethics, 103*(3), 453–467. https://doi.org/10.1007/s10551-011-0873-2.

Sykes, G. M., & Matza, D. (1957). Techniques of neutralization: A theory of delinquency. *Source American Sociological Review, 22*(6), 664–670. Available at http://www.jstor.org/stable/2089195.

Tate, E. D., & Miller, G. R. (1971). Differences in value systems of persons with varying religious orientations. *Journal for the Scientific Study of Religion. JSTOR*, 357–365.

Vitell, S. J. (2009). The role of religiosity in business and consumer ethics: A review of the literature. *Journal of Business Ethics, 90*(Suppl. 2), 155–167. https://doi.org/10.1007/s10551-010-0382-8.

Vitell, S. J., & Paolillo, J. G. P. (2003). Consumer ethics: The role of religiosity. *Journal of Business Ethics, 46*(2), 151–162. https://doi.org/10.1023/A:1025081005272.

Wall, D. S. (2008). Cybercrime, media and insecurity: The shaping of public perceptions of cybercrime1. *International Review of Law, Computers & Technology, 22*(1–2), 45–63. https://doi.org/10.1080/13600860801924907.

Wang, J., Gupta, M., & Rao, H. R. (2015). Insider threats in a financial institution: Analysis of attack-proneness of information systems applications. *MIS Quarterly, 39*(1), 91–U491. Available at http://misq.org/insider-threats-in-a-financial-institution-analysis-of-attack-proneness-of-information-systems-applications.html.

Weaver, G. R., & Agle, B. R. (2002). Religiosity and ethical behavior in Organizations: A symbolic interactionist perspective. *The Academy of Management Review, 27*(1), 77–97. Academy of Management Review.

Welch, K. W. (1981). An interpersonal influence model of traditional religious commitment. *The Sociological Quarterly, 22*(1), 81–92. Wiley Online Library.

Westin, A. F. (1968). Privacy and freedom. *Washington and Lee Law Review, 25*(1), 166.

Wiebe, K. F., & Fleck, J. R. (1980). Personality correlates of intrinsic, extrinsic, and nonreligious orientations. *The Journal of Psychology*, 181–187. https://doi.org/10.1080/00223980.1980.9915149.

Wilford, S. H. (2004). *Information and communication technologies, privacy and Policies: An analysis from the perspective of the individual* (March).

Wilkes, R. E., Burnett, J. J., & Howell, R. D. (1986). On the meaning and measurement of religiosity in consumer research. *Journal of the Academy of Marketing Science*, 47–56. https://doi.org/10.1007/BF02722112.

Witte, K. (1992). Putting the fear back into fear appeals: The extended parallel process model. *Communication Monographs, 59*(4), 329–349. Taylor & Francis Group.

Worthington, E. L. J., et al. (2003). The Religious Commitment Inventory–10: Development, refinement, and validation of a brief scale for research and counseling. *Journal of Counseling Psychology, 50*(1), 84–96. https://doi.org/10.1037/0022-0167.50.1.84.

Xu, H., et al. (2011). Information privacy concerns: Linking individual perceptions with institutional privacy assurances. *Journal of the Association for Information Systems, 12*(12), 798–824.

Yao, M. Z., Rice, R. E., & Wallis, K. (2007). Predicting user concerns about online privacy. *Journal of the American Society for Information Science and Technology, 58*(5), 710–722. Wiley Online Library.

6

Avoiding a cyber world war: rational motives for negative cooperation among the United States, China and Russia

Tomas Janeliūnas, Agnija Tumkevič

Institute of International Relations and Political Science, Vilnius University, Vilnius, Lithuania

117

Introduction

Cyberspace has become a military domain, and cyber instruments have been integrated into all aspects of modern warfare. However, anonymity is the distinguishing feature and one of the most important issue of cyberspace. In cyberspace, it is difficult to attribute actions to specific actors or distinguish hostile attacks from innocent mistakes. A lack of clarity regarding what constitutes a cyberattack under international law and the lack of credible retaliatory threats encourage foes and competitors to plan, initiate and conduct relatively cheap cyberattacks. The state-sponsored weaponization of cyberspace and the engagement of militaries in offensive cyberspace operations heighten the risk of a cyber arms race and cyber warfare.

The prospects for cyberspace conflict and cooperation among the major powers of the United States, China and Russia are changing. The threat of cyberspace conflicts increases the risk of a cybersecurity dilemma inadvertently prompting crisis escalation. The issue of escalation in cyberspace is critical given that the cyber domain lacks binding rules. The existing legal instruments for restraining cyberspace conflicts are modest. As history has revealed in the competitive post-WWII run-up to the nuclear arms race, this could prove a dangerous situation.

However, the same forms of cooperation practiced among potential enemies during the nuclear arms race era, including agreements on nuclear disarmaments, may be unfolding in the current cybersecurity domain. International relations theories, particularly defensive realism, explain how and why security needs can prompt cooperation between adversaries. Cooperation sought under these conditions, negative cooperation, is based on the need to minimize the risk of a direct conflict. Therefore, it is important to examine the United States, China and Russia's cyberspace interactions. Are these states moving toward a global conflict, which could become a cyber world war? Or, are they restraining themselves and regulating the weaponization of cyberspace?

This chapter explores the motives and conditions under which the United States, China and Russia are likely to cooperate on qualitative arms control in cyberspace to improve both their national and international security. The analysis focuses on the 20-year period spanning from 1998 to 2018. The premises of defensive realism serve as the theoretical background for the analysis of the countries' behaviors and motives in cyberspace. This analysis is based on Charles Glaser's theory (1995, 2010), which explains the conditions leading to negative cooperation among potential adversaries.

Theoretical concept: defensive realism and cooperation in the cyberspace

Incentives for cooperation among rivals

Security cooperation poses a challenge for international relations theorists. Harald Müller (2013) writes, 'States opting for security cooperation sacrifice one security asset to gain another which they believe helps them to better provide for their security: the collaboration with their potential enemies and the pursuant agreements and organizations'. Cooperation among states with a common enemy is explained in classic or structural realism. The formation of alliances is addressed comprehensively by Glenn Snyder (1984, pp. 461–95, 1997), Stephen Walt (1987) and Randall Schweller (1994, pp. 72–107). According to the constructivist approach, states with shared values and interests tend to increase their security cooperation efforts and form security communities (Adler and Barnett, 1998). Robert Jervis (1985, 1999) has also explored in detail incentives for cooperation among states from the theoretical perspectives of realism and neoliberalism. Yet, neither these theorists nor other theorists can explain how potential adversaries' interests and perceptions prompt them to enter into security cooperation and self-restriction.

Structural and offensive realists believe that as states compete among themselves for power, cooperation among states lacks meaning (Mersheimer, 2013; Waltz, 1979). During and after the Cold War, most realists ignored obvious displays of cooperation among adversaries. These displays, such as the treaties on disarmament and the limitation of nuclear weapons between the United States and the USSR, reveal that cooperation between competing states is not only possible but also occurs frequently.

Glaser challenges classic neorealistic assumptions on cross-border cooperation and even terms them 'unwarranted' (Glaser, 2014, p.157). In his 2010 book *Rational Theory of International Politics: The Logic of Competition and Cooperation*, Glaser presents his own version of rational choice theory. His normative theory provides models of rational behavior and strategy, which he argues states should adopt (Glaser, 2010, p. 2). Unlike offensive realists, who claim the costs of cooperation are too high, Glaser asserts that the costs of confrontation are much higher and offers a theory of rational security based on policies of disarmament and cooperation.

According to Glaser, the logic of the security dilemma does not pre-suppose the competitive and confrontational nature of the international system (Glaser, 2010). Like Wendt (1992), Glaser (1992) discusses the less confrontational logic of anarchy (1992) in which confrontation between states is seen as irrational as it forces states to use their resources ineffi-ciently, (e.g., by engaging in an arms race), increases the possibility of military conflict and reduces security. Therefore, Glaser proposes three theoretical additions to neorealism.

First, he argues that confrontation is not natural in the international anarchic system. Glaser concedes that states are prone to compete to in-crease their military power, 'If military advantages are extremely valu-able, then military disadvantages can be extremely dangerous' (Glaser, 1995, p. 59). Yet, he adds that the fear of losing such competitions could lead to cooperation:

> Cooperation is valuable if it reduces the adversary's insecurity by reducing the military threat it faces. Moreover, cooperation is valuable if it can reduce the adver-sary's uncertainty, convincing it that the first state is motivated more by insecurity than by greed. (*Glaser 1995, p. 60*).

Second, Glaser writes that states are more motivated to strengthen security and military capabilities than to seek power. Therefore, it is important to differentiate between defensive and offensive capabilities Defensive realism offers two considerations to states as they choose be-tween either a confrontational or a cooperative security strategy:

> First, which will contribute more to its military capabilities for deterring attack, and for defending if deterrence fails? Second, appreciating the pressures created by anarchy and insecurity, the state should ask which approach is best for avoiding ca-pabilities that threaten others' abilities to defend and deter, while not undermining its military capabilities? (*Glaser 1995, p. 60*)

While explaining possible cooperation, Glaser turns to the theory based on military capabilities and strategy. The balance between offensive and defensive capabilities is of great importance to strategic choice. Glaser asserts, 'The defender's power multiplied by the offense-defence balance tells us much more about the defender's prospects for maintaining effective defensive capabilities than does considering power alone' (1995, p. 62).

The possibility of distinguishing between offensive and defensive capabilities is very important to Glaser's explanation:

> When offense and defence are completely distinguishable, the forces that support offensive missions do not support defensive missions, and vice versa; when offense and defence are not at all distinguishable, the forces that support offensive missions can be used as effectively in defensive missions. Therefore, the extent to which military power can be disaggregated, making offense and defence distinguishable, is important for answering a key question — whether defenders can avoid having offensive-mission capabilities while maintaining defensive ones. (*Glaser 1995, p. 62*)

Third, a potential adversary should be informed about the motives and goals of state security policy. Neorealists note that uncertainty about an adversary's motives and goals increases insecurity among states. A state seeking security should inform its adversary of its security goals. However, the international structure limits states' abilities to communicate. An information vacuum further increases uncertainty about goals and tensions among states (Wendt, 1992). Glaser tackles this dilemma with an important variable: information. Glaser's information variable is probably his most important contribution to rational international relations theory (Dingli, 2012). Information is defined as an awareness of an adversary's motives that includes an understanding of how the adversary's motives and goals are perceived.

Glaser (1995) states that communication regarding nonaggressive motives is possible if states execute one of the three security policy forms: arms control, unilateral defense or unilateral restraint. These forms of security policy enable states to differentiate between states seeking security and states seeking military power.

Glaser's theory, however, lacks clarity concerning how states become informed. Does choosing strategic restraint communicate enough information to an adversary? Schweller and Dingli note that the information variable does not evaluate changes in international politics due to the digital information revolution, media and online information leak scandals:

> Every day the National Security Agency alone intercepts and stores nearly two billion separate e-mails, phone calls, and other communications. In *Rational Theory*, however, information has nothing to do with the information age. Instead, it refers to beliefs about others' intentions (*Schweller, 2012, pp. 461–462*).

Despite this critique, it would be interesting to test whether or not Glaser's rational conditions, which should lead to negative cooperation, could exist in cyberspace. If the United States, China and Russia demonstrate the ability to cooperate in cyberspace, global cyberspace conflict would be unlikely. Yet, if the states demonstrate that Glaser's theoretical conditions are unattainable in cyberspace, it would be reasonable to expect an increase in cyberspace confrontations among these three powers.

Cyberspace as a playground for cooperation and conflicts

To ensure their cybersecurity, states often invoke traditional military strategies, such as deterrence or restraint. However, whether the typical rules of military strategy are valid in cyberspace is questionable. The specifics of cyberspace could pose an obstacle to cooperation. Cyberspace is characterized by a different perception of time; cyberattacks can be carried out 'here and now' simultaneously in many places. Moreover, there is a different perception of space. In the cyber domain, the boundaries of a state's legal jurisdiction are extended and cyberattacks have a transboundary effect in which they are not bound to physical borders. Cyberspace also poses accountability and assessment problems. It is often difficult to discern who should be held liable for a cyberattack or even how much damage it has caused. Applying traditional security strategies such as deterrence in cyberspace, given the differences between kinetic and cyber scenarios, yields serious issues. Lan et al. (2010) stress that the anonymous nature, global reach, scattered quality and interconnectedness of information networks greatly reduce the efficacy of traditional security strategies. Yet, the opposite view holds that deterrence or security cooperation could play a crucial role in de-escalating or averting cyber conflicts entirely. For example, many existing rules of law are applicable in cyberspace. Despite the specificities of cyberspace, this chapter follows the state-centric principle, which implies that only states can agree to common rules of conduct in cyberspace. The transfer of military logic to the cyber domain is justified for several reasons. First, cybersecurity is already perceived as an integral part of military security. Although cyberforces are acknowledged as a separate kind of military force, most countries' security strategies emphasize cybersecurity as a key component of their national security. Second, cybersecurity already plays a role in cross-border relations between states and bilateral agendas. Indeed, cybersecurity is as important as traditional military or economic cooperation. Third, multilateral cooperation (e.g., the UN) has led to agreements on cybersecurity and the limitations of cyber capacities. These agreements classify trust building in cyberspace as disarmament. Cybersecurity first appeared on the UN's agenda in 1998, when Russia proposed a resolution to invite countries to exchange the information on cybersecurity threats. The resolution attempted to include cybersecurity as a global security and disarmament issue. However, because of disagreements, the UN's documents on cybersecurity are usually declarative. For example, in June 2017, the UN failed to publish a joint report on international law and the cyber domain due to a lack of consensus and the varying perceptions of cybersecurity among experts representing different states. This reveals that the behaviors of potential adversaries, such as the United States, Russia and China, are analogical to their actions in traditional security areas: they have different perceptions of cybersecurity, tend not to trust each other and are not inclined to negotiate common rules that would bind them to comply with a responsible and transparent nonaggression policy in cyberspace (Bund & Pawlak, 2017).

The purpose of this section is to operationalize Glaser's cooperation conditions to explain the United States, Russia and China's behavior and the potential for their cooperation in cyberspace.

Motives

According to Glaser (2010), motives define a state's dominant security and foreign policy strategy. A state's foreign policy could be either revisionist or oriented toward maintaining the status quo. This corresponds to the state's typically realistic attitude regarding the motives of states in anarchy (Mersheimer, 2013, p. 80). Revisionist states seek to unilaterally strengthen their cyber capabilities, while status quo—seeking states seek cooperation and stability in cyberspace. A state's motives are often revealed in official strategic documents, such as national cybersecurity strategies and action plans and foreign security policy. Understandably, official documents do not always reveal a state's true intentions. Even realists admit, 'Policy-makers sometimes lie about or conceal their true intentions' (Mersheimer, 2013, p. 80). However, to identify initial trends in how states perceive the challenges of cybersecurity, a review of the official discourse is necessary. Does the official discourse emphasize a need for cooperation or does it tend to threaten confrontation? Strategic documents not only reveal a state's perceptions of cybersecurity challenges but also communicate messages to potential adversaries.

The distinction between defensive and offensive cyber capabilities

There is uncertainty regarding whether a distinction can be made at all between defensive and offensive capabilities in cyberspace. States seeking cooperation should be able to distinguish defensive from offensive means and purposefully invest in defensive capabilities to reduce the fears of their potential adversaries. However, if the specifics of cyberspace render this distinction difficult to make or if states deliberately avoid distinguishing between the two means, then an offensive—defensive balance in cybersecurity is not attainable, a condition that would reduce incentive for cooperation. States that cannot differentiate between the offensive and defensive capabilities of their adversaries would not be keen to make their own offensive and defensive capabilities clearly distinguishable and would perceive the development of cyber capabilities as dual-use cyber instruments.

Keeping the specificities of cyberspace in mind, identifying posture in cyberspace is important as a state's intentions and motives reveal whether the state's cyber policies are dominantly offensive or defensive.

Information

The dissemination of information strengthens trust and confidence. At the same time, information exchange comes at a cost. By committing to exchange information with a potential adversary, the state limits its ability to cheat or bluff its opponent. This chapter seeks to identify messages the United States, Russia and China send regarding cybersecurity cooperation. An analysis of statements made by high-ranking officials reveals the official positions of states regarding possible cooperation with potential adversaries. The information variable is important in determining whether official strategies are supported in the speeches of state leaders or, conversely, contradicted by the state's official posture.

The conditions for negative cooperation in cyberspace allow for four possible scenarios for cooperation and conflict in cyberspace:

1. The chances for conflict would be highest when competing states clearly distinguish between defensive and offensive capabilities and an offensive strategy prevails in their cyber politics.
   Respectively, according to rational thinking, hostile states will be in favor of negotiating a limitation of cyber capabilities to reduce escalation and avoid the damage caused by a potential conflict.
2. The likelihood of conflict would remain high if competing states do not distinguish between defensive and offensive capabilities, and their policy is dominated by an offensive posture.
   Accordingly, states should seek agreements to restrict offensive cyber capabilities or, at the very least, issue retaliatory sanctions for cyberattacks. In this case, an agreement is harder to reach because states cannot explicitly assess and compare the costs that would be incurred in choosing one of the strategies. Nevertheless, this scenario could indicate a significant escalation risk.
3. The likelihood of conflict would be low when competing states distinguish between offensive and defensive capabilities and prefer a defensive cyber policy, evidenced by voluntarily choosing to restrain their offensive capabilities. In this case, states would

have less incentive to cooperate, as they would not be significantly disturbed by the possibility of a direct collision or escalation in cyberspace.

4. The lowest probability of a cyber conflict would occur when states fail to clearly distinguish between defensive and offensive capabilities and a defensive policy dominates their strategies. The need for cooperation among states in this case would be minimal. However, this scenario would reflect a situation existing among nonconfrontational states with poorly developed cyber capabilities. Therefore, this scenario is not relevant to discussions concerning the United States, Russia and China's cyber relations.

The United States, China and Russia's strategic posturing in cyberspace

The United States

The United States has a broad legal framework behind its cyber policy. Apart from its national cybersecurity strategies, domestic legislation and executive orders have revised or approved cybersecurity action plans and measures in specific sectors. The United States's most important strategic documents in terms of revealing its strategic position in cyberspace include The National Strategy to Secure Cyberspace (2003), International Strategy for Cyberspace (2011), US Department of Defense Cyber Strategy (2015) and National Security Strategy (2015, 2017).

1998 to 2009: moderately defensive cybersecurity policy

In 1998, President Clinton signed a resolution to protect nationally significant infrastructure. The resolution includes the United States's first official acknowledgment of the risk of cyber threats, 'The United States will take all necessary measures to swiftly eliminate any significant vulnerability to both physical and cyberattacks on our critical infrastructures, including especially our cyber systems' (Presidential Decision Directive 63, 1998). In 2001, an executive order signed by President Bush foresaw the development of a programme to secure information networks and systems (Executive Order 13231, 2001). These decisions initiated regulated cyber policy and reveal the formation of a strategic view of cybersecurity.

The first US cybersecurity strategy was approved in 2003 (NSSC, 2003) in a document that reflects a progressive and consistent approach to cybersecurity. The National Cybersecurity Strategy focuses on internal cybersecurity policies and soft cybersecurity measures, such as strengthening public awareness of cyber threats, establishing private and public sector partnerships and creating a system to consistently respond to cyberattacks. The United States's strategy prioritizes national security and includes active defense measures to ensure cybersecurity. First, to strengthen the United States's intelligence capabilities in cyberspace and prevent cyberattacks in the United States, the strategy promotes identifying adversaries' cyberspace capabilities and motives. Next, the strategy asserts that the United States can choose the most appropriate response to a cyberattack. This provision is important not only because it implies that a cyberattack against the United States will get a response but also because it establishes that the US government is free to choose either a political or a military response. Finally, the strategy reveals an interest in strengthening international cooperation and highlights the United States's commitment to developing an international 'cybersecurity culture' and the creation of a global cybersecurity regime based on the values and principles of the Budapest Convention (NSSC, 2003). In summary, a defensive position dominates the United States's 2003 strategy. However, the document also indicates that the United States is prepared to respond to cyberattacks, a provision that should have served to deter.

In 2009, President Obama instructed the government to assess the politics surrounding cybersecurity. By 2009, international cyberspace had changed. Chinese espionage in cyberspace was increasing and Russia was expanding its own cyberspace capabilities. A 2009 report focused on a decentralized institutional framework, which at the time was not effectively responding to cyber threats (Cyberspace Policy Review, 2009). The development of cyberspace capabilities and the predominant cybersecurity strategy are not mentioned in the document. However, this report emphasizes the importance of international cooperation in stating:

> The Nation also needs a strategy for cybersecurity designed to shape the international environment and bring like-minded nations together on a host of issues, such as technical standards and acceptable legal norms regarding territorial jurisdiction, sovereign responsibility, and use of force (*CPR, 2009*).

However, the report does not mention cooperation with potential adversaries or states with different values. The provisions regarding cooperation can be seen as an attempt to create a cybersecurity alliance among Western powers to counterbalance the influence of China, Russia and other countries on the international cybersecurity regime.

2011 to 2018: the consolidation of the United States's cyberattack deterrence strategy

The United States's ambition to actively influence the international cybersecurity regime is reflected in the International Strategy for Cyberspace, Prosperity, Security and Openness in a Networked World (ISC, 2011), which states

> The United States will, along with other nations, encourage responsible behavior and oppose those who would seek to disrupt networks and systems, dissuading and deterring malicious actors, and reserving the right to defend these vital national assets as necessary and appropriate (*ISC, 2011*).

The American deterrence strategy is oriented toward creating an appropriate legal framework that would allow the United States to investigate, apprehend and prosecute those responsible for organizing cyberattacks. The United States explicitly states a need for international cooperation to create such a system and apprehend the actors responsible for cyberattacks.

The United States's strategy gives priority to defensive capabilities that enhance its resistance to cyberattacks. Since 2003, the United States's cybercrime strategy has been designed to discourage opponents by reducing their ability to launch successful cyberattacks. This deterrence-by-denial model appears nonconfrontational, but an analysis of the United States's strategic documents reveals ambiguity regarding distinctions between defensive and offensive capabilities in cyberspace. The cybersecurity strategies of 2003 and 2011 do not mention the development of offensive capabilities. However, provisions on responding to cyberattacks suggest that such a distinction exists. In 2011, the US Department of Defense Report provided Congress with answers to thirteen questions about the United States's cyberspace policy and its implementation (DoD, 2011). The report explains that cyberattack deterrence is carried out in two stages. First, the security and resilience of the United States's information systems is ensured. Second, the capacities to respond to cyberattacks are expanded. The report recognizes the United States's ability to implement offensive campaigns in cyberspace and assesses the risk of escalation and probability of conflict to be greater in cyberspace than in conventional settings. The Department of Defense Report views threatening to use offensive capabilities as a last resort for ensuring security and prioritizes the defensive strategies of decreasing vulnerabilities, confidence building and international cooperation (DoD, 2011).

The 2015 US Department of Defense Cyber Strategy reveals a change in cybersecurity priorities. One of the main priorities is cyberattack deterrence. Effective deterrence, both in traditional military contexts and in cyberspace, is achieved when an adversary is convinced that an attack will not produce the expected damage and that the aggressor will suffer countermeasures. This logic is reflected in the United States's 2015 cybersecurity strategy, which refers primarily to a need to demonstrate the United States's capabilities and its commitment to responding to cyberattacks (DoD CS, 2015). The updated strategy emphasizes a deterrence-by-punishment model. The expansion of the United States's offensive capabilities is also mentioned in the 2015 strategy. The paper notes that cyberattack deterrence is based on a set of actions and principles including declarative defensive positions, red lines, effectively alerting opponents and increasing the United States's access to information (DoD CS, 2015). A summary of the United States's cybersecurity policy postures and motives in two key time periods, identified through the analysis of the United States's security documents, is summarized in Table 6.1.

China

In China, discussions of digitalization and information as an important aspect of the country's economic development ensued in the 1990s. By 2003, China began to develop its cyberspace security policy. China's cyberspace policy and motives evolved during two distinct time periods: 2003—2012 and 2012—18.

TABLE 6.1 US cyber policy principles, priorities and motives.

Period	Cybersecurity policy posture	Officially declared cybersecurity policy motives
1998—2009	Defensive cybersecurity policy	Ensuring cybersecurity through defensive deterrence International cooperation Creation of a secure international cyberspace community
2011—18	Cybersecurity deterrence through denial and punishment	Ensuring national and international cybersecurity
Offensive—defensive balance	Offensive and defensive capabilities are clearly distinguished	

2003–12: China's emerging cyber doctrine

In 2003, China issued its first official strategic vision for information security and its first information security strategy in Document 27: Opinions for Strengthening Information Security Assurance Work. The 2006-approved Digitization Strategy for 2006 to 2020 outlines the direction of and resources for China's information policy and highlights protecting information technologies (Chang, 2014). During this period, information technology is perceived as both a source of economic opportunity and as a security challenge. China clearly understood and attempted to reduce its information vulnerabilities. In 2010, China's White Paper on Security and Defense expresses concern about the expanding cyberspace capabilities of foreign countries and draws attention to the need for China to strengthen its cyberspace defenses (China's National Defense, 2010). During this period, China's information policy was isolated and dominated by a defensive position; its main objective was to ensure the security of national information technologies. On the other hand, China successfully digitized and matched the West's technological progress. This process could be related to China's expanding cyberspace espionage capabilities, which were increasingly used against the United States and other Western nations (Thomas, 2009).

2012–18: establishing the concept of 'active defense'

Significant changes to China's information policy doctrine took place in 2012 and 2013. In 2012, China's Council of State Information Office published a new Concept of Information Security. As Giles and Hagestad (2013) note, this emphasizes strengthening civilian cyber defense. In 2013, the People's Liberation Army (PLA) published China's Science of Military Strategy, which reflected a more strategic view of cybersecurity (SMS, 2013). The document was not regarded as a military strategy, but it outlines new directions for the development of military doctrine. In the document, cyberspace is introduced, next to land, air, sea and space, as a defense and warfare domain. In 2015, the Chinese Ministry of National Defense approved a cyberspace military strategy (CMS, 2015). Although the strategy does not directly indicate the development of offensive cyberspace capabilities, Elsa Kania, of the cybersecurity firm FireEye, asserts that China's cyberspace policy commitments to 'stem major cyber crises, ensure national network and information security, and maintain national security and social stability' imply the possibility of launching cyberattacks (Kania, 2015). China's 2016 National Cyberspace Security Strategy sends a clear message to foreign adversaries: actors who engage in destructive activities directed against China's cyberspace and national security will be 'lawfully punished' (NCSS, 2016). Other cybersecurity measures include strengthening China's cybersecurity, increasing China's

TABLE 6.2   China's cyber policy principles, priorities and motives.

Time period	Cybersecurity policy posture	Declared cybersecurity policy motives
2003–12	Active defense Cyberspace sovereignty Strengthen defensive and offensive capabilities	Cyberattack deterrence maintains status quo in cyberspace
2012–18	Active defense Cyber sovereignty Nonintervention policy Multilateralism	Maintains status quo Cooperation Cyberattack deterrence
Offensive–defensive balance	Offensive and defensive capabilities are clearly distinguished	

power in cyberspace and wielding greater influence in the international cyberspace arena. See Table 6.2 for a summary of China's cyber policy principles, priorities and motives.

Russia

Russia's information policy is reflected in the following documents: Conceptual Views Regarding the Activities of the Armed Forces of the Russian Federation in Information Space (2011), Information Security Doctrine (2000, 2016), Military Doctrine of the Russian Federation (2014) and Russian Information Policy Guidelines for International Information Space (2013). The motives and measures identified in Russia's first security strategies remained basically unchanged until 2018. It should be noted that Russia does not use the term *cybersecurity*. Like China, Russia prefers the term *information security*. The wider concept of the term includes offensive attacks on information and computer networks, cyberattacks and psychological and information operations.

Russia adopted its first strategic document on information security in 2000 (ISD, 2000). It states Russia's intention to internalize information networks to become a full-fledged and active participant in the international information community. Russia viewed the dominant role of the United States in the management of the global Internet network as a challenge to Russia's national information security. In its 2000 information security strategy, Russia expresses an ambition to become a central power in the international information space. The strategy states that unilateral actions aimed to develop an 'information weapon' not only belittle Russia's role in the international information space but also promote an arms race in the information space (ISD, 2000).

In 2011, the Conceptual Views Regarding the Activities of the Armed Forces of the Russian Federation in the Information Space was approved. It reveals that information security is perceived as an integral part of military security. The objectives and measures of Russia's information policy are essentially to implement its military doctrine. The document also illustrates Russia's readiness to respond militarily to information threats. The document states that Russia reserves the right to issue an acceptable informational, political, economic or military response to avoid conflict escalation or prevent an uncontrollable war (CVRAAF, 2011).

In the Military Doctrine of the Russian Federation (2014), Russia clearly states its intent to expand deterrence capabilities through 'the development of forces and means of information warfare'. The Doctrine also includes a discussion of the development of new information weapons and systems for strategic, operational and tactical warfare (MD, 2014).

Russia presents information and psychological operations in its strategic documents as means for neutralizing an enemy and preventing war. This suggests that Russia approves the use of its information capacities not only in response to an attack but also to prevent attacks during peacetime. This assumption is confirmed in the most recent Information Security Doctrine of the Russian Federation (2016). The doctrine highlights Russia's information security policy motives, to identify and combat the sources of threats, to deter information threats and to strengthen Russia's influence in the international information space (ISD, 2016).

Russia's strategic documents lack a clear distinction between offensive and defensive capabilities. The 2016 Security Doctrine is dominated by a rather strict and combative vocabulary. This suggests that Russia views the information space characterized by aggression, hostility, conflicts of interest and influence battles. The security motives and measures revealed in Russia's strategic documents, summarized in Table 6.3, reliably indicate a primarily offensive posture in cyberspace.

TABLE 6.3 Russia's cyber policy principles, priorities and motives.

Time period	Cybersecurity policy posture	Declared cybersecurity policy motives
2000–18	Offensive deterrence Active restraint	Establishing status as a central power in the information space Ensuring national information security Reducing US dominance in the digital world
Offensive–defensive balance	*Offensive and defensive capabilities are not clearly distinguished*	

Cyberspace capabilities and the offence–defense balances of the United States, China and Russia

The United States

The United States makes a clear distinction between its offensive and defensive capabilities. Although information on the United States's cybersecurity weapons and capabilities is relatively limited, behavioral precedents, political debate and statistics reveal the United States's offensive–defensive balance in cyberspace.

The stated goals of the US Department of Defense demonstrate that the development of offensive and defensive cyberspace capabilities remains a top security priority. Consistent increases in the cybersecurity budget since 2015 confirm this priority. According to Admiral Michael Rogers, former director of both the National Security Agency (NSA) and the US Cyber Command, the United States's commitment to bolstering its offensive and defensive cyberspace capabilities was encouraged by increases in activity and aggressive behavior in Russia, China, Iran and North Korea's digital spaces (Gerden, 2016).

In 2017, US spending on offensive and defensive operations in the general defense budget increased by 6.7 million dollars. In 2017, the cybersecurity budget reached 900 million dollars. Despite reductions to some defense budgets in 2018, cybersecurity remained a budget priority with an allocation of 971 million dollars (Office of the Under Secretary of Defense, 2017).

The United States Cyber Command, the United States's official cybersecurity force, was established in 2009. In 2017, the US Department of Defense assigned 133 units (approximately 5000 armed forces service members) to the Cyber Command. By the end of 2018, the Cyber Command is expected to have 6200 service members (DoD, 2017). A reform of the United States's cyberforces began in 2017 to distinguish between the functions of the Cyber Command and the NSA. The US Cyber Command is a military formation. Therefore, it requires isolated infrastructure to collect intelligence on (and when necessary damage or destroy) the cyber capabilities of the United States's adversaries. According to former director of the NSA, Michael Hayden, the NSA does not foresee American offensive activity in cyberspace. Hayden reports that espionage in cyberspace is more operationally and technologically complex and requires the professional infiltration of information networks, an invisible takeover and the destruction of data (Pomerleau, 2017).

Although the United States has the capacity to counterattack or execute extensive offenses, it prioritizes politically restraining escalation in cyberspace. This emphasis on restraint was illustrated by the President Obama's reactions to Russian cyberattacks in 2015 and Russia's 2016 cyberattacks on and interference in the US presidential elections.

According to John Brennan, a former director of the CIA, President Obama decided to confine the United States's response to verbally warn Putin when sufficient evidence surfaced of Russia's interference in the United States's internal political processes. The US security services created several potential responses, including an offensive attack on Russia. Obama rejected offensive–attack scenarios, as he did not want the escalation of the cyberspace conflict to lead to a cyberspace war between the two countries (Miller, 2017). This situation demonstrates that at least during the Obama administration, the use of the United States's offensive cybersecurity capabilities was assessed with extreme caution, and the risk of a cyber conflict was perceived as both real and threatening.

The United States tends to develop its offensive and defensive cyber-security capabilities equally. The United States's large cybersecurity budget and the precedent the United States set in creating the malicious computer worm Stuxnet demonstrate that the United States is capable of executing effective offensive cyberattacks. Until 2016, the United States's security culture and cyberspace politics were dominated by Obama's political restraint regarding the country's offensive cyberspace capabilities, and priority was given to establishing a defensive advantage.

China

China makes a clear distinction between its offensive and defensive capabilities. An analysis of China's strategic security culture, specific behavioral precedents, cyberspace capability structures and primary actors reveal that offensive measures dominate China's cyberspace policy.

China's actors, who perform both offensive and defensive cybersecurity operations, can be divided into two groups. The first group consists of professional hackers, contracted by the PLA. The second group consists of patriotic hackers, who periodically perform cyberattacks ordered by the state. A general department of the PLA serves as China's cyberattack coordination center. It functions similarly to the United States's NSA and comprises of more than 13,000 experts. China has the largest cybersecurity force in the world (see Table 6.4). Each of its departments is responsible for different missions and operations. One of these departments, PLA Bureau 61398 (revealed by the American information technology company, Mediant) employs experts in the fields of information technology, electrical engineering, mathematics and linguistics. The bureau's main task is to collect intelligence on foreign countries' military and technology innovations and industries. Intelligence on unconfirmed anti-China security, doctrine and defense strategies is frequently collected as well (Kozlowski, 2015).

As Kozlowski (2015) notes, cyber-espionage is a skill China has mastered. China's is one the most active states when it comes to

TABLE 6.4   National cybersecurity spending and size of cyberforces of the United States, China and Russia in 2017.

	Annual budget for cybersecurity in million dollars	Individuals in cyberforce personnel
United States	900	6000
China	1500	20,000
United Kingdom	450	2000
Russia	300	1000
Germany	250	1000
North Korea	200	4000

Sources: Hackers Contracted by the Governments. (January 2017). The Businessman (in Russian - Komersant.ru). US Department of Defense Budget Overview.

performing industrial espionage and intellectual theft in cyberspace (Kozlowski, 2015). US General Keith Alexander, former director of the NSA, estimated that China's cyber-espionage activities cost the United States at least 300 to 400 billion dollars annually (Harrold, Libicki, Cevallos, 2016).

Another form of Chinese cyberattacks aims to physically damage the infrastructure of other countries. Chinese hackers were blamed for electrical disruptions in 2003, which affected 50 million in the United States. Tim Bennet, former Chairman of the Cyber Security Industry Alliance, reported that malware developed by China's PLA programmers caused the disruptions (Kozlowski, 2015).

Although China is developing its offensive cyber capabilities, it is paying little attention to its defensive capabilities and remains one of the countries most vulnerable to cyberattacks. The so-called Great Firewall could be a defensive tool, but instead of using it as a means for preventing cyberattacks, the China's government uses it primarily to control the flow of foreign information to China's public spaces. The promotion of offensive cyberspace measures is dominant in China's security policy. Considering China's need to compete with the United States technologically, this is a rational choice.

Russia

Although Russia does not make a clear distinction between its defensive and offensive capabilities in its strategic documents, Russia's behavioral precedents provide insights into its defensive—offensive balance.

Since 2011, the Russian Army has prioritized strengthening its ability to carry out and maintain 'informational confrontation'. This concept reflects Russia's emphasis on securing an informational advantage that is perceived as a collection of diplomatic, economic, political, military, informational and cultural measures aimed at creating technical and psychological impact in the information space.

According to a Defense Intelligence Agency assessment (2017) of Russia's military power, Russia is attempting to use its information and psychological operations to prevent its enemies from acting in a precautionary manner. Given this, the principle of informational confrontation implies the weaponization of information policy, which a priori generates offense-oriented information policy. Furthermore, by conducting psychological operations during peacetime, Russia's demonstrates an offensive information space position. In other words, both cyber and psychological operations in information space should be seen as exclusively offensive acts.

Although Russia's government denies its affiliations with hackers, hacking groups are among Russia's most effective information warfare tools. Because it is relatively easy to navigate cyberspace anonymously, assigning responsibility for cyberattacks is problematic, yet there are a number of groups known to serve the Kremlin's political goals. Russia's intelligence officers and hired cybercriminals often carry out cyberattacks jointly. In March 2017, the US Department of Justice indicted two members of Russia's intelligence agency, FSB, and two hackers hired by Russia's government for their coordinated roles in the heist of 500 million Yahoo user accounts in 2014, marking the first time the United States pressed cybercrime charges against Russian government officials. In July 2018, Special Counsel Robert Mueller indicted twelve Russian intelligence officers for hacking the Democratic National Committee and Hillary Clinton's presidential campaign in 2016.

Although Russia's official information security budget is much lower than the United States or China's, Russia prioritizes the development of its offensive capabilities. Since 2015, Russia has spoken of strengthening its offensive information space capabilities to create an effective system of cyber deterrence. Russia plans to allocate between 200 and 250 million dollars a year for this purpose (Gerden, 2016).

The United States, China and Russia's communications regarding cooperation and confrontation in cyberspace

The United States

US officials' messages regarding cyberspace have become more specific since 2009, when President Obama first mentioned cybersecurity issues in his annual report to Congress. In his address, Obama listed cybersecurity with nuclear weapons and terrorism among 21st century threats to security. In response to these threats, President Obama vowed to 'strengthen old alliances, forge new ones, and use all elements of our national power' (Jackson & Tsui, 2016).

Although US officials have known of China's hacking of American institutional and corporate bases since the first decade of the 21st century, they did not publicly react until the scope and costs of the cyberattacks set new precedents. In 2014, China allegedly hacked into the US Department of Homeland Security databases, and in 2015, China was suspected of launching the attack on the US Office of Personnel Management (OPM). President Obama described the hacking of US offices as 'an act of aggression that has to stop' (Rampton & Lambert, 2015). He also warned that should the United States take offensive measures, its victory would be guaranteed, 'We're still the best at this. If we wanted to go on offense, a whole bunch of countries would have some significant problems' (Fabian, 2015).

However, Obama did not name China, or any particular state, as responsible for the cyber-espionage. During the 2015 G7 Summit, when asked about the OPM attack and its impact on the United States's bilateral relations with China, Obama responded that *some* states are testing the vulnerability of the United States's systems, 'And that means that we have to be as nimble, as aggressive, and as well-resourced as those who are trying to break into these systems' (The White House Office of the Press Secretary, 2015a).

The president's indirect threats were likely issued to encourage China to agree to common rules of conduct in cyberspace. During President Xi's 2015 visit to the United States, Obama said

> China and the United States are two major cyber countries and we should strengthen dialogue and cooperation. I think it's going to very important for the United States and China, working with other nations and the United Nations to start developing an architecture to govern behavior in cyberspace that is enforceable and clear' (*The White House Office of the Press Secretary, 2015b*).

After this meeting and the signing of a cyber cooperation treaty between the United States and China in 2015, the Obama administration and security experts announced that the cyber cooperation agreement between the United States and China was achieved, thanks to the United States's strict rhetoric.

The United States's communication with Russia regarding cybersecurity was minimal until 2015. However, allegations that Russia intervened in the United States's 2016 presidential elections changed the rhetoric between the two states. American political discourse in 2015 and 2016 was marked by rather controversial messages. President Obama did not comment on Russia's interference into American political processes until 2016. For example, at the 2015 G20 Summit, while talking about malicious activities in cyberspace, he did not mention Russia's role in these activities. Instead he stated, 'Our goal is not to suddenly, in the cyber arena, duplicate a cycle of escalation that we saw when it comes to other arms races in the past, but rather to start instituting some norms so that everybody is acting responsibly' (The White House Office of the Press Secretary, 2016). President Obama mentioned that during the G20 Summit he warned Putin, behind the scenes, to halt interference in US political processes, 'or there would be some serious consequences' (Dyer, Sevastopulo, & Weaver, 2016). During an interview for NBC's Meet the Press, Mr. Biden was asked whether the United States was preparing to send a message to the Russian president, Vladimir Putin. US Vice President Biden warned that the United States would 'retaliate under the circumstances that have the greatest impact' (Sanger, 2016).

On the other hand, the United States's threats to use its offensive cyberspace capabilities have been rare and fragmented. There has been a lack of precision and securitization regarding cyberattacks in the United States's political discourse. Former CIA Director John Brennan, while commenting on Obama's refusal to use offensive capabilities against Russia, stated that the president had limited himself to issuing verbal warnings to Putin (Berrier, 2018). Despite verbal warning, sanctions and the 2018 expulsion of 35 Russian diplomats, the United States has essentially neglected its cyber deterrence posture. The United States not only failed to use its offensive cyber capabilities but also failed to communicate clear messages to Russia and failed to effectively deter Russia from committing malicious actions in cyberspace.

China

In speeches delivered by China's high-ranking officials, China is presented as a state that seeks to use international cyberspace peacefully. During President Xi's visit to the United States in 2015, he presented China as a staunch defender of cybersecurity and a victim of cyberattacks. He acknowledged the United States as the most powerful cyber state and reminded the United States that China hosts the world's largest number of Internet users. Xi stated that the two countries should cooperate to ensure a maximum cybersecurity level. He also noted that bilateral dialogue can be maintained if there is a trust between the two states and practical means of cooperation exist (The White House, 2015b).

After the election of President Trump, China's officials informed Washington that they were ready to maintain dialogues regarding cybersecurity with the new administration. In 2016, China's Public

Security Minister Guo Shengkun expressed his wish to maintain China's relations with the United States in the field of cybersecurity based on their established trust and cooperation, 'Both sides should treat this dialogue mechanism as the chief channel for communication over cyber issues to focus on cooperation, manage disputes and respond to each other's concerns in a timely and effective way' (South China Morning Post, 2016).

China's rhetoric of the United States has not always been peaceful. Following each major cyberattack that the Americans blamed on China, China responded with similar allegations. In 2014, when the United States arrested PLA soldiers for data theft and espionage, China cited the United States as the primary source of cyberattacks against China. The Chinese Ministry of National Defense published a statement stating that the United States's accusations were unjustified and would negatively affect bilateral relations, 'The United States, by this action, betrays its commitment to building healthy, stable, reliable military-to-military relations and causes serious damage to mutual trust' (McDonald, 2014).

Russia

Russia is actively following US officials' statements regarding Russia's activities in cyberspace. Recently Russia's leaders responded to US accusations that Russia interfered in the United States's 2016 presidential elections. Vice President Biden's aforementioned threat to use countermeasures against Russian interference in the United States's political processes prompted strong reactions from Russia's officials. Press Secretary Dmitry Peskov, spokesperson for President Putin, declared that Russia would protect its national cybersecurity, 'As US unpredictability and aggression grow, Russia is forced to take precautionary measures, aimed at reducing the risk of these attacks' (Mamontov, 2016). President Putin's advisor Yuri Ushakov confirmed that Russia would launch counteractions if the United States followed through on its threats (Ibid.).

To avoid being accused of escalating tensions and conflict, Russia often employs a blaming tactic. In this regard, Russia and China's communication strategies are similar. In a 2017 interview with the American news channel NBC News, President Putin claimed that either American hackers or the US military was to blame for the cyberattacks the US government has accused Russia of orchestrating. In Russia's view, the United States is threatening an arms race in cyberspace, implementing aggressive cyber policy and refusing invitations to cooperate. In March 2018, President Putin stated that Russia is willing to negotiate a new bilateral treaty for cybersecurity with the United States. According to Russia's president, the US government is simply not willing to cooperate and is thus escalating political and cyberspace confrontations between Russia and the United States (1Prime.ru, 2018). Russia's stated willingness to cooperate with the United States, however, is insincere. Krutskich's response to the US Ambassador to Russia's statement that the United States is waiting for guarantees that Russia will not interfere in the United States's domestic politics shows that Russia is not ready to cooperate. As the US diplomat noted, cooperation between the two countries would only be possible in this case. Krutskich named similar demands as ultimatum and strictly rejected any possibility of 'unilateral statements or confessions about alleged faults of Russia' (Topcor.ru, 2018).

Conclusion

The risk of a cyberspace conflict escalating between these three major cyber powers is still high. The United States, China and Russia fully understand the cost of a potential cyber war, but their strategic and political postures regarding cyberspace confrontations differ significantly.

Each of the three states invests large amounts of resources into maintaining competitive cyber capabilities. The United States and China clearly distinguish between offensive and defensive cybersecurity capabilities in their strategic documents and practical arrangements. This establishes, at least theoretically, grounds for a rational calculation of whether to pursue a cooperative strategy or engage in deliberate confrontation. Of the three states, the United States possesses the most powerful cyberspace forces, but its extensive cyber infrastructure is also the most vulnerable to cyberattacks. The United States has relied on a deterrence strategy in cyberspace and has signaled clearly that it is for negative cooperation and would like to forge agreements to avoid offensive actions.

The United States's strategy has been partially successful with China. China also officially demonstrates a defensive posture toward its cyberspace infrastructure and toward the security of China's information space. Following Obama and Xi's meeting in September 2015, during which the two countries agreed they would not knowingly support or conduct cybercrimes targeting trade secrets, analytical institutions reported a dramatic drop in the cyber-espionage of 72 suspected cybercrime groups in China (Fireeye, 2016). This improvement, even if temporary, establishes a precedent for bilateral cooperation to restrict offensive actions. From a defensive realism perspective, the United States and China's relations exhibit the necessary theoretical components to attain negative cooperation in cyberspace and avoid a large-scale cyber conflict.

However, the United States's deterrence strategy did not work with Russia. On the contrary, it provoked large-scale and complex intrusions of the United States's cyberspace before the 2016 presidential election. President Obama's refusal to respond with coercive cyber measures against Russia, despite having evidence of Russia's breaches, illustrates the

United States's cyber deterrence failure. Russia, like China, is using offensive cyber instruments to gain a competitive advantage over the United States. While China is deploying its cyber capabilities to conduct commercial and military espionage, Russia is using its cyber capabilities to provoke a political confrontation with the United States and impact politics within the United States. By choosing not to differentiate between its offensive and defensive capabilities and by sending confrontational messages, Russia is refusing to establish grounds for cooperation. This elevates the risk for the escalation of a cyber conflict between the United States and Russia, should the United States decide to respond with cyberattacks against Russia.

Despite some dangerous cyber conflict escalation developments, logic and rational motives suggest that the desire to minimize potential destruction should lead to de-escalation attempts, especially following a crisis. Examples from history, such as the Cuban crisis of 1962, indicate that a critical near clash can initiate cooperation, even between the bitterest of enemies.

References

Adler, E., & Barnett, M. (Eds.). (1998). *Security communities*. Cambridge: Cambridge University Press.

Berrier, H. (2018). Brennan admits Obama refused to retaliate for Russian cyber-warfare against U.S. making nice with the Russians. *The DailyWire*. Available from https://www.dailywire.com/news/29537/brennan-admits-obama-refused-to-retaliate-russian-hank-berrien.

Bund, J., & Pawlak, P. (2017). *Multilateralism and norms in cyberspace*. European Union Institute for Security Studies (EUISS).

Chang, A. (2014). *Warring state: China's cybersecurity strategy*. China's cybersecurity strategy. Center for New American Security.

China's Military Strategy. (2015). *The state Council information office of the PRC*. Available from https://news.usni.org/2015/05/26/document-chinas-military-strategy.

China's National Defense. (2010). *Information office of the state council*. Available from http://www.nti.org/media/pdfs/1_1a.pdf?_=1316627912.

Conceptual views regarding the acitivities of the armed forces of the Russian federation in the information space. (2011). Ministry of Defense of RF.

Cyberspace policy review, assuring a trusted and resilient information and communications infrastructure.(2009).

Defense Intelligence Agency. (2017). *Russia military power. Building a military to support great power aspirations*. Available from https://assets.documentcloud.org/documents/3891752/Defense-Intelligence-Agency-RussianMilitary.pdf.

Department of Defense Cyberspace Policy Report to Congress Pursuant to the National Defense Authorization Act for Fiscal Year 2011, Section 934. Available from https://nsarchive2.gwu.edu/NSAEBB/NSAEBB424/docs/Cyber-059.pdf.

Department of Defense (DoD). (Feb. 9, 2016). *Releases Fiscal Year 2017 President's Budget Proposal*. Available from https://dod.defense.gov/News/News-Releases/News-Release-View/Article/652687/department-of-defense-dod-releases-fiscal-year-2017-presidents-budget-proposal/.

Dingli, S. (2012). Book review: Charles L. Glaser, rational theory of international politics: The logic of competition and cooperation. *Millennium: Journal of International Studies, 40*(3), 679—681.

Dyer, G., Sevastopulo, D., & Weaver, C. (2016). Obama vows to hit back at Russia over election hacks. *Financial Times*. Available from https://www.ft.com/content/087fcd40-c35a-11e6-9bca-2b93a6856354.

Executive Order 13231. (2001). *Critical infrastructure protection in the information age.*

Fabian, J. (2015). Obama says he's prepared to retaliate against China. *The Hill*. Available from http://thehill.com/policy/cybersecurity/253826-obama-says-hes-prepared-to-retaliate-against-china-for-cyberattacks.

Fireeye. (2016). *Red line drawn: China recalculates its use of cyber espionage.* Available from https://www.fireeye.com/content/dam/fireeye-www/current-threats/pdfs/rpt-china-espionage.pdf.

Gerden, E. (2016). *Russia to spend $250 m strengthening cyber-offensive capabilities. SC Media UK.* Available from https://www.scmagazineuk.com/russia-to-spend-250m-strengthening-cyber-offensive-capabilities/article/531418/.

Giles, K., & Hagestad, W. (2013). Divided by a common language: Cyber definitions in Chinese, Russian and English. In *Proceedings of 5th international conference on cyber conflict, NATO CCDCOE, Tallinn.*

Glaser, C. L. (1992). Nuclear policy without an adversary: U.S. planning for the post-Soviet era. *International Security, 16*(4).

Glaser, C. L. (1995). Realists as optimists: Cooperation as self-help. *International Security, 19*(3), 50—90.

Glaser, C. L. (2010). *Rational theory of international politics: The logic of competition and cooperation.* Princeton University Press.

Glaser, C.h. L. (2014). The necessary and natural evolution of structural realism. In C. Elman, & M. Jensen (Eds.), *The realism reader.* Routledge.

Harold, W. S., Libicki, M. C., & Cevallas, R. S. (2016). *Getting to yes with China in cyberspace.* Santa Monica, California: RAND Corporation.

Information security doctrine of the Russian federation.(2000).

Information security doctrine of the Russian federation. (2016). MFA.

International Strategy for Cyberspace. (2011). *United States white house.*

Jackson, R., Tsui C-K., (2016) War on Terror II: Obama and the adaptive evolution of US counterterrorism. In Bentley M., Holland M. (Eds.), *The Obama Doctrine: a Legacy of Continuity in US Foreign Policy?*

Jervis, R. (1985). From balance to concert: A study of international security cooperation. *World Politics, 38*(1), 58—79.

Jervis, R. (1999). Realism, neoliberalism, and cooperation. Understanding the debate. *International Security, 24*(1), 42—63.

Kania, E. (2015). *China's military strategy: Cyber perspective.* Real Clear Defence.

Kozlowski, A. (2015). *The "cyber weapons gap". The assessment of the China's cyber warfare capabilities and its consequences for potential conflict over Taiwan.* University of Lodz.

Lang, T., Xin, Z., Raduege, H., Grigoriev, D., Duggal, P., & Schjolberg, S. (2010). *Global cyber deterrence views from China, the US, Russia, India and Norway.* EastWest Institute. Available from https://www.files.ethz.ch/isn/115239/2010-04_GlobalCyberDeterrence.pdf.

Mamontov, C. (2016). Кремль: России Придется Принимать меры После заявлений США об ответныч кибератакач. BBC. Available from https://www.bbc.com/russian/news-37666658 (in Russian).

McDonald, J. (2014). China warns US cyber spying charges could damage ties. *Global News.* Available from https://globalnews.ca/news/1341141/china-warns-u-s-cyber-spying-charges-could-damage-ties/.

Mersheimer, J. (2013). Structural realism. In T. Dunne, K. Kurki, & S. Smith (Eds.), *International relations theories: Discipline and diversity* (3rd ed., pp. 77–93). Oxford: Oxford University Press.

Military doctrine of the Russian federation.(2014).

Miller, L. (2017). Facing a Russian cyber attack, Obama officials struggled to respond. *Frontline.* Available from https://www.pbs.org/wgbh/frontline/article/facing-a-russian-cyber-attack-obama-officials-struggled-to-respond/.

Müller, H. (2013). Security cooperation. In W. Carlsnaes, T. Risse, & B. A. Simmons (Eds.), *Handbook of international relations* (pp. 607–634). Sage Publications Inc.

National cyberspace security strategy.(2016). Available from https://chinacopyrightandmedia. wordpress.com/2016/12/27/national-cyberspace-security-strategy.

National Security Strategies. (2015). *United States white House.*

National Security Strategies. (2017). *United States white House.*

Pomerleau, M. (June 29, 2017). *Here's what cyber command's war-fighting platform will look like.* Fifth Domain. Available from https://www.c4isrnet.com/home/2017/06/29/hereswhat-cyber-commands-war-fighting-platform-will-look-like/.

Presidential decision directive 63. (1998). Critical Infrastructure Protection.

Rampton, R., & Lambert, L. (2015). *Obama warns China on cyber spying ahead of Xi visit.* Reuters. Available from https://www.reuters.com/article/us-obama-roundtable-cybersecurity/ obama-warns-china-on-cyber-spying-ahead-of-xi-visit-idUSKCN0RG2AS20150916.Sanger.

Remarks by president Obama and president Xi of the people's Republic of China in joint press conference. (2015). The White House Office of the Press Secretary. Available from https:// obamawhitehouse.archives.gov/the-press-office/2015/09/25/remarks-president-obamaand-president-xi-peoples-republic-china-joint.

Remarks by president Obama in press conference after G7 Summit. (2015). The White House, Office of the Press Secretary. Available from https://obamawhitehouse.archives.gov/the-pressoffice/2015/06/08/remarks-president-obama-press-conference-after-g7-summit.

Russian Information Policy Guidelines for International Information Space.(2013). Available from http://static.government.ru/media/files/41d49f3cb61f7b636df2.pdf.

Sanger, D. E. (2016). *Biden hints at U.S. Response to Russia for cyberattacks, The New York Times* October 15. Available from https://www.nytimes.com/2016/10/16/us/politics/bidenhints-at-us-response-to-cyberattacks-blamed-on-russia.html.

Schweller, R. L. (1994). Bandwagoning for profit: Bringing the revisionist state back in. *International Security, 19*(1), 72–107.

Schweller, R. L. (2012). Debating Ch. L. Glaser's Rational theory of international politics. Rational theory for a bygone era. *Security Studies, 20*(3), 460–468.

Snyder, G. H. (1984). The security dilemma in alliance politics. *World Politics, 36*(4), 461–495.

Snyder, G. H. (1997). *Alliance politics.* Ithaca: Cornell University Press, London.

South China Morning Post. (2016). *China willing to work with Trump on cybersecurity.* Available from http://www.scmp.com/news/china/diplomacy-defence/article/2052881/chinawilling-work-trump-cybersecurity.

The DOD cybersecurity strategy.(2015).

The National Strategy to Secure Cyberspace. (2003). *United States department of homeland security.*

The Science of Military Strategy. (2013). *People's liberation Army.* Available from https://fas. org/nuke/guide/china/sms-2013.pdf.

The White House, Office of the Press Secretary. (2016). In *Press conference by president Obama after G20 Summit.* Available from https://obamawhitehouse.archives.gov/the-press-office/2016/09/05/press-conference-president-obama-after-g20-summit.

Thomas, T. (2009). Nation-state cyber strategies: Examples from China and Russia. In F. Kramer, H. S. Stuart, & L. Wentz (Eds.), *Cyberpower and national security.* National Defense University Press and Potomac Books Inc.

Topcor.ru. (2018). Москва ответила на ультиматум ВашинГтона. Available from https://topcor.ru/1047-zapad-snova-oshibsya-stranoy.html (in Russian). National security documents, official statements, reports etc.

US department of defense cyber strategy.(2015).

Walt, S.M. (1987). *The origins of alliances*. Ithaca: Cornell University Press, New York.

Waltz, K. N. (1979). *Theory of international politics*. London: Addison-Wesley.

Wendt, A. (1992). Anarchy is what states make of it: The social construction of power politics. *International Organization, 46*(2), 391—425.

1Prime.ru. (2018). Путин: Москва Готова ПодПисать доГовор о кибербезоПасности с ВашинГтоном. 1Prime.ru. Available from https://1prime.ru/News/20180310/828585424.html (in Russian).

Further reading

Defense Budget Overview, Office of the under Secretary of Defense, Chief Financial Officer, 2017. All cyber mission force teams achieve initial operating capability. DOD Press Release, 2016. Available from https://www.defense.gov/News/Article/Article/984663/all-cyber-mission-force-teams-achieve-initial-operating-capability/.

Ernst, D. (2010). *Indigenous innovation and globalization — the challenge for China's standardization strategy*. East-West Center.

Obama, B. (2009). *Address before a joint session of the congress*. Available from http://www.presidency.ucsb.edu/ws/index.php?pid=85753.

Standard operating procedures for cybercrime investigations: a systematic literature review

Stephen Jeffries, Edward Apeh

Department of Computing and Informatics, Bournemouth University, Poole, United Kingdom

OUTLINE

Emerging Cyber Threats and Cognitive Vulnerabilities
https://doi.org/10.1016/B978-0-12-816203-3.00007-1

Introduction

Over recent years, there has been a large increase in the use of computers, tablets and mobile phones with their users being much more active in buying and selling items online and the use of social networks (Laudon, Traver, & Elizondo, 2007). According to the Office for National Statistics (2014), 38, million adults (76%) in Great Britain accessed the Internet every day, 21 million more than in 2006, when directly comparable records began. Access to the Internet using a mobile phone more than doubled between 2010 and 2014, from 24% to 58% and 74% of all adults bought goods or services online, up from 53% in 2008 with clothes (49%) being the most popular online. This massive increase in the use of the Internet and the growth of the digital economy has led to advancements for society but has also created new areas of threat and risk. Increasingly, the Internet is being used to facilitate a new avenue for crime to be committed (McGuire, 2013). Cybercrimes are commonly considered as falling into one of two categories (Home Office, 2010):

(i) new offences committed using new technologies, such as hacking or breaking into computer systems to steal or alter data, offences against computer systems as dealt with in the Computer Misuse Act 1990 (Legislation.gov.uk, 1990),

(ii) old offences committed using new technology, such as the transfer of illegal images or fraud where networked computers and other devices are used to facilitate the commission of an offence.

Irrespective of the category of the cyber offences, the proliferation of mobile devices and computers has not only resulted in an increase in the number of cyber-related crimes but most traditional crime scenes now having some form of digital evidence (McGuire, 2013). This growth of offences and increase in devices has afforded an opportunity for the police to access large amounts of new data which can assist in the investigation process (Bell, 2002). However, this large volume of data has not been matched by the reporting of cybercrime offences. Companies are often reluctant to report breaches or attacks' for reputational and economic reasons (Richards, 2009). The large volume of data and the lack of reporting have led to an illusion that those involved in cybercrime are unlikely to be identified and prosecuted. The National Crime Agency believes that this applies to those involved in organized crime as they perceive this to be a low-risk, high-yield activity (National Crime Agency, 2015).

Various techniques and policies have been introduced by police and government agencies across the world to combat this growing cybercrime trend. For instance, the UK Government produced its contest paper: *the*

United Kingdom's Strategy for Countering Terrorism in which it launched the four Ps (HM Government, 2011):

- Pursue — To stop terrorist attacks
- Prevent — To stop people becoming terrorists or supporting terrorism
- Protect — To strengthen the protection against a terrorist attack
- Prepare — To mitigate the impact of a terrorist attack.

In the United States, the Federal Bureau for Investigation strategy focuses on (FBI, 2011)

- Intelligence-Driven Operations — Through the use of threat focus cells
- Leadership and Collaboration — National Cyber Investigative Joint Task Force
- Partnerships — With industry and academia
- International — Retaining responsibility inside and outside borders for attacks on US citizens and its critical infrastructure

Legislation has been introduced in the United Kingdom to help reduce the growing trends on cybercrime. However, whilst improvements in the proposed new Counter-Terrorism Bill will obligate Internet service providers (ISPs) to retain information linking Internet protocol (IP) addresses to individual users, which will be available to UK law Enforcement through applications made under the Regulation of Investigatory Powers Act (HMG, 2015), there is no recommended best practice for the UK police on how to investigate online crimes in a similar manner to those in which they investigate traditional crime types. This chapter presents a systematic literature review to identify techniques, policies, legislation and best practice for the investigation and gathering of evidence for cybercrime.

The problem of investigating cybercrime

The UK police are trained and competent at the investigation and gathering of evidence of traditional crimes. Initial police training is coordinated by the College of Policing through the Initial Police Learning and Development Programme (IPLDP) (Police.uk, 2015). During this training, they are instructed in basic investigation techniques that follow the traditional police investigation process.

For example, the standard process for a case in which a member of the public leaves a bank with cash and is robbed on the street is for police officers to attend the scene and take a statement of evidence from the victim and any witnesses and search for an offender using dogs, other officers and possibly a helicopter. They will locate and review CCTV images, seek to recover any potential DNA and fingerprints and potentially release an image to the public of the suspect they wish to interview. This collectively increases the likelihood of the offender being identified, arrested and prosecuted.

However, if we take the same example to cyberspace, we find that cybercrime tends to involve a number of intricate connections which makes the investigation more complicated (Broadhurst, Grabosky, Mamoun, & Chon, 2014). Thus, using the same example, if the victim attends their bank to withdraw a sum of money and finds that the account has been emptied via an online attack, the victim is likely to be informed to report this matter to action fraud online and is not likely to even see a police officer. Therefore, the likelihood of any suspect being identified, arrested and prosecuted is very low.

As shown by the two examples despite the offences involving the same victim, bank and money, the levels of service provided vary vastly. This is compounded by a lack of standard operating procedures for officers to follow in investigating the online example, as well a lack of knowledge as to what data are available and how that data can be used. This is further exasperated by the government's comprehensive spending review and the extensive cuts to police budgets which have resulted in fewer police officers (Millie & Bullock, 2012). Furthermore, any additional officers that the police seek to employ to combat cybercrime will require training not only in the respect of cybercrime but the basics of UK law and the traditional police investigation processes. Even when training is made available, the legislation needs to be in place to support the investigation techniques and the evidence-gathering processes.

Effective cybercrime investigations are usually undertaken using best practice approaches such as evidence-based policing. In an evidence-based policing approach, police officers and staff create, review and use the best available evidence to inform and challenge policies, practices and decisions. Such best practice tends to help in effective and efficient investigations and evidence gathering. For traditional policing, the training and sharing of best practice is managed through the College of Policing. Training for new recruits is controlled through the IPLDP. Additional training for detectives is provided through the Initial Crime Investigators Development Programme and for experienced managers through the Senior Investigating Officers programme (College of Policing, 2015). The courses are designed to instruct officers in the investigation of traditional crime types. Recently, the College of Policing have started to develop the following training standards for cybercrime:

- Level 1 'Cyber Awareness' — Target audience being all police employees who may have some involvement in cybercrime reporting and investigation. The aim of this course is to cover identification of a cybercrime, preservation of evidence, basic legislation and signpost who to escalate reports to.

- Level 2 'Cyber for Investigators' — Target audience being all police employees who will be investigating cybercrimes. Level 1 will be a prerequisite for Level 2, with the aim of Level 2 being to increase the ability of investigators to understand and respond to cybercrime effectively (College of Policing, 2015).

However, these training programmes have not yet been implemented. It is envisaged that these packages will be delivered via National Centre for Learning Technologies. However, in a recent survey by the Police Federation, it was stated that officers had expressed real concerns about the contents and style of the packages used for training (Weinfass, 2015). This highlights the need for a carefully thought-out approach to developing and deploying cybercrime investigation techniques. Best practice is shared through seminars and conference with Senior Police Investigators sharing their experiences in dealing with a complex investigation or identifying a new technique. These conferences count towards the Continual Professional Development points required to maintain accreditation. However, whilst there are conferences available that discuss strategies across the Internet, none are focused on the sharing and developing of best practice at a practical investigators level.

This chapter presents an approach for conducting a systematic literature review for investigating and gathering evidence for cybercrimes that is based on utilizing traditional policing techniques. The aim is to identify any shortcoming in existing techniques and identify new opportunities that can be used in the investigation of cybercrimes.

Therefore, the following questions are sought to be answered in relation to the covert and overt methods used to investigate online cybercrime:

- Techniques — What traditional techniques can be adopted to investigate cybercrime? What new techniques need to be adopted?
- Policy/strategy — What are the existing policies/strategies for tackling cybercrime? What are their shortcomings?
- Legislation — What legislation exists for traditional surveillance? Can this legislation be used for cybercrime investigations and prosecutions?
- Best practice — What best practice exists in the investigation of cybercrime? How is this best practice shared?

Research methodology

To address these questions, the research takes the approach of a systematic literature review which consists of the following steps:

1. Specifying the research questions — This step defines the objective of the systematic literature review and resulted in the following research questions:
   - Techniques — What traditional techniques can be adopted to investigate cybercrime? What new techniques need to be adopted?
   - Policy/strategy — What are the existing policies/strategies for tackling cybercrime? What are their shortcomings?
   - Legislation — What legislation exists for traditional surveillance? Can this legislation be used for cybercrime investigations and prosecutions?
   - Best practice — What best practice exists in the investigation of cybercrime? How is this best practice shared?
2. Develop a review protocol — These are the steps undertaken to show how the data for the review is selected. These include the following:
   - Identifying the relevant search sources — Databases were selected on the basis that they are most likely to contain material that will assist in the literature review. These include the following:
     - Elsevier
     - SpringerLink
     - Google Scholar
     - Taylor and Francis
     - Emerald Insights
     - UK and International Government websites
     - Google (as a final capture check)
   - The selection of the most relevant dates to conduct the search — Publications with dates from 2005 to 2015 will be considered given that the increase in online crimes and their investigation are a relatively new phenomenon.
   - The selection language — Only publications in English will be reviewed from the selected databases.
   - Stating selection criteria so that studies can be included and excluded.

     The search criteria were based on the questions that were raised and sought to be answered through this review. In searching for techniques, then words used were based on a direct comparison with the techniques used in traditional proactive organized crime investigation techniques. So search phrases included

- Surveillance online
- Intelligence gathering online
- Interception online
- Undercover online

Policies/strategies, Legislation and Best Practice were reviewed in this initial review, and where nothing specific was found, then additional searches were made with these phrases included. Papers that related only to digital forensic were excluded on the basis that at the point of digital recovery it is apparent that the offender is known or the malicious software is being removed from the victim's hardware, and this relates only to the recovery of the data and not to the investigation.

- Assess the data quality.
  - Peer-reviewed journals were considered the highest
  - Peer-reviewed conference papers
  - Peer-reviewed workshop papers
  - Non−peer-reviewed papers were considered the lowest

Initial results using the online surveillance were produced in 1690; this process was then refined as outlined in Fig. 7.1.

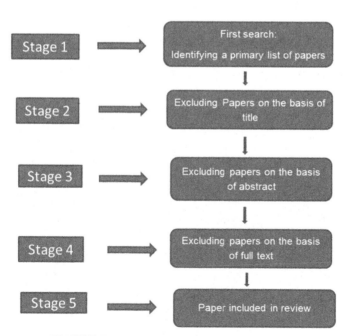

FIGURE 7.1   Systematic literature review process.

Results and discussion

The work undertaken has focused on the research questions for techniques, legislation, policy/strategy and best practice/training, and their impact or encouragement on cybercrime investigations. The findings of the systematic literature review are depicted as follows in Fig. 7.2, and the results are described in the following section.

Techniques

In researching the concept of traditional police techniques being applied to the investigation of cybercrime, it is apparent that there is little previous research that relates directly to this process. There are a number of papers that relate to digital forensics but very few that relate to the initial investigation of the cybercrime.

Zanasi (2009) considers the use of online intelligence gathering methods that can be used in the fight against terrorism; these techniques can also be applied to the investigation of organized crime. He explains that those involved in acts of terrorism are organized in small and dispersed units coordinating their activities online and using the Internet to recruit followers and donors to funds their cause. In a traditional intelligence gathering process, the police would seek to identify a potential Covert Human Intelligence Sources (CHIS) close to the subject of the investigation. To proceed with either of this option, the organized crime group must be understood so that any CHIS may be identified and the hierarchy of the group mapped. This process should now be considered

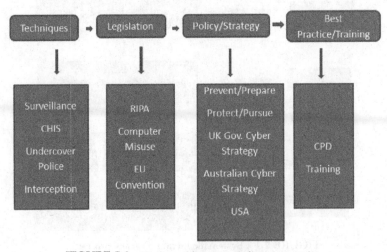

FIGURE 7.2   Findings of systematic literature review.

and applied online using technology that can be applied to open source intelligence analysis. Police could seek to analyze the data from emails, chat rooms, forums, blogs and social media sites to gather intelligence on these groups of criminals. This will involve the analysis of large amounts of data which will exceed the capability of a human but whilst the technology created can be exploited by the criminals it can similarly be used to support police investigations. He further explains the use of 'text mining' to create investigative opportunities from these data.

Text mining is described as information extraction in linguistic processing, where semantic models are defined according to the user requirements, allowing the user to extract the principal topics that are of interest to them. For example, the extraction of organization names, people's names, emails addresses, phone details and bank accounts can be done using text mining techniques from social media which lends itself to the use of text mining for the gathering of evidence (Zander, Nguyen, & Armitage, 2005).

Furthermore, Tokunaga (2010) argues that social networking sites can be used as a tool for interpersonal electronic surveillance not by the police but by those using the social networking sites to gain an awareness of their partners, friends and business associates offline and/or online behaviours. These sites are an important way for lots of individuals to communicate with friends, associate and the wider world and thereby impart a wealth of information through social networking sites, e.g., Twitter, Facebook, blogs, etc. Whilst this chapter considered this methodology as a means of keeping watch on those you know, a similar process can be adopted by the police to identify the locations, associates and activities of those involved in organized crime. For example, Ali (2014) proposes an experimental framework to discover and predict suspicious messages that are sent via social networking sites as a means of identifying the threat activity and the offender's details. This framework is based on ontology-based information extraction techniques and association mining (a data mining technique with a set of predefined knowledge-based rules). Although this technique is yet to be applied by law enforcement to establish its values, there is a consensus from this literature review that these techniques can be successfully applied by the police as a means of gathering intelligence and investigating crime online.

An alternative technique is the interception of communications. Branch (2003) describes lawful interception as the process of covertly intercepting communications between parties that are of interest to law enforcement. He explains the difficulty in Internet interception is due to Internet traffic being transmitted using the IP. This transfers the communication via a number of separate packages each with their own destination address and once routed by different routes they are at the destination and are reassembled. He describes the process of using 'sniffers' being installed at key points within the network to monitor passing traffic which can be programmed to listen for specific IP addresses and capture the packets containing the relevant IP addresses for onward transmission or later recovery. He also suggest as an alternative including a lawful intercept function within a router but recognizes that routers are used by corporations and not just ISP, and therefore there will be a difficulty in restricting the functions just to the ISPs. However, in its conclusion, the paper does not suggest any trials or solutions just an acknowledgement of the difficulties in intercepting Internet communications.

Furthermore, another traditional technique that lends itself to cyber investigations is the use of an undercover police officer. A review of online undercover investigations identified papers that relate to the grooming and sexual exploitation of children where officers purport to be children and pose as such online to identify those who seek to exploit children for a sexual reason. Tetzlaff-Bemiller (2011) conducted a survey of police officers involved in this activity in the finding the paper identified that officers felt the training was weak and covered more on child pornography and less on the role of an undercover officer and the current terminology used online. Training was provided in relation to forensic recovery, chatting techniques and information technology together with the techniques used by sex offenders. The training was varied depending on where the officers were working. This identifies that law enforcement needs to agree some agreed standards in the deployment, use training of online officers as they could be interacting with a sex offender or criminal from any location in the world when they are operating online. Whilst these techniques proposed can lend themselves to cybercrime investigation, the legislation needs to be in place to facilitate their lawful use.

Legislation

Legislation exists to support the techniques used in the investigation of traditional organized crime. For example, the Regulation of Investigatory Powers Act 2000 (HMG, 2000):

- Part I of the legislation covers Interception and the acquisition and disclosure of communications data.
- Part II covers Human Intelligence that covers the use of surveillance and CHIS (this includes the deployment of undercover police officers).
- Part III covers the investigation of electronic data protected by encryption.

The Chief Surveillance Commissioner Sir Christopher Rose (2013) in his annual report stated that he was encouraged by the increasingly mature debate relating to the use of the Internet for investigative purposes, especially the use of social networking sites. He acknowledged that there were points of detail to work out, particularly in relation to repeated viewing of a publicly available site but was comfortable to acknowledge in the main, RIPA Part II (Directed Surveillance) could be used effectively. RIPA for the deployment of an undercover officer has been used for a number of years in both the real world and online worlds. Undercover policing in the United Kingdom is currently subject to a public enquiry led by Lord Justice Pitchford. The purpose of the inquiry is to consider the deployment of police officers as CHIS, the undercover policing practices, identify lessons learned and make recommendations about the future of undercover policing (Home Office, 2015). This enquiry may lead to a change in the legislation.

However, interception is yet to reach the same level of trial and usage as undercover policing in cyberspace. Ward and Horne (2015) in a report for the Home Affairs committee outline the process for intercept and identif' confusion in the legislation over what constitutes 'in the course of transmission' and argue that this could include data that are held on a communication system before their transfer to the intended recipient. The report identifies the impact of the European court's ruling on a 2006 directive on data retention which resulted in the UK government introducing the Data Retention and Investigatory Powers Act 2014. This was a hurried piece of legislation that was passed with a sunset clause, and it expires at the end of 2016. Legislation is currently being drafted to replace the Data Retention Act.

The main police of legislation that relates directly to the criminal use of a computer is the Computer Misuse Act which created offences of (Legislation.gov.uk, 1990):

- Unauthorized access to computer material.
- Unauthorized access with intent to commit or facilitate commission of further offences.
- Unauthorized acts with intent to impair, or with recklessness as to impairing, operation of computer.
- Making, supplying or obtaining articles for use in offence under Introduction section or Research methodology section

Mac Ewan (2008) in a review of the act stated that it suffered a premature birth, which left it weak and vulnerable when the Internet, as we know it, arrived. In this review, there are highlights of a number of cases where a wide interpretation of the act has been taken to encompass hacking offences and denial of service. In 2015, this act was amended by the Serious Crime Act 2015 which introduced two additional offences to close gaps and extended the scope of the act to include computer crime committed by British Nationals in foreign countries (HMG Legislation, 2015):

- Unauthorized acts causing, or creating risk of, serious damage
- Obtaining articles for purposes relating to computer misuse

Broadhurst (2006) acknowledges that cybercrime is often traditional crimes (frauds, child pornography, etc.) executed swiftly and to vast numbers of potential victims across the world. Furthermore, cyberspace is a world without borders. Traditional crime tends to be committed with the victim and the offender being in the same location. Cybercrimes can be committed across vast divides with the victim and offender never meeting. Brenner, Lee, Cox, & Siber, 2006) state with crimes being committed across international borders, it is not always possible to determine the 'locus comissi delicti' (the place where the offences were committed). This creates difficulty in deciding who has primacy in any investigation. There is a need for a process for information sharing, deciding jurisdiction and the ability to rapidly deploy to secure evidence and identify offenders. In seeking solutions for the global law enforcement of cybercrime, the paper identifies current conventions from the Council of Europe and the United Nations that may be of assistance.

The United Nations convention against transnational organized crime was introduced in 2000 and although not specific to cybercrime it can be a useful instrument in this process. The convention enables mutual legal assistance between states and establishes several offence categories; participation in an organized criminal group; money laundering; trafficking of people and methods for combating computer misuse.

The Council of Europe Cybercrime Convention lays down three objectives:

- To lay down definitions of certain criminal offences
- To define common types of investigative powers better suited to the information technology environment
- To determine both traditional and new types of international cooperation.

Whilst the convention encourages cooperation to investigate these offences, the difficulty remains when attacks occur across multiple jurisdictions each having their own laws and methods of preserving evidence (Choo, 2011; Kshetri, 2006). This suggests that given the speed and complexity of these attacks, traditional methods of law enforcement in the securing and preserving of evidence are no longer adequate.

Furthermore, Marion states in Marion (2010), that because the Convention is largely symbolic, its long-term effectiveness must be brought into question. There are problems relating to the definitions of terms in the treaty, privacy issues and the investigatory powers created in the document. Furthermore, international laws requiring cooperation between nations are difficult to enforce. Overall, the treaty leaves too many holes in terms of the lack of definitions and inconsistencies. Watney (2012) suggests that many nation-states favour regulation by the United Nations in a belief that it will promote transparency and ensure that all states are involved in the negotiations. There needs to be an acceptance that cyberspace ultimately belongs to the global world and all nation-states should be in agreement or cybercrime may end the economic and social advantages for generations to come.

Policy/strategy

To support the investigation techniques and legislation to work effectively in combating cybercrime, there need to be effective policy and strategy. The Cabinet Office (2014) reports on the UK government progress on delivery of its 2011 Cyber Security Strategy. The document focuses on the progress with small business, the critical infrastructure and the funds that have been allocated to the setting up of the National Cyber Crime Unit, Regional Cyber Units and the Metropolitan police Falcon team. These units contain a small number of specialist officers and there is no acknowledgement in this document of any strategy to support the mainstream investigation of cybercrime. The Home Office Strategy on Cybercrime (2010) highlights the need of a classification for the recording of cybercrimes, but 5 years later law enforcement still does not have classification codes so there remains no central collation of any statistics. The strategy does no focus on the generic police investigators, their training and any required legislation changes.

Furthermore, strategy needs to be shared to be effective. In the United States Department of Defence Cyber Strategy (2015), it states as a matter of first principle, cyber security is a team effort within the US Federal government and Defence Department operates in partnership with other Agencies, international allies, states and local governments and, most importantly, the private sector. The document outlines its five strategic aims as follows:

• Build and maintain ready forces and capabilities to conduct cyberspace operations;
• Defend the Department of Defence (DoD) information network, secure DoD data, and mitigate risks to DoD missions;
• Be prepared to defend the US homeland and US vital interests from disruptive or destructive cyberattacks of significant consequence;
• Build and maintain viable cyber options and plan to use those options to control conflict escalation and to shape the conflict environment at all stages; and

- Build and maintain robust international alliances and partnerships to deter shared threats and increase international security and stability.

This document does not comment on current legislation or a strategy for investigations.

In Australia's Cyber Crime Strategy (2009), the government seeks to carry out the following:

- providing additional resources for security and law enforcement agencies to enhance operational capabilities for combating cybercrime
- ensuring that linkages are in place between cyber security and law enforcement efforts to combat specific related crime types, through the sharing of information and intelligence
- ensuring Australia's criminal and civil legal framework is robust and keeps pace with developments in technology and criminal behaviour
- providing Australian legal professionals with access to information and resources to provide them with the requisite level of technological knowledge and understanding to effectively administer these laws, and promoting the harmonization of Australia's legal framework for cyber security with other jurisdictions and internationally to facilitate information sharing and law enforcement cooperation across borders

There is an acknowledgement in the Australian strategy that the resources and the correct legislation must be in place to achieve the objectives.

All these strategies considered partnerships, information sharing, correct legislation and access to the right resources with the right skills to be key in achieving their delivery; however, none of these approaches has considered how to ensure that the investigative skills required are mainstreamed into policing and what is required by the officers.

Developing a training regime and delivering the training and learning from its implementation and application will take a long period and may only be suitable for new recruits, this leave 130,000 police officers in the United Kingdom which will need some form of additional up skilling to tackle these crimes.

Best practice/training

One such way of introducing best practice is through training and developing front-line police officers but such approaches have not yet been adopted by the constabularies as evidenced by the UK Governments Home Office Cyber Strategy document published in 2011. However, there were no recommendations to address the way that police officers were trained (Home Office, 2010).

Research identifies numerous training recommendations and academic papers that provide advice and guidance on the digital forensic process (Casey, 2011; Katos & Bendar, 2008), but very little that relates to traditional investigative techniques and how they can be applied to cybercrimes.

In the United Kingdom, training for new police officers is controlled through the IPLDP. The courses are designed to instruct officers in the investigation of traditional crime types. Recently, the College of Policing have started to develop the following training standards for cybercrime:

Level 1 'Cyber Awareness' — Target audience being all police employees who may have some involvement in cybercrime reporting and investigation. The aim of this course is to cover identification of a cybercrime, preservation of evidence, basic legislation and signpost who to escalate reports to.

Level 2 'Cyber for Investigators' — target audience being all police employees who will be investigating cybercrimes. Level 1 will be a prerequisite for Level 2 (College of Policing, 2015).

However, these training programmes are yet to be implemented.

In a survey conducted in the United States by Holt and Bossler (2011), they identified that patrol officers had little training or experience with computer crime cases. As a consequence of their research, they concluded there was clear need for comprehensive training and educational programs to be implemented in police training schools to increase officer awareness of computer crimes and improve their efficacy as first responders to cyber. They formed the opinion that an ability to identify common patterns across street and computer offences, whilst at the same time recognizing some of the distinct characteristics of computer crimes, would substantively improve the ability of law enforcement agencies to investigate these offences.

In the United States, the investigation of the cybercrime is mainly carried out by the Federal Bureau of Investigations. They promote the National Cyber-Forensics and Training Alliance, based in Pittsburgh as an international model for bringing together law enforcement, private industry and academia to share information to stop emerging cyber threats and mitigate existing ones (Federal Bureau for Investigation, 2011).

For businesses in the United Kingdom, the Centre for the Protection of National Infrastructure provides a range of guidance documents and technical notes aimed at improving practices and raising awareness of current issues relating to information security (Centre for Protection of National Infrastructure, 2015), but there is no similar exchange of best practice with policing.

Summary, conclusions, and future work

The absence of clearly defined techniques, effective policies, legislation and best practice all add up to make investigation and the gathering of evidence of such offences as online child exploitation, fraud and organized crime very difficult. This review has been the first steps in proposing a new standard operating procedure for investigating cybercrime. This systematic literature review was undertaken in which initial results and discussions were undertaken around the themes of investigative techniques, legislation, policy/strategy and best practice/training.

Initial results show traditional policing techniques can lend themselves to cybercrime investigations, but for them to be used effectively, legislation must be in place to support online surveillance, data mining and interception.

Whilst there are strategies in place that promote the international sharing of information, training of officers and the classification of recording for cybercrimes, these need to be implemented. There also needs to be recognition that to investigate cybercrime there need to be effective partnerships between the police, private industry and academia supported by the correct legislation.

This was highlighted by Chung, Chen, Chang, and Chou (2006). Their research concluded that the following needed to be in place for the future to be effective in combating cybercrime:

- update and continually review existing laws,
- enhance specialized task forces,
- utilize civic resources,
- promoting cybercrime research.

The systematic literature review also investigated best practices and training. It was established that training is well established for traditional investigations but identified that a lot of work still needs to be done for the investigation of cybercrime and the up skilling of existing police officers and new police recruits. There is clearly a change required in the dynamics of policing of online activities to monitor, control, deter, deflect, detect, prevent or preempt risky and potentially malicious activities. At the core of any new policing system are proactive tactics of policing. Instead of waiting for a crime to be committed and reacting to it, online policing will need to shift the initiative from the criminal to the constabulary.

References

Ali, M. M. (2014). *Framework for surveillance of instant messages in instatnt mesangers and social networking sites using data mining ontology* (pp. 297–302). IEEE.

Bell, R. E. (2002). The prosecution of computer crime. *Journal of Financial Crime, 9*(4), 308–325.

Branch, P. A. (2003). *Lawful intercept of the internet.* Melbourne: Citeseerx.

Brenner, S., Lee, J. H., Cox, N., & Siber, U. (2006). Cybercrime and jurisdiction a global survey. In , Vol. 11. *Information technology and law series* (pp. 227–239).

Broadhurst, R. (2006). Developments in the global law enforcement of cyber-crime. *Policing: An International Journal of Police Strategies and Management, 404–433.*

Broadhurst, R., Grabosky, P., Mamoun, A., & Chon, S. (2014). Organisations and cybercrime: An analysis of the nature of groups engaged in cybercrime. *International Journal of Cyber Criminology, 8*(1), 1–20.

Cabinet Office. (2014). *The UK cybersecurity strategy – report on progress and forward plans.* London: HMSO.

Casey, E. (2011). *Digital evidene and computer crime* (3rd ed.). San Diego: Elsevier.

Centre for Protection of National Infrastructure. (2015). *Centre for protection of national infrastructure.* Available at http://www.cpni.gov.uk/advice/cyber/.

Choo, K.-K. R. (2011). The cyber threat landscpae: Challenges and future research. *Computer and Security, 30*(8), 719–731.

Chung, W., Chen, H., Chang, W., & Chou, S. (2006). Fighting cybercrime: A review and the Taiwan experience. *Decision Support Systems, 41*(3), 669–682.

College of Policing. (2015). *Mainstreaming cybercrime training.* Available at http://www.college.police.uk/What-we-do/Learning/Curriculum/Investigation/cyber%20crime/Pages/Cyber-crime.aspx.

Federal Bureau for Investigation. (2011). *The NCFTA combining forces to fight cyber crime.* Available at https://www.fbi.gov/news/stories/2011/september/cyber_091611.

HM Government. (2011). *Contest: The United Kingdom's strategy for countering terrorism.* London: HMSO.

HMG. (2000). *Regulation of investigatory powers act 2000.* legislation.gov.uk. Available at.

HMG. (2015). *Counter-terrorism and security act 2015.* Available at http://www.legislation.gov.uk/ukpga/2015/6/contents/enacted/data.htm.

HMG Legislation. (2015). *Serious crime act 2015.* London: HMG.

Holt, T. J., & Bossler, A. M. (2011). Police perceptions of computer crimes in two southern cities: An examination from the viewpoint of patrol officers. *Souther Criminal Justice Association, 37,* 396–412.

Home Office. (2010). *Cybercrime strategy.* HMSO.

Home Office. (2015). *News story.* Available at https://www.gov.uk/government/news/home-secretary-announces-statutory-inquiry-into-undercover-policing.

Katos, V., & Bendar, P. M. (2008). A cyber-crime investigation framework. *Computer Standards and Interfaces, 30*(4), 223–228.

Kshetri, N. (2006). The simple economics of cybercrimes. *Security and Privacy, 4*(1), 33–39.

Laudon, K. C., Traver, C. G., & Elizondo, A. V. (2007). *E-commerce business.technology.society* (4th ed.). Boston: Pearson Addison Wesley.

Legislation.gov.uk. (1990). *Computer misuse act 1990.* London: National Archives.

MacEwan, N. (2008). The Computer Misuse Act 1990: Lessons from its past and predictions for its future. *Criminal Law Review, 12.*

Marion, N. E. (2010). The Council of Europe cybercrime treaty: An exercise in symbolic legislation. *International Journal of Cyber Criminology, 4*(1 & 2).

McGuire, M. (2013). *Cyber crime: A review of the evidence.* London: HMSO.

Millie, P. A., & Bullock, D. K. (2012). Re- Imagining policing post austerity. *British Academy Review,* (19), 16–18.

National Crime Agency. (2015). *National Crime Agency – Cyber Crime.* Available at http://www.nationalcrimeagency.gov.uk/crime-threats/cyber-crime.

Office for National Statistics. (2014). *Internet access – households and individuals 2014.* Available at http://www.ons.gov.uk/ons/dcp171778_373584.pdf.

Police.uk (2015). [Online]. Available at https://www.college.police.uk/What-we-do/Learning/Curriculum/Initial-learning/Pages/Initial-learning.aspx.

Richards, K. (2009). *The Australian business assessment of computer user security: A national survey.* Canberra: Australian Institute of Criminology.

Rose, S. C. (2013). *Annual report of chief surveillance commissioner.* London: Office of Surveillance Commissioners.

Tetzlaff-Bemiller, M. J. (2011). Undercover Online: An extention of traditional policing in the United States. *International Journal of Cyber Criminology, 5*(2), 813–824.

Tokunaga, R. S. (2010). Social networking site or social surveillance site. *Computers in Human Behavior, 26*(3), 277–287.

United States Department of Defence. (2015). *Department of defence cyber strategy.*

Ward, P., & Horne, A. (2015). *Interception of communications.* London: HMG.

Watney, M. (2012). The way forward in addressing cybercrime regulation a global level. *Internet Technology and Secured Transactions, 1*(1/2), 61–67.

Weinfass, I. (2015). *Police oracle.* Police Oracle, 15th July.

Zanasi, A. (2009). Virtual weapons for real wars: Text miningfor national security. *European Security Research and Innovation Forum, 53,* 53–60.

Zander, s., Nguyen, T., & Armitage, G. (2005). *Automated traffic classification and application identification using machine learning.* IEEE.

Further reading

Australian Goverment. (2009). *Cyber security strategy.*

FBI. (n.d.). Federal Bureau of Investigation. [Online]. Available at https://www.fbi.gov/about-us/ten-years-after-the-fbi-since-9-11/just-the-facts-1/cyber-1.

Hogan-Howe, B. (2015). *Police skimming the surface on cybercrime* [Interview].

Jang, J. (n.d.). Best practices in cybercrime investigation in the Republic of Korea: Department of Police Service Korea.

Leppard, A. (2015). *Cybercrime could become more lucrative than drug, police chief warns.* London: Telegraph.

O'Connell, R. (2003). *A Typology of child cybersexploitation and online grooming practices.* University of Lancashire.

Spalek, B., & Lambert, R. (2008). Muslim communities, counter-terrorism and counter-radicalisation: A critically reflective approach to engagement. *Journal of Law, Crime and Justice, 36*(4), 257–270.

Veldhuis, T., & Staun, J. (2009). *Islamist radicalisation: A root cause model.* Den Haag: Karin van Egmond.

Information and communication technologies: a curse or blessing for SMEs?

Anne-Marie Mohammed[1], Bochra Idris[3], George Saridakis[2], Vladlena Benson[3]

[1] Department of Economics, The University of the West Indies, St. Augustine, Trinidad and Tobago; [2] Kent Business School, University of Kent, Canterbury, United Kingdom; [3] Aston Business School, Aston University, Birmingham, United Kingdom

Emerging Cyber Threats and Cognitive Vulnerabilities
https://doi.org/10.1016/B978-0-12-816203-3.00008-3

163

Introduction

Over the last few decades, there has been an increase in the development of computing and telecommunication technologies, which has enabled, in a significant way, the development of an advanced global business and commerce (Andrijcic & Horowitz, 2006). The continuous advancement of information technology (IT) impacts all sectors of the economy, both positively and negatively. The implementation of the Internet into business operations creates a paradigm shift from the traditional ways in which firms operated and interacted with customers and employees. However, it also increases the vulnerability to information security breaches (Arcuri, Brogi, & Gandolfi, 2017). The Internet, coupled with advancement in IT, makes virtual management of business possible and this allows for quicker and more efficient transactions. It also allows for online databases, which significantly reduce the time it takes to retrieve information while creating the possibility for linkages across them. With the escalating globalization forces and the added pressure of competition around the world, companies are increasingly applying the Internet as a strategic tool (Ching & Ellis, 2004; Pezderka & Sinkovics, 2011). The proliferative usage of information and communication technology (ICT) applications acts as a source for competitiveness and allows firms to grow (Higón, 2011; Jorgenson & Stiroh, 2000), enables them to control their processes (Jean, Sinkovics, & Cavusgil, 2010) and also allows them to expand their international activities (Sinkovics & Penz, 2005). Because small- and medium-sized enterprises (SMEs) play an important role in the economy, through their contribution to job creation and stimulating innovation, it is anticipated that SMEs may adopt new technologies to create more innovative products, compete in more effective ways and enhance their growth and survival (Bruque & Moyano, 2007; Higón, 2011; Nguyen, 2009; Smith, 2008; Steinfield, LaRose, Chew, & Tong, 2012).

This chapter discusses some positive performance aspects of the growing use of information and communication technologies by firms, especially SMEs, but also to highlight potential security threats that can affect the life span of the firm through, for example, financial losses and damage of the firms' reputation. In particular, The role of information and communication technologies on performance and internationalization activities of SMEs section discusses the effect of ICT on firms' performance and international expansion. Section SME security challenges and cybercrime risks associated with the use of information and communication technologies reviews the security risk associated with the increasing adoption and reliance of the ICT Section. The costs of cybercrime to firms' financial performance and reputation provides some aspects related to the costs of cybercrimes to firms and customers. Finally, the last section concludes this chapter and provides some recommendations for building a safer online environment.

The role of information and communication technologies on performance and internationalization activities of SMEs

The advantages of adopting ICT in SMEs have been widely explored in the current literature (Afolayan, Plant, White, Jones, & Beynon-Davies, 2015). For instance, integration of IT enables firms to reduce their cost (e.g., Oluwatayo, 2014; Singh, 2011), apply more efficient methods of communication (e.g., Ajayi & Olayungbo, 2014; Pickernell et al., 2013), respond to their business partners and customers' requirements (e.g., Raymond, Bergeron, & Blili, 2005), reduce delivery time, improve decision-making (Beheshti, 2004) and allow engagement in entering multiple foreign markets (Pezderka & Sinkovics, 2011). However, by adopting the Internet into business operations, this allows for the employees to use the Internet for personal purposes, which causes them to postpone their duties and reduce their productivity (Sharma, Shrivastava, & Marimuthu, 2016). The contribution of ICT to firm performance has been documented in previous literature at the macro- (e.g., Oliner & Sichel, 2000) and the microlevels (e.g., Brynjolfsson & Hitt, 2003). Smith (1999), for instance, provides statistical evidence showing that when firms adopt a greater use of IT, their performance is higher for a sample of new and small firms. Baldwin and Lin (2002), on the other hand, show that highly productive SMEs in Canada are more likely to adopt advanced technologies, while Ollo-Lopez and Aramendia-Muneta (2012) find that the effect of adopting ICT can have a positive relationship on firms' productivity in direct and indirect ways. These effects also depend on the sector in which the firm operates (Tarutèa & Gatautis, 2014).

Moreover, the development of IT and the digital age is changing the way in which international business activities are being conducted (Alcacer, Cantwell, & Piscitello, 2016). Undoubtedly, the use of ICT and the Internet provides small firms with new methods to conduct their businesses, exchange ideas, gain information and communicate with their customers and suppliers in more efficient ways (Loane, 2006; OECD, 2001; Weill & Vitale, 2001). Many researchers have argued that the Internet enables small firms to expand their businesses aboard and reach customers there via the use of websites (Hamill, 1999). The acquisition of foreign market knowledge which is needed for internationalization and which is also the foundation of different internationalization theories such as Uppsala Internationalization Model (Johanson & Vahlne, 1992; Johanson & Wiedersheim-Paul,

1975) can be obtained through the application of these technologies and thus the Internet can enhance firms' internationalization opportunities. For instance, formal and informal Internet collaborations enable firms to develop new products and enhance their innovative activities (Loane, 2006). In more simple words, Internet and ICT may enable firms to obtain a specific set of knowledge, collaborate with different types of customers and suppliers which will enable the acquisition of the foreign market knowledge needed for internationalization.

It is strongly suggested that the use of e-commerce, emails and social media networks have generated positive effects on firms by enabling a better and more efficient way in sending mails, conducting financial transactions, buying products and advertising (Manochehri, Al-Esmail, & Ashrafi, 2012). Wang, Pauleen, and Zhang (2016) argue that the application of social media such as Facebook, Whatsapp, etc., witnessed an increased adoption by companies recently. Companies are using social media applications to achieve different business objectives such as communicating with their customers and suppliers, establishing relationships and identifying potential trading partners (Nath, Singh, & Iyer, 2010; Shih, 2009; Wang et al., 2016). For example, it can be argued that firms' interaction with customers allows them to extract information about their existing products and services (e.g., through monitoring customers' data and online feedback) and potential ways of improvements (Castriotta, Floreddu, Di Guardo, & Cabiddu, 2013; Fernandes, Belo, & Castela, 2016; Floreddu, Cabiddu, & Evaristo, 2014; Manyika, Roberts, & Sprague, 2008; Schniederjans, Cao, & Schniederjans, 2013) as well as to identify new and cross-border opportunities. Moreover, it is implied that the introduction of tablets and smart mobile phones is also changing the way small firms conduct their businesses and compete (Harris & Patten, 2014). For instance, employees in small firms increase their individual performance at a lower cost of services by using smartphones to engage with their customers through social media platforms.

SME security challenges and cybercrime risks associated with the use of information and communication technologies

As with the advancement of the Internet and ICT system enabling firms to improve their performance, growth and entrance into foreign markets, the same period of advancement has witnessed an increased number of cyber-based crimes. These have resulted in an increase in different types of cyberattacks that are disrupting businesses, breaching data and causing various types of business problems which can result in economic losses to both businesses and the national economy as a whole (Andrijcic & Horowitz1, 2006; PricewaterhouseCoopers, 2018). Firms may experience greater expenses, reduction in future profits and dividends, decreases in sales revenue, deteriorating reputation and reduction in the market value of these firms as a result of cybercrimes (Gordon, Loeh, & Lucyshyn, 2003). The risk that cyber-based crimes pose to the profitability and performance of a firm grows steadily with the increasing reliance on technology for efficiency and reliability. According to Hamilton Place Strategies (2015), the median cost of a cyberattack tripled between 2010 and 2015. Firms incur these increasing losses due to cyber-based crimes and as a result the current global cost of cyber-based crimes is approximately 600 billion USD (McAffee, 2018).

Just as with large firms, SMEs are also subject to cyberattacks and security breaches. However, there is the implication that SMEs are more vulnerable to such attacks due to the fact that they have limited financial resources and limited expertise to implement an inclusive information security system (Gupta & Hammond, 2005). It is also implied that a cyberattack can affect the business in a negative way especially financially through the loss of bank account details and customers' data (Ponemon, 2005; Valli, Martinus, & Johnstone, 2014). Security attacks and threats can cost firms significant amounts of money each year (Gordon, Loeh, Lucyshyn, & Richardson, 2004); therefore, SMEs are required to protect their data from such attacks (Romano & Fjermestad, 2007). However, earlier studies argued that owner-managers of SMEs were not aware of the security risks associated with their IT applications (Bradbard, Norris, & Kahai, 1990) and did not understand what actions should have been taken to minimize these risks (Harris & Patten, 2014). It is inferred that owner-managers of SMEs do not perceive that their firms are targets for cyber-based crimes (Sangani & Vijayakuma, 2012). Gupta and Hammond's (2005) study shows that small firms are less likely to experience cyberattacks, and this can be attributed to the value of the information stored by these firms as it might not be of great value for hackers. However, a cyber-based crime embodies a 'ricochet effect' whereby a business can be impacted by merely sharing the same industry sector with a victim (Hamilton Place Strategies, 2015). Therefore, no industry is immune or invulnerable to cyber-based crimes or the impact of cyber-based crimes (Benson, 2017; Hamilton Place Strategies, 2015).

The probability of being a victim of a cyber-based crime varies depending on the firm size and the sector under which the firm operates. The financial sector is the most attacked sector globally (Benson, McAlaney, & Frumkin, 2018). A study by NTT Security (2018) found that 26% of all cyberattacks were aimed at the financial sector, where these cybercriminals were motivated by financial gains or espionage. Therefore, firms in the financial sector experience the highest occurrence of cyber-based crimes and hence must invest heavily on cyber security to reduce the cost and damages associated with a cyberattack. The technology sector experiences 19% of all cyberattacks and the business and professional service sector experiences 10%, thus making them the second and third most attacked sectors globally by cyber-based crimes (NTT Security, 2018). Furthermore, their study also found that there was an increase in the percentage of cyber-based crimes aimed at the financial sector from 15% in 2016 to 43% in 2017. In the Americas, however, there was a decrease from 46% to 26% in the Asian Pacific region. Therefore, this shows that firms that operate in a specific sector will experience different probabilities of being a victim of a cyber-based crime depending on which region they operate their business.

The costs of cybercrime to firms' financial performance and reputation

Cyberattacks have been found to affect firms in significant ways. For instance, a study by Saridakis, Mohammed, and Sookram (2015) find that the losses which firms encounter due to a crime have both immediate and long-term negative effects on the firms' innovative activities. Additionally, the Information Security Breaches Survey commissioned by the Department of Business, Innovation and Skills (BIS, 2013), in the United Kingdom, showed that 87% of participant firms in all sectors had experienced at least one attack or breach in the previous year (Hayes & Bodhani, 2013). On the other hand, the recent Cyber Security Breaches survey (2018), commissioned by the Department for Digital, Culture, Media and Sport (2018), showed that 42% of micro and small firms in the United Kingdom experienced at least one attack or breach in the previous years. A recent study by Romanosky (2016) showed that the total cost from cyberattacks was 8.5 billion USD yearly. In addition, their results showed that firms experienced lower annual revenues (by 0.4%) as a result of these cyberattacks. According to Cambell, Gordon, Loeb, and Zhou (2003), a firm's performance is significantly and negatively affected by cyber-based crimes due to the market reaction when there is a security breach that allows unauthorized individuals to access confidential information. A study by Cavusoglu, Mishra, and Raghunathan (2004) found that firms that had information breaches lose on average 2.1% of market value within 2 days of the announcement. Another study by Acquisti, Friedman, and Telang (2006) found that on the day of a data breach announcement, the firms' market value is significantly and negatively impacted. Furthermore, a recent study by Arcuri, Brogi, and Gandolfi (2017) found that negative market returns always follow the announcement of a cyberattack.

When firms are victims of cyber-based crimes, the reputational risk associated with these crimes extends far beyond monetary damages

(Hamilton Place Strategies, 2015). For example, if a firm in the financial sector, such as a bank, experiences a cyberattack where their clients' sensitive and personal information were to be obtained by unauthorized individuals, then these clients will lose trust in that bank and therefore transfer to a more secure bank. It can also expose these clients to other types of crimes because their home addresses, job addresses and account details are no longer kept confidential, thus giving criminals financial motivation to commit a crime. The direct cost of a cyberattack can be quite substantial depending on the type of data acquired by the attackers as well as the firm size and reputation. Although the reputational risk can be difficult to measure, the damage to reputation from a cyberattack sometimes far exceeds the direct cost of the cyberattack. For example, the damage of target's data breach of 2013 cost the company 252 million USD in data breach—related expenses. However, only 90 million USD of that was offset by insurance recoveries (Hamilton Place Strategies, 2015).

Conclusions and future directions for research

The use of information and communication technologies is increasingly adopted by new entrepreneurial ventures and existing SMEs (Alam & Noor, 2009). The use of new technologies has made the establishment of a firm easier at a low start-up cost, moving from the traditional physical form to firms operating entirely on Internet or hybrid business models (Teece, 2018). Additionally, new technologies have improved communication across business owners, employees and customers (Chen & Popovich, 2003), improved supply chain distribution channels (Santarelli & D'Altri, 2003) and efficiency, enhanced collaboration at regional, national and international levels, and increased firms' international activities. With all these benefits emerging from the use of technology, information security becomes a crucial aspect of firms and individuals (see Saridakis et al., 2015; Smith, Grabosky, & Urbas, 2004). The increase in cybercrime and the cost associated with it require firms to build a secure environment in which they can protect themselves and their customers from potential cyberattacks. The rise in cybercrimes incidents consequently increases the demand for cyber security by firms; therefore, it opens a market for cyber insurance and security services. Companies demand cyber insurance to protect their businesses against network interruption and data breaches (PricewaterhouseCoopers, 2018). In a survey by PricewaterhouseCoopers (2018), it was found that 61% of the companies in Singapore had cyber insurance, with 62% in the Asian Pacific region and 58% globally claiming to have cyber insurance. In addition to continuous updating of cyber security and ensuring that employees are adequately trained to prevent or minimize cyberattacks, another strategy put forward by Hamilton Place Strategies (2015) is for firms to have a prepared contingency plan of action for potential cyber-attacks which can save the company millions in damages.

As cyberattacks become more sophisticated and complex, more collaboration will be needed between institutions (e.g., business, governments, insurance and academia) to combat cyber-based crimes and prevent major cyber incidents such as those that occurred in the recent past (e.g., WannaCry and Petya) (see Choo, 2011). Currently, 69% of firms globally confirm that they are collaborating with other firms and institutions for the improvement of their security in an attempt to reduce the risk of future cyberattacks (PricewaterhouseCoopers, 2018).

We suggest that the academic community should address the process of cyber insurance support for SMEs. As the governance, risk and compliance processes become more complex and the liabilities for falling a victim of cybercrime grow (such as with the recent introduction of the GDPR), SMEs are more prone to cyberattacks and more susceptible to their consequences. We propose for the future research agenda to look into formulating a structured governance framework for SMEs. The framework will help align their cyber insurance needs to their circumstances, aspirations for growth, small business ecosystems and ultimately should promote engagement with other SMEs and government agencies in standing up to cybercrime.

References

Acquisti, A., Friedman, A., & Telang, R. (2006). Is there a cost to privacy breaches? An event study. In Workshop on the Economics of Information Security (Cambridge, UK).

Afolayan, A., Plant, E., White, G. R. T., Jones, P., & Beynon-Davies, P. (2015). Information technology usage in SMEs in a developing economy. Strategic Change, 24, 483–498.

Ajayi, A., & Olayungbo, D. (2014). ICT adoption in small and medium scale enterprises in Nigeria: An assessment. International Journal of Research, 1(9), 889–897.

Alam, S. S., & Noor, M. K. M. (2009). ICT adoption in small and medium enterprises: An empirical evidence of service sectors in Malaysia. International Journal of Business and Management, 4(2), 112–125.

Alcacer, J., Cantwell, J. A., & Piscitello, L. (2016). International in the information age: A new ear for places, firms, and international business networks? Journal of International Business Studies, 47(5), 499–512.

Andrijcic, E., & Horowitz, B. (2006). A macro-economic framework for evaluation of cyber security risks related to protection of intellectual property. Risk Analysis: An International Journal, 26(4), 909–923.

Arcuri, M. C., Brogi, M., & Gandolfi, G. (2017). How does cyber crime affect firms? The effect of information security breaches on stock returns. In ITASEC (pp. 175–193). http://ceur-ws.org/Vol-1816/paper-18.pdf.

Baldwin, J., & Lin, Z. (2002). Impediments to advanced technology adoption for Canadian manufacturers. Research Policy, 31, 1–18.

Beheshti, H. M. (2004). The impact of IT on SMEs in the United States. *Information Management and Computer Security, 12*(4), 318−327.

Benson, V. (2017). *The state of global cyber security: Highlights and key findings*. London, UK: LT Inc. https://doi.org/10.13140/RG.2.2.22825.49761.

Benson, V., McAlaney, J., & Frumkin, L. A. (2018). Emerging threats for the human element and countermeasures in current cyber security landscape. In *Psychological and behavioral examinations in cyber security* (pp. 266−271). IGI Global.

Bradbard, D. A., Norris, D. R., & Kahai, P. H. (1990). Computer security in small business: An empirical study. *Journal of Small Business Management, 28*(1), 9−19.

Bruque, S., & Moyano, J. (2007). Organisational determinants of information technology adoption and implementation in SMEs: The case of family and cooperative firms. *Technovation, 27*(5), 241−253.

Brynjolfsson, E., & Hitt, L. (2003). Computing productivity: Firm-level evidence. *Review of Economics and Statistics, 85*(4), 793−808.

Campbell, K., Gordon, L., Loeb, M., & Zhou, L. (2003). The economic cost of publicly announced information security breaches: Empirical evidence from the stock market. *Journal of Computer Security, 11*(3), 431−448.

Castriotta, M., Floreddu, P., Di Guardo, M., & Cabiddu, F. (2013). Disentangling the strategic use of social media in the insurance industry: A value co-creation perspective. *Advanced Series in Management, 11*, 63−86.

Cavusoglu, H., Mishra, B., & Raghunathan, S. (2004). The effect of internet security breach announcements on market value: Capital market reactions for breached firms and internet security developers. *International Journal of Electronic Commerce, 9*(1), 69−104.

Chen, I. J., & Popovich, K. (2003). Understanding customer relationship management (CRM): People, process and technology. *Business Process Management Journal, 9*(5), 672−688.

Ching, H. L., & Ellis, P. (2004). Marketing in cyberspace: What factors drive e-commerce adoption? *Journal of Marketing Management, 20*(3,4), 409−429.

Choo, K.-K. R. (2011). The cyber threat landscape: Challenges and future research directions. *Computers and Security, 30*, 719−731.

Department for Business, Innovation and Skills (BIS). (2013). *Information security breaches survey 2013*. Technical report. Department for Business, Innovation and Skills. Available at https://assets.publishing.service.gov.uk/government/uploads/system/uploads/attachment_data/file/200455/bis-13-p184-2013-information-security-breaches-survey-technical-report.pdf.

Department for Digital, Culture, Media and Sport. (2018). *Cyber security breaches survey 2018: Micro/small business findings visualisation*. Department for Digital, Culture, Media and Sport. available at https://assets.publishing.service.gov.uk/government/uploads/system/uploads/attachment_data/file/701841/CSBS_2018_Infographics_-_Micro_and_Small_Businesses.pdf.

Fernandes, S., Belo, A., & Castela, G. (2016). Social network enterprise behaviours and patterns in SMEs: Lessons from a Portuguese local community centred around the tourism industry. *Technology in Society, 44*, 15−22.

Floreddu, P., Cabiddu, F., & Evaristo, R. (2014). Inside your social media ring: How to optimise online corporate reputation. *Business Horizons, 57*(6), 737−745.

Gordon, L. A., Loeh, M. P., & Lucyshyn, W. (2003). Information security expenditures and real options: A wait-and-see approach. *Computer Security Journal, 19*(2), 1−7.

Gordon, L. A., Loeh, M. P., Lucyshyn, W., & Richardson, R. (2004). *Ninth annual CSI/FBI computer crime and security survey*. Computer Security Institute. available at www.theiia.org/iia/download.

Gupta, A., & Hammond, R. (2005). Information systems security issues and decisions for small businesses: An empirical examination. *Information Management and Computer Security, 13*(4), 297−310.

Hamill, J. (1999). Internet editorial: Export guides on the net. *International Marketing Review, 15*(5), 434–436.

Hamilton Place Strategies. (2015). *Cybercrime costs more than you think.* https://www.hamiltonplacestrategies.com/wp-content/uploads/2016/09/HPS20Cybercrime2_0.pdf.

Harris, M. A., & Patten, K. P. (2014). Mobile device security considerations for small- and medium-sized enterprise business mobility. *Information Management and Computer Security, 22*(1), 97–114.

Hayes, J., & Bodhani, A. (2013). Cyber security: Small firms under fire. *Engineering and Technology, 8*(6), 80–83.

Higón, D. A. (2011). The impact of ICT on innovation activities: Evidence for UK SMEs. *International Small Business Journal, 30*(6), 684–699.

Jean, R.-J. B., Sinkovics, R. R., & Cavusgil, S. T. (2010). Enhancing international customer-supplier relationships through it resources: A study of Taiwanese electronics suppliers. *Journal of International Business Studies, 41*(7), 1218–1239.

Johanson, J., & Vahlne, J. E. (1992). Management of foreign market entry. *Scandinavian International Business Review, 1*(3), 9–27.

Johanson, J., & Wiedersheim-Paul, F. (1975). The internationalization of the firm-four Swedish cases. *Journal of Management Studies, 12*(3), 305–322.

Jorgenson, D. W., & Stiroh, K. (2000). Raising the speed limit: US economic growth in the information age. *Brookings Papers on Economic Activity, 1*, 125–235.

Loane, S. (2006). The role of internet in the internationalisation of small and medium sized companies. *Journal of International Entrepreneurship, 3*, 263–277.

Manochehri, N. N., Al-Esmail, R., & Ashrafi, R. (2012). Examining the impact of information and communication technologies (ICT) on enterprise practices: A preliminary perspective from Qatar. *The Electronic Journal on Information Systems in Developing Countries, 51*(3), 1–16.

Manyika, J. M., Roberts, R. P., & Sprague, K. L. (2008). Eight business technology trends to watch. *McKinsey Quarterly, 1*, 60–71.

McAffee. (2018). *Executive summary: The economic impact of cybercrime—No slowing down.* https://www.mcafee.com/enterprise/en-us/assets/executive-summaries/es-economic-impact-cybercrime.pdf.

Nath, A. K., Singh, R., & Iyer, L. S. (2010). Web 2.0: Capabilities, business value and strategic practice. *Journal of Information Science and Technology, 7*(1), 22–29.

Nguyen, T. H. (2009). Information technology adoption in SMEs: An integrated framework. *International Journal of Entrepreneurial Behavior and Research, 15*(2), 162–186.

NTT Security. (2018). *Global threat intelligence report 2018.* https://www.nttsecurity.com/docs/librariesprovider3/resources/gbl-ntt-security-2018-global-threat-intelligence-report-v2-uea.pdf?sfvrsn=c761dd4d_10.

Oliner, S. D., & Sichel, D. E. (2000). The resurgence of growth in the late 1990s: Is information technology the story? *Journal of Economic Perspectives, 14*, 3–12.

Ollo-Lopez, A., & Aramendia-Muneta, M. E. (2012). ICT impact on competitiveness, innovation and environment. *Telematics and Informatics, 29*, 204–210.

Oluwatayo, I. B. (2014). *Information and communication technologies as drivers of growth: Experience from selected small-scale businesses in rural southwest Nigeria.* Nigeria: Department of Agricultural Economics, University of Ibadan. http://www.nai.uu.se/ecas-4/panels/141-156/panel-150/Isaac-Oluwatayo-Full-paper.pdf.

Organization for Economic, Cooperation and Development. (2001). *ECD science, technology and industry scoreboard 2001: Towards a knowledge-based economy.* Paris: OECD Publishing. https://doi.org/10.1787/sti_scoreboard-2001-en.

Pezderka, N., & Sinkovics, R. R. (2011). A conceptualization of e-risk perceptions and implications for small firm active online internationalization. *International Business Review, 20*, 409–422.

Pickernell, D., Jones, P., Packham, G., Thomas, B., White, G., & Willis, I. (2013). E-commerce trading activity and the SME sector: An FSB perspective. *Journal of Small Business and Enterprise Development, 20*(4), 866–888.

Ponemon, L. (2005). *Lost customer information: What does a data breach cost companies?* Tucson, AZ: Ponemon Institute. available at www.securitymanagement.com/library/Ponemon_DataStudy0106.pdf.

PricewaterhouseCoopers. (2018). *The global state of information security survey 2018*. PwC. https://www.pwc.com/sg/en/publications/assets/gsiss-2018.pdf.

Raymond, L., Bergeron, F., & Blili, S. (2005). The assimilation of E-business in manufacturing SMEs: Determinants and effects on growth and internationalization. *Electronic Markets, 15*(2), 106–118.

Romano, N. C., & Fjermestad, J. (2007). Privacy and security in the age of electronic customer relationship management. *International Journal of Information Security and Privacy, 1*(1), 85–106.

Romanosky, S. (2016). Examining the costs and causes of cyber incidents. *Journal of Cybersecurity, 2*(2), 121–135.

Sangani, N. K., & Vijayakuma, B. (2012). Cyber security scenarios and control for small and medium enterprises. *Informatica Economică, 16*, 58–71.

Santarelli, E., & D'Altri, S. (2003). The diffusion of E-commerce among SMEs: Theoretical implications and empirical evidence. *Small Business Economics, 21*(3), 273–283.

Saridakis, G., Mohammed, A.-M., & Sookram, S. (2015). Does crime affect firm innovation? Evidence from Trinidad and Tobago. *Economics Bulletin, 35*(2), 1205–1215.

Schniederjans, D., Cao, E.,S., & Schniederjans, M. (2013). Enhancing financial performance with social media: An impression management perspective. *Decision Support Systems, 55*(4), 911–918.

Sharma, M., Shrivastava, A., & Marimuthu, P. (2016). Internet use at workplaces and its effects on working style in Indian context: An exploration. *Indian Journal of Occupational and Environmental Medicine, 20*(2), 88–94.

Shih, C. (2009). *The facebook era: Tapping online social networks to build better products, reach new audiences, and sell more stuff.* Upper Saddle River, NJ: Prentice Hall.

Singh, R. (2011). Developing the framework for coordination in supply chain for SMEs. *Business Process Management Journal, 17*(4), 619–638.

Sinkovics, R., & Penz, E. (2005). Empowerment of SME websites: Development of a web-empowerment scale and preliminary evidence. *Journal of International Entrepreneurship, 3*(4), 303–315.

Smith, J. (1999). Information technology in the small business: Establishing the basis for a management information system. *Journal of Small Business and Enterprise Development, 6*(4), 326–340.

Smith, R. (2008). *Where do they find the time? Research technology management* (Vol. 51, pp. 67–68). Industrial Research Institute, Inc.

Smith, R. G., Grabosky, P., & Urbas, G. (2004). *Cyber criminals on trial.* Cambridge: Cambridge University Press.

Steinfield, C., LaRose, R., Chew, H. E., & Tong, S. T. (2012). Small and medium-sized enterprises in rural business clusters: The relation between ICT adoption and benefits derived from cluster membership. *The Information Society, 28*, 110–120.

Tarutèa, A., & Gatautis, R. (2014). ICT impact on SMEs performance. *Procedia – Social and Behavioral Sciences, 110*, 1218–1225.

Teece, D. J. (2018). Business models and dynamic capabilities. *Long Range Planning, 51*(1), 40–49.

Valli, C., Martinus, I. C., & Johnstone, M. N. (2014). Small to medium enterprise cyber security awareness: An initial survey of western Australian business. In *Proceedings of international conference on security and management* (pp. 71–75). Las Vegas, USA: CSREA Press.

Wang, W. Y. C., Pauleen, D. J., & Zhang, T. (2016). How social media applications affect B2B communication and improve business performance in SMEs. *Industrial Marketing Management*, *54*, 4–14.

Weill, P., & Vitale, M. (2001). *From place to space: Migrating to ebusiness models*. Cambridge, MA: Harvard Business School Press.

Cyber personalities in adaptive target audiences

Miika Sartonen[1], Petteri Simola[2], Lauri Lovén[3], Jussi Timonen[4]

[1] Department of Leadership and Military Pedagogy, National Defence University, Helsinki, Finland; [2] Finnish Defence Research Agency, Tuusula, Finland; [3] Center for Ubiquitous Computing, University of Oulu, Oulu, Finland; [4] National Defence University, Helsinki, Finland

OUTLINE

Emerging Cyber Threats and Cognitive Vulnerabilities
https://doi.org/10.1016/B978-0-12-816203-3.00009-5

Introduction

Cyber domain is today used in many ways as a platform for military operations. The digital battlespace has emerged from the fringes of science fiction to the frontline of modern military conflict. From a historical point of view, cyber is a relative newcomer within the domains in which the militaries operate. Although in recent years there has been an awakening to the advancing cyber threats, the wider understanding of those threats that emerge from using the cyber domain as a platform for other than purely technical means of war is a relatively new phenomenon in the Western hemisphere. The obvious use of cyber weapons to destroy, disable or deceit digital systems is already being tackled in various ways. However, the digital environment has other less obvious threats that are now beginning to emerge. As the digital world has transformed from a curiosity to hard reality, it is now being understood that digitalization produces many new military problems, in addition to the solutions it provides.

Militaries perform both the functions – use technology and drive it. Many technological innovations (including the Internet itself) have been introduced to find a solution to a military threat. The global cyber domain allows, among its other uses, new means of influence for militaries that are willing and capable of using them. Such means include the global reach of digital communications, new intelligence gathering capabilities and the reciprocal nature of social media, allowing for obfuscation of truth and transforming the role of gatekeepers.

The information that people and organizations give away in their daily business, both directly and indirectly, can be valuable to anyone with the means of obtaining it. It is now possible to gather mission-relevant data almost in real time, often with the willing help of the subjects themselves. On the other hand, both individuals and organizations obtain much of their information from the Internet, meaning that anyone with means of either directly or indirectly influencing that information has a global reach of operations. Thus, the fast and reciprocal nature of the Internet provides real-time opportunities for both data mining and message dissemination in support of influence operations. Von Clausewitz's famous statement, of war being a continuation of politics with the admixture of other means, finds new relevance with these opportunities provided by the digital revolution. If military objectives can be achieved without use of force or without accountability, the threshold for clandestine military influence operations is lowered. In this chapter, we argue that the emergence of the cyber domain within the information battlespace allows for intelligence gathering in ways that may seem illegal, unethical or unimaginable today. It is, however, the duty of both the scientist and the soldier to look at the possible futures to prepare for them.

In this chapter, we present the idea of cyber personalities as the target audience (TA) for military influence operations in addition to a concept of adaptive TAs. Following the introduction, the second section looks at cyber personalities from the viewpoint of influence operations and how digital cyber personalities can be found in a Libicki's five-layer framework (Libicki, 2007) as presented by Sartonen, Huhtinen, and Lehto (2016). The third section presents an idea of adaptive TAs for cyber personalities, followed by conclusion and discussion in sections fourth and fifth.

Military influence operations

Cyber domain as a battlespace

The concept of influencing others is probably as old as the human culture. Similarly, militaries have always sought ways of influencing opponent behaviour to even the odds at the physical battlefield. New technologies and domains have always been adapted for military use, with the cyber domain being no exception. As was the case with the introduction of flight in the early 20th century, it can be expected that adapting to this new domain of military activity requires a review of the other domains as well. Thinking of how the introduction of the air domain transformed naval or ground war, one understands how thorough and long lasting the effects of digitalization in the future battlefields will be.

As is typical with new phenomena, familiar terminology and concepts are used to understand the changing battlefield. Very often, however, old concepts eventually lack the explanationary power needed to understand the changing battlefield and will be replaced by new ones. The same goes for rules and laws used to govern human behaviour in conflict, both in domestic and international framework. Typically in the Western hemisphere, influence operations have been held in a supportive role, subordinate to the activities of the physical battlefields. War, even information war, is still mostly conceptualized by the realities of the physical battlefield, with the exception of emerging rules concerning cyberattacks and defence.

The idea of militaries wielding weapons of information within the cyber domain, among the billions of daily civilian activities, is a frightening one. One argument is that militaries have no role in the cyber domain at all, that the only role for a military is to remain as the ultimate watchdog in the physical world. This is, however, a choice every nation will make on their own, meaning that there will be a various degree of military involvement in the goings-on of the cyber domain. The global reach of this interconnected domain means that within this operational theatre, there will be different national solutions, different roles for militaries and as such there will be variation within the level of engagement and rules of engagement between various nation's armed forces. The fact remains, however, that the various cyber threats need to be confronted by some appropriate means. It should be pointed out that the line between what is military and what is not in the cyber domain is not always clear. As such, it can be concluded that unless there will be a new 'Tallinn Manual' concerning military influence operations in the cyber, for the time being the restrictions concerning military operations in the cyber are obfuscated at best.

Ultimately, if advancing technologies will allow military operations' targets to be achieved in the cyber domain alone, it is plausible to expect militaries to operate in the cyber domain much in the way they control the skies today, with technologies of intelligence, attack and defence. Although this idea may appear too far-reaching, it can be argued that any technology that can we weaponized typically ends up as being such, and thus the militaries should not prepare for today's but for tomorrow's wars. In the end, it only takes one actor to claim dominance in a military domain, forcing others either to admit defeat or to engage in new frontiers and with new weapons.

Target audience analysis in influence operations' framework

To look at the plausibility of military influence operations within the cyber domain, we examine the intelligence part of such operations, namely the investigation and selection of suitable audiences. This procedure is often called target audience analysis (TAA), within the framework of psychological operations (PSYOPS). As a reference for conduction of psychological operations, we use U.S. Field Manual 3-05-301, Psychological Operations Tactics, Techniques and Procedures, which provides one example of the TAA process.

According to FM3-05-301, TAA is a detailed and systematic process of selecting the most viable TAs that can be reached and influenced and whose behavioural change will effectively produce results that support the overall military operation (FM3-05-301, 5-1).

According to FM3-05-301, TAA seeks to answer five key questions:

- What TAs will be most effective in accomplishing the Psychological Operations objectives
- What are the reasons for the TA's current behaviour?

- What are the best means of communication to reach the TA?
- How can the TA be influenced to achieve the desired behaviour?
- What are the appropriate criteria to assess changes in behaviour?

As pointed out in FM3-05-301, for a set of messages to be effective, a TA typically needs to consist of a homogenous group of people with similar conditions and vulnerabilities. There are various ways of building these homogenous groups, such as looking for common demographic or geographic features. Centres of gravity (people or small groups that have large degree of power over others) or key communicators or other high-value individuals (HVIs) are also desirable, although such TAs are typically small (FM3-05-301, 5-3—5-4). These TAs can be most effective, regardless of their small size. In these situations, TAA should be more detailed than what is described in FM3-05-301. To understand and influence such TAs, it is possible to gather far more detailed information than it is from larger TAs, which are always more general in nature. When dealing with HVIs or small groups, the requirements for information can be very detailed. Taylor, Furnham, and Breeze (2014) have proposed six key dimensions necessary for understanding and influencing a single individual. These elements are (1) culture, clan, (2); biography, family; (3) intelligence; (4) personality; (5) dark side of personality and (6) motivation. Most of the information in these dimensions can be extracted from the cyber domain.

Once initial TAs have been selected, a more detailed scrutiny is applied, beginning with the conditions that the TA has to cope with. Conditions, according to FM3-05-301, are the life-affecting elements over which the TA has little or no control. In an ideal TA, common conditions within the group lead to similar needs. These unfulfilled or perceived needs are manifested as vulnerabilities, as the TA's desire to fulfil, alleviate or eliminate the needs acts as motivation to change behaviour. A successful TAA provides the most effective means of satisfying the TA's needs in a way that allows the psychological operation's objectives to be reached (FM3-05-301, 5-4—5-9).

The TAA described above is built for a military process and requires the TAs to be approved by an appropriate command structure before executing the influence activities. Thus, a requirement of identifying the members of the TA is built into the process. This, in turn, is required to ensure only legal targets are engaged by the military and to streamline the influence activities with other, typically kinetic activities. A feedback loop is also included in the process, in the form of setting impact indicators that are monitored to find out whether or not the set objectives are being achieved (FM3-05-301, 5—18).

As pointed out in Sartonen et al. (2016), the cyber domain is vast, fast and reciprocal. In a complex and constantly changing environment, traditional means of conducting TAA may not be fast and comprehensive enough to utilize the full potential of global reach, advanced automatic analysis methods and the potential of unleashing the power of masses of content producers. In addition, the anonymity provided by current application of digitalization is another challenge to the abovementioned process. TAs are not present as such but presented by various aliases or avatars, behavioural patterns and behavioural effects. The requirement of influencing only positively identified TAs runs quickly aground once the realities of the cyber domain are acknowledged.

However, there are several approaches beyond this point. The most arduous solution is to work out the identities behind various aliases and identity obfuscation methods to ensure only approved TAs are the recipients of influence messages. Quite obviously, this method may cause more legal issues than it solves. In addition, the interconnected nature of the cyber domain means that one cannot control the streams of information, making the idea of reaching only approved audiences unviable.

Another approach is to use the data already available, for example, from other branches of government or from a third party. Using this type of data for military intelligence has its own legal and practical challenges. The relevant question in these cases is how to define military activity in the cyber domain, or rather at which stage does an intelligence gathering activity change its colour and become a military activity, in essence to be governed by rules of military conflict. Given the current plethora of opinions concerning the nature of information war and whether it's activities can be treated as an act of armed conflict, different actors can orchestrate various influence operations in the cyber domain in a relative safety of not being accused of using military force. It has to be pointed out that it is exactly these difficulties of attribution that encourage the use of the cyber domain for influence purposes as an alternative for using force in the physical domains.

The third option is to ignore the requirement for positive identification of individuals within a TA. It is not the option for the legally restricted, but has to be observed, nevertheless, we argue, for two reasons: (1) It presents a theoretical understanding of how military TAA process can be performed in the cyber domain, helping to further understand the role of cyber domain in the military operations. (2) As there will eventually be militaries not concerned with the individual privacy, this approach will help to understand these influence attack vectors and how to defend against such attacks and their influence-gathering methods. It has to be remembered that soldiers are also citizens and thus provide relevant data for those digitally and legally agile, even when not wearing their uniform.

It is for the abovementioned reasons we look beyond what is currently feasible, for the theoretical possibilities of military TAA in the cyber domain, and propose a way of looking at influence operations' TAs. We suggest that as air war could not be appropriately described by the concepts of land or naval warfare, conducting influence operations in the digital age requires fresh approaches and concepts. Our approach is an attempt to enable the emerging digital powers of the cyber domain to be utilized in a more effective way. Given the possibilities of Artificial Intelligence and deep fake technologies, however, we can only assume that even what we examine in this chapter will fall short of the future realities of influence activities.

Cyber personalities as a target audience

Five-layer model

When conducting TAA in cyber domain, we need to know what to look for and where to look for it. Whether a TAA is based on a traditional model, such as presented in US field manual (FM3-05-301, 5-1), on a more detailed model proposed by Taylor et al. (2014), or on a cyber domain–specific one, such as proposed by Suler (2016) (which will be discussed later on) or any other, one thing remains the same: we need sources of information. As mentioned earlier, cyber domain is vast, complex, boundless and constantly changing. Therefore, we need a cyber domain–specific framework for data collection and utilization. Libicki's (2007) five-layer model as presented in Sartonen et al. (2016) provides a useful framework for data collection and utilization.

One important feature of the five-layer model is that communication between humans in the cyber domain will typically pass through all the layers, meaning that communication both leaves residue to be collected and analyzed in all layers and also provides means of influence. It has to be pointed out that in addition to easily acknowledgeable means, such as sending direct influence messages, there are multiple, subtle ways of altering one's interpretation of his or her surroundings. As an example, instead of trying to alter the content in all the relevant web pages a user typically visits, an alternative way could be to gain access to user's browser to change the search engine's parameters, distorting search results and thus affecting the interpretation of user's reality.

Cyber personalities

To understand cyber personalities and their possible use as a TA, we need to understand how individuals present themselves in cyberspace as psychological entities. As Suler (2016) points out, cyberspace is a psychological space; '*It is an extension of our individual and collective minds. It is a space "out there" where the minds of self and other converge*' (Suler, 2016). To conceptualize this space and its psychological aspects, Suler has proposed eight dimensions of cyber psychology. These dimensions are (1) Identity; (2) Social; (3) Interactive; (4) Text; (5) Sensory; (6) Reality; (7) Temporal and (8) Physical dimension. Identity dimension includes self-presentation in particular online environment, whereas Social dimension includes the relationships with individuals and groups. Interactive dimension entails how well a person can understand, navigate and control a digital environment (human—computer interaction). Text dimension includes all text-based communication and the psychological effects of communicating via text. Sensory dimension entails how the cyberspace activates senses (mainly auditory and visual). Temporal dimension is the use and experience of time. Reality dimension entails how much of the experience in cyberspace is grounded to everyday life and reality and how much of it is mere fantasy (such as presenting oneself via exotic avatar in massive multiplayer online role-playing game). Physical dimension involves the physical existence, including bodily sensations and movements.

Through these dimensions, it is possible both to understand and to anticipate behaviour of individuals in cyberspace, and they can serve as a useful framework when we have enough information of or when we can interact with these individuals (for instance, ask questions from them). The challenge is that when conducting TAA in the cyber domain, it is not often possible to have close interaction with TAs. There have, however, been numerous studies on the behavioural residue humans leave behind when they operate in the cyber domain. Studies show various correlations between data collectable from interactions within the cyber domain and behaviour. Such data includes, but is not limited to, digital pictures, audio and video files, social media posts, social media activity (such as liking, linking or commenting), browsing and location data history and topographic analysis of both physical and virtual networks. The idea of a cyber personality in the form we propose in this chapter is to combine this data collected from various sources. In other words, it is an attempt to conceptualize a theoretical model for utilizing data collected from the five layers of the cyber domain. While single sources of data can predict behaviour to a certain extent, combining the data of multiple sources into a single entity can provide a more complete (although possibly conflicting) picture and therefore provide information necessary for conducting TAA in cyberspace. A cyber personality also helps to overcome the limitation of not being able to identify actors, as it encompasses the idea of meaningful (in the viewpoint of the military objective) behavioural factors above identifying actors for its own sake.

A cyber personality can, of course, consist of nonhuman actors (such as bots or AI) as well, as their activities leave behavioural residue in their wake as well. An additional benefit the concept of a cyber personality allows for is looking for 'what is not there', e.g., human components that artificial actors lack. Artificial entities may also express components that people generally do not have, such as constant activity devoid of any resting periods or overwhelmingly prolific creativity. These factors may help in making the distinction between human and artificial actors, which in turn helps to avoid false or biased observations based on volumes of information produced by the latter. As it is likely that advances in AI technology will make the distinction between human and machine in the cyber domain harder, this approach of looking for missing human components in other layers may provide some solutions.

As shown above, a cyber personality interacts with the layers of the cyber domain in various ways. Fig. 9.1 illustrates the complex relations between the different aspects of a cyber personality and the cyber domain layers at large.

	Context data	Interaction data
Cognitive level	- the "bubble" - contents of all media in close reach	- N/A
Service level	- user lists - links, followers, friends, address books	- timestamps of user actions: sign-in, login, context-specific - timestamps and subjects of actions targeting user: friend requests, follows, etc.
Semantic level	- service system architectures - service system logs	- user documents - user added content: reactions, links, tweets, comments, status updates, blog posts, ... - actions targeting user: comments, likes etc.
Syntactic level	- IP addresses, DNS names and their mappings	- local protocol data: system logs, network traffic dumps
Physical level	- maps, address lists - census data - network topologies, switching diagrams - MAC addresses	- public and private records of personal history - GPS locations

FIGURE 9.1   Cyber personality aspects in relation to the five layers of the cyber domain.

Physical layer

The physical layer includes all the physical devices and networks of the cyber domain (Sartonen et al., 2016). For example, mobile devices with location services double as surveillance assets, and combined with the information provided by digital maps, they can provide constant information about the location of a physical identity of a cyber personality. The same applies to network topologies and switching diagrams together with the network traffic generated by the virtual identity of a cyber personality. With a long enough surveillance time, and provided that the user keeps the location services on, this information reveals geographic information, behavioural patterns and even lifestyle choices. Where a cyber personality lives and works, how many hours, which stores are visited daily or weekly, what recreational locations the cyber personality visits etc., can all be established with information from the physical layer.

Conversely, when provided a physical trajectory of a cyber persona as well as the corresponding service or semantic level activities, it is possible to analyze whether there are any discrepancies, omissions or conflicts between the levels. These could point to possible fabrication or a fraudulent cyber personality belonging to an artificial construct. For the cyber personality to be convincing, the location information needs to correlate with the personality's activities.

Syntactic layer

The syntactic layer consists of the software that operates the devices of the physical layer (Sartonen et al., 2016). The corresponding cyber personality aspect is a virtual identity: a local user account on a computer or device. In other words, once a cyber personality starts using a new device (computer, mobile phone), a virtual identity has been created in the syntactic layer. A single virtual identity can provide access to multiple network identities, such as e-mail addresses or cloud-based user IDs, and can thus be the means of connecting multiple network identities to a single cyber personality. Linking a physical device, such as a computer on a campus or in a working place, to a virtual identity also provides demographic information about the physical identity of a cyber personality. The browser used by the cyber personality is also a good source of information. It can leave traces of past browsing and other information (such as user agent and operating system) (Wang, Lee, & Lu, 2016).

Again, conversely, supposing we have established a possible connection between the physical as well as the virtual identities of a cyber personality, we can assess the likelihood of the connection being real by comparing the information on both levels. Is the network usage pattern as expected and does it correspond with the physical trajectory? If there are discrepancies, it is possible that the cyber personality is fraudulent, such as an automated social media bot that is not utilizing a browser and is only focussing on application programming interface (Chu, Gianvecchio, Wang, & Jajodia, 2012). Discrepancies can also occur if a cyber personality uses different techniques, such as encryption (Gupta, Gupta, & Singhal, 2014) and TOR network (Haraty & Zantout, 2014), to avoid detection.

Semantic layer

The semantic layer consists of data and information provided by the cyber personalities (Sartonen et al., 2016). This information includes images, text and audio files that people use to communicate and share their views of the world. The semantic layer may in many cases be the most useful in terms of TAA, as personality is manifested in everyday life, in our behaviour and interaction with others (Mehl, Gosling, & Pennebaker, 2006). Along with Facebook, other social media platforms such as Twitter, VKontakte, Renren and Weibo updates provide a great deal of information about individuals and their personalities. To illustrate this, Qiu and colleagues named their article as 'you are what you tweet', as they were able to identify several aspects of personality from twitter tweets. They also showed that some of the content that they analyzed was more specifically related to gender and age than personality (Qiu, Ramsay, & Yang, 2012). More recently, Pandya, Oussalah, Monachesi, Kostakos, and Lovén (2018) further studied Twitter user age prediction by including also previously overlooked contextual information.

A significant proportion of behaviour research in the past years has focused on personality (mainly on Five Factor Model). Personality-related information can be extracted from both text-based and online social media information (Tskhay & Rule, 2014). For example, extroverted people use positive words more often, whereas the use of positive words is negatively correlated with neuroticism (Pennebaker & King, 1999; Yarkoni, 2010). In addition to personality traits, factors such as sexual orientation, ethnicity, religious and politic views, intelligence, happiness, use of substances, parental separation, age and gender have been assessed from social media inputs (Kosinski, Kholi, Stillwell, & Graepel, 2013), as well as dysfunctional dispositions and stress (Akhtar, Winsborough, Ort, Johnson, & Chamorro-Premuzic, 2018; Kandias, Grizalis, Stavrou, & Nikolous, 2017). In a similar manner, criminals behind digital personas can be tracked using vast amounts of text data sets from social media (Rashid et al., 2013). Insider threats can be recognized from social media feeds by using a natural language processing system and combined with risk assessment (Symonenko et al., 2004). It is also possible to perform sentiment analysis on Twitter feeds. Along with this analysis, devices and other entities can be extracted from the data set (Saif, He, & Alani, 2012).

Service layer

The service layer consists of public and commercial digital services, with various social media platforms as the main focal point of psychological operations (Sartonen et al., 2016). In the past few years, an increasing amount of studies have focused on understanding how our actions in social media reflect our personality and behaviour in the physical world. There is evidence showing that personality traits relate to the content of status updates and choice of profile pictures on Facebook (Winter et al., 2014; Wu, Chang, & Yuan, 2014), showing that people, adding a particular post or picture, also reveal more than they anticipate.

Ikeda, Hattori, Ono, Asoh, and Higashino (2013) proposed a method for demographic estimation of Twitter users. Demographics such as age, gender, area, hobby, occupation and marital status were estimated by tracking the tweet history and clustering of followers/followees. Although the proposed model failed to recognize gender, it provides a good baseline for future research. Although most of the content extracted from different social media platforms and digital services falls under semantic layer, there are unique and useful information from service layer alone. When analyzing service layer, it is beneficial to ask questions such as why this service exists, what does it do and what is its value proposition? Each public and commercial digital service exists for certain reason, and that reason reveals useful information about customers using that service.

Furthermore, whole social networks may be analyzed to find and target fraudulent, artificial (such as social botnets) or 'troll' networks. A natural social network follows the shape of a certain type of random graph. Divergences from this shape indicate nonnaturalness: the greater the divergence, the higher the probability of fraud (Zhang, Lü, Wang, Zhu, & Zhou, 2013).

It has to be noted that, concerning social media, the semantic and service layers are often intertwined. What someone says, how it is said and to whom, what links are used, the overall behavioural pattern of the writer, etc., fall under different categories of semantic, network, demographic and other analysis types. The main difference, however, is the digital tools used for analyzing different aspects of a cyber personality.

Cognitive layer

The cognitive layer is the ultimate target of influence operations in the cyber domain. This layer consists of rational and emotional human processes that direct the information flow through all the layers of the cyber domain (Sartonen et al., 2016). Successful influence attempts affect this layer, producing a change in behaviour that can be observed through the data obtained from in the other layers.

Although we interact with digital representations of personalities on the Internet, behind a social media account, there typically still is a person (although the number of bots and other algorithms is increasing). This person exists in the physical world and interacts with other entities both in the physical world and the cyber domain — he or she is not just bits in cyberspace. This person has a unique personality, motivations and desires that direct his or her behaviour and interaction with others. One may be overly extrovert or may want to keep to oneself (McCrae & John, 1992); similarly, one may be motivated by gaining power and dominance above anything else or maintaining positive social relationships at the expense of one's own needs (McClelland, 1988). To understand a personality we must understand both the environment that he or she lives in and the personality and motivations that mediate behaviour in that environment (Funder, 2006, 2009).

Once the necessary characteristics of personality have been identified, this information can be used to create approach vectors and strategies for influence operation, which may include basic elements of influence psychology (Cialdini, 1984). For example, if we identify individuals as extroverts, we can use influence methods that exploit the principles of liking, reciprocation, social proof and scarcity (Alkış & Temizel, 2015; Uebelacker & Quiel, 2014). Similarly, agreeable individuals, in other words individuals who are amicable, compassionate and trust others (McCrae & John, 1992), are the most vulnerable to influencing attempts such as phishing (Parrish, Bailey, & Courtney, 2009). They are also the most vulnerable to influence methods using the principles of authority, reciprocity and liking (Alkış & Temizel, 2015).

On the other hand, individuals who are identified as highly conscientious tend to follow safety and security regulations (Darwish, Zarka, & Aloul, 2012; Parrish et al., 2009) and as such are less likely to react to influence attempts that try to make them break these regulations. However, it has been suggested that conscientious individuals may be vulnerable to influence methods using principles of reciprocity, authority, commitment and consistency (Alkış & Temizel, 2015; Uebelacker & Quiel, 2014).

Cultural aspects, identified through demographic and geographic data in addition to behavioural information, can also indicate successful means of influence. As an example, Orji (2016) demonstrated that collectivists and individualists vary with respect to their responsiveness to influence. For individuals living in a collective culture authority, reciprocity, consensus and liking-based influence seems to be somewhat more effective than on individuals living in individualist cultures (Orji, 2016).

Although correlations between data obtained from cyber domain and individual aspects such as personality have been confirmed, those

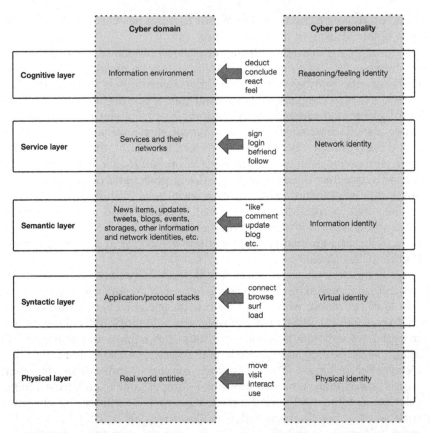

FIGURE 9.2   Cyber personalities and their different identities in cyber domain.

correlations do not outright predict behaviour, meaning that targeting a single individual as a TA may not be the best approach. However, using data for selecting suitable TA groups and appropriate influence methods may provide desired outcomes. In marketing research, this has been understood (for example, see Buettner, 2017; Myers, Sen, & Alexandrov, 2010).

The interactions in each abovementioned layer leave traces that can be used for data analysis and creating a layer-specific identity. This is illustrated in further detail in Fig. 9.2.

Cyber personalities in adaptive target audiences

Once an artificial construct of combined behavioural indicators, a cyber personality, has been built, a new question arises. How to build a TA based on abstract indicators of behaviour? Traditionally, as in FM3-05-301, the TA is basically a target of influence messages and retaining the same composition once approved by a proper authority. We argue that in the fast-paced cyber domain, this approach is not optimal. Combining fast or even real-time feedback from the digital personalities' observed behaviour with the possibilities provided by the sheer amount of information mined from extensive data requires rethinking the concept of a TA. We suggest a new concept of adaptive TAs. These audiences are based on behavioural indicators that suggest a certain aspect of need and/or predictive behaviour. An adaptive TA will ultimately consist of nonconflicting behavioural indicators which when combined can be assumed to indicate means of altering the overall behaviour of a target population. A single cyber personality can belong to multiple TAs, as long as the influence attempts of these different audiences are coherent with each other.

In addition to changing how TAs are comprehended, successful influence operations in the cyber domain may need more than just the composition of the TA to be adjusted. The rhizomatic nature of this environment means that the information flows and the integrity of data cannot be controlled. A message, once sent, may or may not end up being read by the intended TA in the form it was written. In addition, other messages may suddenly gain wide audiences and approval, possibly colliding with existing themes and creating something entirely new. This leads to sudden, abrupt changes in how matters are viewed and thus may lead to friendly parts of TA becoming hostile and vice versa (Sartonen et al., 2016). Thus, an essential aspect of an adaptive TA is that it is allowed to change in volume and in some of the aspects, as long as the additional behavioural indicators of a cyber personality do not conflict with the elementary factors that define the TA. This enables the influence operation to adapt quickly to the fast-paced nature of the cyber domain. This, in turn, demands a constant and effective feedback loop that can provide accurate information to the process. The requirement for speed also means that the whole operational process has to be redefined with information gathering, decision-making, influence actions and feedback following each other in a constant loop.

Reacting (preferably faster than adversaries) to these changes in global digital moods requires changing the messages and their recipients, in other words, changing the TAs. This cannot, however, be done without a feedback mechanism, i.e., without knowing how to change messages and which members to include or exclude in a TA. For this purpose alone, the authors of this chapter argue that the input − feedback loop has to be both constant and very fast. Constancy requires supervision, which in turn means that authority for making decisions about the composition of a TA and thus the targets of a psychological operation has to be very low hierarchically.

Typically, any psychological operation has to begin with predefined initial TAs as the base of operations. There are, however, two main ways of applying adaptive TAs to these initial groups. One would be to allow new adaptive TAs to be created outside the initial groups and to let them be populated by new cyber personalities in addition to those already inside an initial TA. Another would also be allowing the initial TAs to become dynamic in nature (and possibly nonexistent in the long run), but this would mean greater risk of losing the scope of the operation. However, as cyber personalities are transient by definition, a static TA is an oxymoron to begin with. More aptly, the initial TA should reflect the preferred initial state of cyber personalities to be included in the TA, whereas the actual personalities included are allowed and even expected to change. Indeed, it is the change in the TA, caused by the ongoing psychological operations as well as external factors, that becomes its most important characteristic.

In summary, the concept of adaptive TA needs to take into consideration three separate entities: the initial state of individuals to be included, the actual cyber personalities adhering to that initial state, and the direction towards which the cyber personalities are desired to be moved, in accordance to the psychological operations targets.

The nudges or changes required in the TA to first change their perception and, consequently, their actions would then be executed by way of controlling or influencing the information flows to the cyber personalities included in the adaptive TA. As controlling the information flows on each of the five layers of cyber personalities is very demanding, one of the first operational targets then should be to nudge the personalities into reflective control of their information environment, voluntarily preferring information sources in agreement with the final targets of the operation. The operation itself, rather than static, individual one-shots per TA, becomes an ongoing, dynamic process of nudges towards a target state, with the adherence of the cyber personalities in the TA constantly measured and the nudges adjusted accordingly. Fig. 9.3 further illustrates the concept of an adaptive TA in relation to a psychological operation.

In essence, we propose the following definition for an adaptive TA:

> An adaptive TA, corresponding to an ongoing psychological operation, is composed of 1) an initial collection of behavioural indicators, signifying vulnerability to the psychological operation, and manifested as a feature vector in the space of behavioural indicators; 2) a desired collection of behavioural indicators, signifying compliance to the next step in the ongoing psychological operation, and manifested as another feature vector in the space of behavioural indicators and 3) a collection of cyber personalities adhering to the indicators signifying vulnerability, manifested by close proximity of their individual behavioural feature vectors to the initial one.

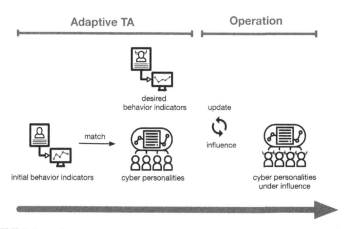

FIGURE 9.3   Adaptive target audience (TA) in relation to a psychological operation.

The abovementioned concept means that many such TAs would be temporal in nature, utilized as long as the requirement of supporting the PSYOPS objectives is met. The concept would also require the influence channels linked to the TA to be flexible, allowing for messages to be sent by the means that are currently the most effective. The usability and effectiveness of different channels would be a constantly changing variable, updated either through the same feedback loop as the TA or by external analysis.

Conclusion

Many digital tools are capable of providing specific information on different subjects of interest. The five-layer model used in this chapter is just one framework, and many services and digital platforms contribute many layers. Our main point is that the meaningful combination of the information from all the five layers of the cyber domain makes it possible to conduct a more effective TAA. Therefore, focus should not be in one layer or one feature but on collecting the behavioural indicators that manifest themselves in different forms in all the layers. As noted above, combining information allows gathering data about digital TAs' geographic information, demographics, personality, behaviour and conditions, all of which are requirements for an effective TAA.

The type of TAA we suggest here is an attempt to utilize the emerging possibilities provided by a global, digital environment. It serves also as a warning of emerging cyber threats that do not come in the purely technical form that cyber threats are often perceived. Although militaries typically adapt to any new environment eventually, we believe that influence operations or 'information war' is a phenomenon whose importance is not yet fully appreciated. One of the reasons may be that militaries are very aware of the obfuscate lines of authority in the cyber domain. Militaries typically operate within very strict legal guidance and are careful not to cross any lines of authority. It is our suggestion, however, that it is important also for militaries to explore all the emerging possibilities of the cyber domain. The possibilities are there, and eventually, some actors will use them. It is always unfortunate if militaries have to learn new technologies 'the hard way', fighting enemies with superior understanding of the environment.

Attaching cyber personalities to adaptive TAs, as suggested in this chapter, would require the mindset of accepting the rhizomatic nature of the cyber domain as an undeniable part of operations. In order words, all the messages in the cyber domain that shape the information environment would be accepted as an environmental factor, rather than a possible disruption of ongoing operations. Thus, our concept also includes the mindset of influencing, instead of controlling, the information environment. This means that instead of seeking controlled and evaluated cause–effect changes, a more holistic approach should be applied, with only the end result in mind. For a western military thinker such an approach may sound haphazard in its uncontrollability, but the authors of this chapter argue that the cyber domain has a level of chaos built in as a feature.

Discussion

This chapter joins the debate on the cyber domain as a platform for influence operations. The authors argue that although advances in understanding human psychology take place in a relatively careful pace, changes in the digital environment are rapid and revolutionary. Stepping from the industrial into the information age may require entirely new approaches, instead of trying to adjust current processes to work in a new environment. Perhaps, the concept of war itself needs to be defined. Or rather, perhaps, there has to be new concepts and definitions to describe the new types of war fighting the emerging technologies will enable.

Using personal data in the form described in this chapter may breach many laws concerning privacy. It is our intent, however, to examine the potential threats and opportunities in what we see as a new front or warfare, driven by advances in technology. If one truly wishes to understand the evolving digital battlespace, it is impossible to stay away from the shades of grey. Then again, whether dealing with activities described in this chapter is a military matter or not is a decision each nation will make individually. Nevertheless, we suggest that the roles of the military and civilian authorities within the legally obscure cyber domain must be defined clearly, if there ever is intention to keep the military and civilian activities separate in the digital battlespace as well. If the idea that militaries only engage hostile militaries is to prevail, there must be techniques of separation, instead of keeping militaries out of the cyber domain entirely.

An obvious challenge in combining different types of data from various sources is that of commensurating the indicators of behaviour. This, we assess, can only be done by further research on the combined effects that different selections of data have on the end result, the overall behavioural change of the TA. This, we suggest, is one special field of further research on this subject. Although single studies can provide correlation between data collectable from the cyber domain and actual behaviour, testing conflicting results against each other requires a large body of studies. Ultimately, though, these types of studies could yield information on what are the most predictive sources of information concerning behaviour. In turn, it most probably would be within these subjects that most effective influence operations could be performed. Although it can be argued that marketing studies most probably are way ahead in such studies, it should be understood that there are crucial differences on the approach between civilian and military influence approaches. Both are regulated by law, but militaries have to prepare for adversaries not following national laws and thus must prepare defending against far more sinister attempts than their civilian counterparts. It is against this background that militaries should prepare for what is possible, not against what is currently legal.

Another challenge to the operations described in this chapter is that the usability of TAs consisting entirely of cyber personalities depends on their representation of the overall target group in the real world. In other words, the critical question is whether the cyber TAs have the capability of conveying the desired behavioural change in the overall population. This probability depends on many factors, such as the percentage of Internet users in the target population and cultural differences in the use and importance of the digital environment. These factors may be difficult to estimate reliably in advance. Further studies are thus needed to assess the real world usefulness of the theoretical approach presented here.

To verify the theoretical approach presented in this chapter, the authors suggest three methods. The first would simply test the ability of this approach to deliver the desired behavioural changes in a TA. However, as with any other psychological operation's evaluation, the problem with this approach is that the causalities behind observed behavioural changes are very difficult to prove.

The second approach would be to compare the results from two influence operations, performed on similar audiences but with different

TAA methods. The first method would be the more traditional model of seeking out human identities through the cyber interface, while the other would suffice with the cyber personalities only. Comparing the results and the overall practicality (such as time consumed) of these methods would show whether or not human identification is necessary for satisfactory results. To conduct several tests with various audiences with different percentages of Internet access would yield additional information on the applicability of different methods. To have reliable results, the properties of the TAs would have to be known, which may present the greatest challenges of this approach. To make the test in laboratory conditions may lack the real world complexity of TAs, while tests with real audiences seldom have clear cause and effect correlations.

The third method would be to access data from an already conducted TAA and perform the TAA with cyber personality approach on the same TA. The challenge with this approach is that the conditions of the TA may have changed and thus the results may not be comparable.

Disseminating and analyzing a cyber personality through the five layers in the way presented in this chapter may also include the benefit of recognizing bots and other algorithms more easily. One suggestion for further studies would be to look at what features artificial cyber personalities lack in comparison to humans in the five cyber layers and whether these differences are platform-specific. The lack of human qualities would thus enable the identification of artificial entities.

References

Akhtar, R., Winsborough, D., Ort, U., Johnson, A., & Chamorro-Premuzic, T. (2018). Detecting the dark side of personality using social media status updates. *Personality and Individual Differences, 132*, 90−97.

Alkış, N., & Temizel, T. T. (2015). The impact of individual differences on influence strategies. *Personality and Individual Differences, 87*, 147−152.

Buettner, R. (2017). Predicting user behavior in electronic markets based on personality-mining in large online social networks. *Electronic Markets, 27*, 247−265.

Chu, Z., Gianvecchio, S., Wang, H., & Jajodia, S. (2012). Detecting automation of twitter accounts: Are you a human, bot, or cyborg? *IEEE Transactions on Dependable and Secure Computing, 9*, 811−824.

Cialdini, R. B. (1984). *Influence: The psychology of persuasion*. New York: HarperCollins.

Darwish, A., Zarka, A. El, & Aloul, F. (2012). Towards understanding phishing victims' profile. *ICCSII 2012 Proceedings*. Sharjah, Arab Emirates.

Funder, D. C. (2006). Towards a resolution of the personality triad: Persons, situations, and behaviors. *Journal of Research in Personality, 40*, 21−34.

Funder, D. C. (2009). Persons, behaviors and situations: An agenda for personality psychology in the postwar era. *Journal of Research in Personality, 43*(2), 120−126.

Gupta, R., Gupta, S., & Singhal, A. (2014). Importance and techniques of information hiding: A review. *International Journal of Computer Trends and Technology, 9*(5), 260−265.

Haraty, R. A., & Zantout, B. (2014). The tor data communication system. *Journal of Communications and Networks, 16*, 415−420.

Ikeda, K., Hattori, G., Ono, C., Asoh, H., & Higashino, T. (2013). Twitter user profiling based on text and community mining for market analysis. *Knowledge-Based Systems, 51*, 35–47.

Kandias, M., Grizalis, D., Stavrou, V., & Nikolous, K. (2017). Stress level detection via OSN usage pattern and chronicity analysis: An OSINT threat intelligence module. *Computer & Security, 69*, 3–17.

Kosinski, M., Kholi, P., Stillwell, D., & Graepel, T. (2013). Private traits and attributes are predictable from digital records of human behavior. *Proceedings of the National Academy of Sciences, 110*(15), 5802–5805.

Libicki, M. (2007). *Conquest in cyberspace – national security and information warfare*. Cambridge: Cambridge University Press.

McClelland, D. (1988). *Human motivation*. Cambridge: Cambridge University Press.

McCrae, R. R., & John, O. P. (1992). An introduction to the five-factor model and its applications. *Journal of Personality, 60*, 175–215.

Mehl, M. R., Gosling, S. D., & Pennebaker, J. W. (2006). Personality in its natural habitat: Manifestations and implicit folk theories of personality in daily life. *Journal of Personality and Social Psychology, 90*(5), 862–877.

Myers, S., Sen, S., & Alexandrov, A. (2010). The moderating effect of personality traits on attitudes toward advertisements: A contingency framework. *Management and Marketing Challenges for Knowledge Society, 5*(3), 3–20.

Orji, R. (2016). Persuasion and culture: Individualism-collectivism and susceptibility to influence strategies. *CEUR Workshop Proceedings, 1582*, 30–39.

Pandya, A., Oussalah, M., Monachesi, P., Kostakos, P., & Lovén, L. (2018). On the use of URLs and hashtags in age prediction of twitter users. In *IEEE international conference on information reuse and integration (IRI)*. Salt Lake City, UT: IEEE.

Parrish, J. L., Jr., Bailey, J. L., & Courtney, J. F. (2009). A personality based model for determining susceptibility to phishing attacks. *SWDSI 2009 Proceedings*. Oklahoma City, United States.

Pennebaker, J. W., & King, L. A. (1999). Linguistic styles: Language use as an individual difference. *Journal of Personality and Social Psychology, 77*(6), 1296–1312.

Qiu, L., Ramsay, J., & Yang, F. (2012). You are what you tweet: Personality expression and perception on Twitter. *Journal of Research in Personality, 46*(6), 710–718.

Rashid, A., Baron, A., Rayson, P., May-Chahal, C., Greenwood, P., & Walkerdine, J. (2013). Who am I? Analyzing digital personas in cybercrime investigations. *Computer, 46*(4), 54–61.

Saif, H., He, Y., & Alani, H. (2012). Semantic sentiment analysis of twitter. In *International semantic web conference* (pp. 508–524). Springer.

Sartonen, M., Huhtinen, A.-M., & Lehto, M. (2016). Rhizomatic target audiences of the cyber domain. *Journal of Information Warfare, 15*(4), 1–13.

Suler, J. (2016). *Psychology of the digital age: Humans become electric*. UK: Cambridge University Press.

Symonenko, S., Liddy, E. D., Yilmazel, O., Del Zoppo, R., Brown, E., & Downey, M. (2004). Semantic analysis for monitoring insider threats. In *International conference on intelligence and security informatics* (pp. 492–500). Springer.

Taylor, J., Furnham, A., & Breeze, J. (2014). *Revealed. Using remote personality profiling to influence, negotiate and motivate*. UK: Palgrave Macmillian.

Tskhay, K. O., & Rule, N. O. (2014). Perceptions of personality in text-based media and OSN: A meta-analysis. *Journal of Research in Personality, 49*(1), 25–30.

U.S. Joint Publication 3-05-301. (2003). *Psychological operations tactics, techniques and procedures.* Viewed retrieved January 7, 2017, from https://www.fas.org/irp/doddir/army/fm3-05-301.pdf.

Uebelacker, S., & Quiel, S. (2014). The social engineering personality framework. *STAST 2014 Proceedings*. Wien, Austria.

Wang, L., Lee, K.-C., & Lu, Q. (2016). Improving advertisement recommendation by enriching user browser cookie attributes. In *Proceedings of the 25th ACM international on conference on information and knowledge management* (pp. 2401–2404).

Winter, S., Neubaum, G., Eimler, S. C., Gordon, V., Theil, J., Herrmann, J., et al. (2014). Another brick in the Facebook wall - how personality traits relate to the content of status updates. *Computers in Human Behavior, 34,* 194–202.

Wu, Y.-C. J., Chang, W.-H., & Yuan, C.-H. (2014). Do Facebook profile pictures reflect user's personality? *Computers in Human Behavior, 51,* 880–889.

Yarkoni, T. (2010). Personality in 100,000 words: A large-scale analysis of personality and word use among bloggers. *Journal of Research in Personality, 44*(3), 363–373.

Zhang, Q.-M., Lü, L., Wang, W.-Q., Zhu, Y.-X., & Zhou, T. (2013). Potential theory for directed networks. *PLoS One, 8*(2), e554377. https://doi.org/10.1371/journal.pone.0055437.

CHAPTER

10

Privacy issues and critical infrastructure protection

Jussi Simola

Department of Information Technology, University of Jyväskylä, Finland

OUTLINE

Emerging Cyber Threats and Cognitive Vulnerabilities
https://doi.org/10.1016/B978-0-12-816203-3.00010-1

197

Introduction

European Public Protection and Disaster Relief (PPDR) services such as law enforcement, firefighting, emergency medical and disaster recovery services have recognized that the lack of interoperability of technical systems limit the cooperation between the PPDR authorities. The military (MIL) and critical infrastructure protection (CIP) face similar challenges.

Cyberthreats have increased in spite of formal integration in Europe and the world. Therefore, authorities need to respond to growing challenges. As major terror attacks, hybrid warfare and major accidents, for example in Belgium, France, Ukraine and the United States have shown, preparation for different kind of threats is challenging. Recent major accidents have indicated that lack of human resources affects disaster recovery.

Due to the terrorist attacks that have occurred, public safety authorities are convinced that network traffic control is a good way to proactively prevent acts that threaten peace of society, but it is only one way to protect the citizens or control the situation.

There is an issue concerning privacy because most mobile user/end-users of web-based services or applications do not know where and to whom personal information is transmitted and how social media behaviour is analyzed for different purposes. It has been seen that data, which are collected from social media, are tradable goods that may violate an individual's privacy.

In the market economy, customer profiling or tracking is seen only from the point of view of data exploitation in Internet marketing. Marketing people and advertisers try to focus on services and products more efficiently for the right target audience. Location-based services rely on a combination of technologies to pinpoint the location of a user with contextual data to provide more value to a mobile user. For example,

Geo-targeting or Geo-fencing with Wi-Fi, cell towers and beacons create a privacy-restricting advertisement atmosphere that aims to influence consumer behaviour.

The main purpose of this chapter was to find local- and state-level factors concerning privacy issues, which affect the utilization of proposed smart hybrid emergency response model (Simola & Rajamäki, 2017). Privacy issues with ethical aspects are an important part of continuity management because the government cannot accept and produce services that are illegal.

The rest of this chapter is divided as follows. Section 2 handles the overview of legislation concerning privacy issues in the United States and Europe. Section 3 proposes central concepts and framework of this article. Sections 4 handles the organizational and management perspective of situational awareness. Section 5 presents location-based technologies. Section 6 handles the research process of this study. Section 7 presents findings. Section 8 presents discussion about usage of the proposed Hybrid Emergency Response Model. Section 9 handles expectations of implementation when the proposed model is applied on CI.

Legislation concerning privacy issues

European Data Protection Reform (EDPR) partly harmonizes data protection regulation in European Union (EU) countries. The EU General Data Protection Regulation (GDPR) replaces the Data Protection Directive 95/46/EC and was designed to harmonize data privacy laws across Europe, to protect and empower all EU citizens' data privacy and to reshape the way organizations across the region approach data privacy. GDPR applies to all businesses offering goods and/or services to the EU. That means that the organizations do not have to reside in the EU area or even in Europe; if you are holding private information about an EU citizen whom you provide services, GDPR applies (European Commission, 2016a). The regulation introduces stronger citizens' rights as new transparency requirements. It strengthens the rights of information, access and the right to be forgotten. Regulation gives all data protection authorities the right to impose fines up to EUR 20 million or 4% of the worldwide annual turnover on companies (European Commission, 2016a).

The EU's new GDPR regulates the processing by an individual, a company or an organization of personal data relating to individuals in the EU. For this purpose, personal data are comprised of any information that relates to an identified or identifiable living individual. Different pieces of information, which is collected together and can lead to the identification of a particular person, also constitute personal data. Personal data that have been encrypted or pseudonymized but can be used to re-identify a person remains personal data and fall within the scope of the law. Personal data that have been rendered anonymous in such a way that the individual is not or no longer identifiable are no longer considered personal data. For data to be truly anonymized the anonymization must be irreversible (European Commission, 2016a).

The GDPR protects personal data regardless of the technology used for processing that data. The law is technology neutral and applies to both automated and manual processing if the data are organized in accordance with pre-defined criteria (European Commission, 2016a). It also does not matter if the data are stored in an IT system through video surveillance or on paper. In all these cases personal data are subject to the protection requirements set out in the GDPR.

Personal data consist of, for example, name, address, email address, an Internet protocol address, location data on a mobile phone and a cookie ID, and the advertising identifier of your phone. In some cases, there is a specific sectoral legislation regulating, for instance, the use of location data or the use of cookies. Directive presents mostly a continuation of earlier Data Protection Directive efforts (European Commission, 2016a).

EU directive named the ePrivacy 2002/58 (European Commission, 2002) deals with the regulation of a number of important issues such as confidentiality of information, treatment of traffic data, spam and cookies. This directive has been amended by Directive 2009/136, which introduces several changes, especially in what concerns cookies, that are now subject to prior consent. The ePrivacy directive presents mostly a continuation to earlier Data Protection Directive (European Commission, 2002).

The directive does not apply to Titles V and VI (second and third pillars constituting the EU). Also, it does not apply to issues concerning criminal law and state security, public security and defence. The interception of data is covered by the new EU Data Retention Directive, the purpose of which is to amend ePrivacy Directive (IBP, 2014). In the future, Regulation on Privacy and Electronic Communications will repeal the ePrivacy Directive 2002/58/EC (European Commission, 2017).

The EU Data Protection Directive 2016/680 or Law Enforcement Directive regulate the protection of natural persons with regard to the processing of personal data by competent authorities for the purposes of the prevention, investigation, detection or prosecution of criminal offences or the execution of criminal penalties, and on the free movement of such data. This proposal applies cross-border and national processing of data by member states' competent authorities for the purpose of law enforcement. This comprises, for example the prevention, investigation, detection and prosecution of criminal offences and the safeguarding and prevention of threats to public security (European Commission, 2016b).

Information exchange

The exchange of information between the EU and the United States has been regulated, among other things, as follows: The European Commission and the US government reached a political agreement on a new framework for transatlantic exchanges of personal data for commercial purposes named the EU—US Privacy Shield. The European Commission adopted the EU—US Privacy Shield on July 2016 (European Commission, 2016c).

The framework protects the fundamental rights of anyone in the EU whose personal data are transferred to the United States as well as bringing legal clarity for businesses relying on transatlantic data transfers.

The EU—US Privacy Shield is based on the principles like obligations on companies which handle data. (a) The US Department of Commerce will conduct regular updates and reviews of participating companies to ensure that companies follow the rules they submitted themselves to. (b) Clear safeguards and transparency obligations on US government access: The United States has given the EU assurance that the access of public authorities for law enforcement and national security is subject to clear oversight mechanisms. (c) Effective protection of individual rights: citizens who think that collected data have been misused under the Privacy Shield scheme will benefit from several accessible dispute resolution mechanisms. It is possible for a company to resolve the complaint by itself or give it to the alternative dispute resolution (ADR) to be resolved for free. Citizens can also go to their national data protection authorities, who will work with the Federal Trade Commission to ensure that complaints by EU citizens are investigated and resolved. The Ombudsperson mechanism means that an independent senior official within the US Department of State will ensure that complaints are properly investigated and addressed in a timely manner (European Commission, 2016c).

All of this regulation reflects the need for privacy protection in the Western world.

Central concepts

Situational awareness

According to Endsley (1988), a general definition of situational awareness (SA) is 'the perception of the elements in the environment within a volume of time and space, the comprehension of their meaning and the projection of their status in the near future'. From a technical viewpoint, SA comes down to compiling, processing and fusing data, and such data processing includes the need to be able to assess data fragments as well as fused information and provide a rational estimate of its information quality (Franke & Brynielsson, 2014). The cognitive side of SA concerns the human capacity of being able to comprehend the technical implications and draw conclusions in order to come up with informed decisions (Franke & Brynielsson, 2014). According to Endsley (1988, 2015) humans are not as good at processing large volumes of data, quickly and consistently, nor of sustaining attention for long periods of time. The level of autonomy increases as the capability of the system increases for performing various components of any given function. Flexible autonomy should provide smooth, simple, seamless transition of functions between a human and the system (Endsley, 2015).

Cyber situational awareness

According to Franke and Brynielsson (2014), cyber SA is a subset of SA, that is cyber SA is the part of SA that concerns the 'cyber' environment. Such SA can be reached, for example, by the use of data from IT sensors (intrusion detection systems, etc.) that can be fed to a data fusion process or be interpreted directly by the decision-maker (Franke & Brynielsson, 2014). SA is a prerequisite for CPS to be resilient. According to Franke and Brynielsson (2014), cyber SA cannot be treated in isolation, but it is intertwined with and a part of the overall SA. Cyber SA concerns awareness regarding cyber issues but these need to be combined with other information to obtain full understanding regarding the current situation.

Public protection and disaster relief functions

The term PPDR or public safety organization implies that those groups are responsible for the prevention of and protection from events that could endanger the safety of the general public (Baldini, 2010). According to Baldini (2010), the main public safety functions include law enforcement, emergency medical services, border security, protection of the environment, firefighting, search and rescue (SAR) and crisis management. PPDR is used to describe critical public services that have been created to provide primary law enforcement, firefighting, emergency medical services and disaster recovery services for the citizens of the political sub-division of each country. These individuals help to ensure the protection and preservation of life and property. Public safety organizations are responsible for the prevention of and protection from events that could endanger the safety of the general public. Such events could be natural or man-made.

One major challenge in defining a classification of public safety organizations at the European level is that, due to the non-homogenous historical development of public safety, similar organizations have different roles in different countries (Baldini, 2010).

Structural and organizational changes in Finnish PPDR

Structural changes within the public sector, such as the regional administration reform, the Emergency Response Centre (ERC) reform and so-called social welfare and health-care reform have influenced the public sector employee's work processes over the past 10 years. In addition, technological development has occurred rapidly (Hanni, 2013). Changes in PPDR organizations due to legislation have developed a need to create special operational working methods (Aine et al., 2011). The Finnish Security Intelligence Service (Supo) is an operational security authority engaged in close cooperation with international security and intelligence services. Supo moved directly under the Ministry of the Interior in 2016. Earlier the Finnish Secure Intelligence Service operated under the National Police Board (The Finnish Security Intelligence Service, 2015).

Command and control system

A command centre is any place that is used to provide centralized command for some purpose. An Incident Command Centre would be located at or near an incident to provide localized on-scene command and support of the Incident Commander. Mobile command centres may be used to enhance emergency preparedness and back up fixed command centres. Command centres may include emergency operations centres (EOCs) or transportation management centres (TMCs) as well.

Supervisory Control and Data Acquisition (SCADA) systems are basically process control systems (PCSs) that are used for monitoring, gathering and analyzing real-time environmental data from a simple office building or a complex nuclear power plant. PCSs are designed to automate electronic systems based on a predetermined set of conditions, such as traffic control or power grid management (Gervasi, 2010).

According to Gervasi (2010), SCADA systems can be described with the following components: operating equipment which can include but are not limited to valves, pumps and conveyors controlled by energizing actuators or relays. Local processors communicate with site's instruments and operating equipment including programmable logic controller (PLC), remote terminal unit (RTU), intelligent electronic device (IED) and process automation controller (PAC). A single local processor may be responsible for dozens of inputs from instruments and outputs to operating equipment. SCADA also consists of instruments in the field or in a facility with or which sense conditions such as power level, flow rate or pressure. Short-range communications mean wireless or short cable connections between local processors, instruments and operating equipment. Long-range communications between local processors and host computers cover a wide area using methods such as satellite, microwave, frame relay and cellular packet data. Host computers act as the central point of monitoring and control. The host computer is where a human operator can supervise the process, as well as receive alarms, review data and exercise control. The system may consist of automated or semi-automated processes. A networked control system (NCS) is a control system where the control loops are closed through a communication network. The defining feature of an NCS is that control and feedback signals are exchanged among the system's components in the form of information packages through a network (McLarty and Ridge, 2014; Rosslin & Tai-hoon, 2010).

Integration of safety functions

Decision support engine (DSE) is a facilitator intended to help authorities and other decision-makers that compiles key information from raw data using system rules and knowledge. It captures data from different sensors, for example surveillance cameras (Ahmed et al., 2012). Face detection camera (FDC) is also a decision support engine itself. Data processing for event detection follows next in order to identify events in current surveillance context (NEC Corporation, 2016). To understand the current surveillance state depends on the output of combined event detection units.

Distributed systems intercommunication protocol

Distributed systems intercommunication protocol (DSiP) forms multiple simultaneous communication channels between the remote end and the control room: if one communication channel is down, other channels will continue operating. DSiP makes communication reliable and unbreakable by using various physical communication methods in parallel. Applications, equipment and devices can communicate over a single unbreakable data channel. Satellite, TETRA, 2G/3G/4G, VHF-radios and other technologies can be used simultaneously. DSiP is simultaneously a protocol-level and routing-level traffic engineering software solution for intelligently handling data routing, using all kinds of physical media, including IP and non-IP communication (Ahokas, Guday, Lyytinen, & Rajamäki, 2010).

Critical infrastructure protection

Critical Information Infrastructure means any physical or virtual information system that controls, processes, transmits, receives or stores electronic information in any form including data, voice or video that is vital to the functioning of CI. CI includes energy production, transmission and distribution networks, ICT systems, networks and services (including mass communication), financial services, transport and logistics, water supply, construction and maintenance of infrastructure, and waste management in special circumstances. The smart network will integrate information and communication technologies with the power-delivery infrastructure (Ahokas et al., 2010; Ministry of the Interior, 2016).

Examples of cyberattacks

Cyber threats include denial of service (DoS), unauthorized vulnerability probes, botnet command and control, data exfiltration, data destruction and physical destruction via alternation of critical software/data. These attacks can be initiated and maintained by a mixture of malware, social engineering or highly sophisticated advanced persistent threats (APTs) that are targeted and continue for long periods of time. Channel jamming is one of the most efficient ways to launch physical-layer DoS attacks, especially for wireless communications (National Institute of Standards and Technology, 2014).

According to the National Institute of Standards and Technology (2014) cyber-physical attacks can be classified into three broad sections:

- Physical attacks informed by cyber
  The use of information gathered by cyber means that an attacker is allowed to plan and execute an improved or enhanced physical attack. For example, if an enemy has decided to destroy components within a substation though are not sure which substation or components would have the greatest impact. They could access confidential information or aggregate unprotected information by cyber and they could then physically attack that specific substation and lines.
- Cyberattacks enhancing physical attacks
  An enemy uses cyber means to improve the impacts of a physical attack by either making the attack more successful (e.g. greater

consequences) or interfering with restoration efforts (thereby increasing the duration of the attack). Inadvertent actions could also cause such an attack. One example is an enemy tampering with the integrity of protective relay settings prior to a physical attack on power lines. Although the original settings were designed to contain the effects of a failure, the tampered settings allow the failure to cascade into impacts on a wider segment of the grid.

• Use of a cyber system to cause physical harm

An enemy uses a cyber system that controls physical equipment in such a manner to cause physical damage. An example of this is the burner management system for a natural gas generator. In this case, an enemy or a careless operator could attempt to turn on the natural gas inflow without an ignition source present. As the burner unit fills with natural gas, the enemy could turn on the ignition source, potentially causing an explosion.

Good cyber, physical and operational security planning and implementations can minimize the impacts of cyber-physical attacks. Defensive measures that can be used to minimize the likelihood of successful cyberattacks and physical attacks will also work to minimize the impacts of a cyber-physical attack. The attacker can also be the state. This type of cyberattacker is politically motivated and may try to use several tools to affect the state's vital functions.

Intelligence solutions for public safety organizations

OSINT is defined as the systematic collection, processing, analysis and production, classification and dissemination of information derived from sources openly available to and legally accessible by the public in response to particular government requirements serving national security. It is any unclassified information, in any medium, that is generally available to the public, even if its distribution is limited or only available upon payment (Glassman and Kang, 2012; Morrow & Odierno, 2012; Nurmi, 2015).

Most information has geospatial dimensions. Examples of geospatial open source include maps, airborne imagery, atlases, gazetteers, port plans, gravity data, aeronautical data, navigation data, geodetic data, human terrain data (cultural and economic), environmental data, commercial imagery, LIDAR, hyper and multi-spectral data, geo-names and features, urban terrain, vertical obstruction data, boundary marker data, geospatial mashups, spatial databases and web services. Most of the geospatial data mentioned above are integrated, analyzed and syndicated using geospatial software such as a geographic information system (GIS) (Morrow & Odierno, 2012; Nurmi, 2015; Trottier, 2015; Vetter, 2015; Wood, 2016).

Social Media Intelligence (SOCMINT) identifies social media content in particular as a challenge and opportunity for open-source investigations (Trottier, 2015). Big data includes processes of analysis, capture, research, sharing, storage, visualization and safety of information. Associated with OSINT, Big Data is the ability to map standards of behaviour and tendencies (Dos Passos, 2016). The availability of worldwide satellite photography, often of high resolution, on the web (e.g. Google Earth Pro) has expanded open-source capabilities into areas formerly available only to major intelligence services.

Emergency communications in Europe

The Emergency Response Centre Administration provides emergency response centre services throughout Finland. The duty of the Emergency Response Centre Administration is to receive emergency calls from all over the country for the rescue, police and social and health services; handle communications relating to the safety of people, property and the environment and relay the information they receive to the appropriate assisting authorities or partners.

European authorities communicate with each other in VIRVE network. There is a need to create a new trusted network with a wide bandwidth. The transmission capacity is often limited in an overload situation. The needs of data transmission must be classified. Classification can be used for the benefit of message traffic prioritizing the entire transmission chain. Therefore, it is important to reduce unnecessary data communications between the authorities (Simola & Rajamäki, 2016).

Emergency communications in the United States

Importance of enhancing common operational picture between public safety actors has been noticed also in the United States. The need to transmit live video but also different kinds of sensor data from the scene of an accident has become a main area for development of information systems. The National Emergency Number Association (NENA) and the Association of Public-Safety Communications Officials (APCO) recognize the fundamental need to update the North American 9-1-1 system and are addressing the challenge with a system design called "Next Generation 9-1-1". i3 is the NENA architecture for a system of 9-1-1 services, functional elements and databases that run on an Emergency Service IP Network ESInet. The 9-1-1 centre of the future with First Responder Network Authority (FirstNet) systems will receive incoming data calls from the machines and sensor systems including automatic crash notification (ACN), break-in alarms and body health monitors. Use of both systems ensures multi-media capabilities throughout the entire call process (National Emergency Number Association (NENA) and the Association of Public-Safety Communications Officials (APCO), 2016; National Public Safety Telecommunications Council, 2015).

The US Congress established an independent government authority with a mandate to provide specialized communication services for public safety called FirstNet. It will be connected to the state-level ESinet. The service package consists of NG9-1-1 emergency services, Commercial Mobile Alert System. The dispatcher can utilize a combination of computer-assisted dispatch (CAD) and radio resources to relay information to the appropriate responder resources. FirstNet capable NG9-1-1—PSAP system would be used to relay the appropriate data. For example, processed video or picture material can be transmitted to the first responders via the FirstNet broadband network. In this way NG9-1-1 and FirstNet systems are highly complementary and both are required to ensure a seamless flow of information from the public, to the PSAP and to the responders. Use of both systems ensures multi-media capabilities throughout the entire call process (National Public Safety Telecommunications Council, 2015).

A smart grid system and internet of things

Internet of Things (IoT) connects systems, sensors and actuator instruments to the broader internet. IoT allows the things to communicate, exchange control data and other necessary information while executing applications towards the machine goal (Electrical Technology, 2016).

The idea of IoT was developed in parallel to Wireless Sensor Networks (WSN). Sensors are now everywhere. In our vehicles, in our smartphones, in factories controlling CO_2 emissions and even in the ground monitoring soil conditions in vineyards. A WSN can generally be described as a network of nodes that cooperatively sense and may control the environment, enabling interaction between persons or computers and the surrounding environment. The development of WSNs was inspired by MIL applications, notably surveillance in conflict zones (Bröring et al., 2011).

IoT is an emerging paradigm of Internet-connected things that allow the physical objects or things to connect, interact and communicate with one another similar to the way humans talk through the web in today's environment. It connects systems, sensors and actuator instruments to the broader Internet.

IoT allows things to communicate, exchange control data and other necessary information while executing applications towards machine goal. The IoT has also impacted the industrial sector, especially for industrial automation systems in which Internet infrastructure makes extensive access to sensors, controls and actuators, with a goal of increasing efficiency (Electrical Technology, 2016).

Cybersecurity risks should be addressed as organizations implement and maintain their smart grid systems. According to the National Institute of Standards and Technology (2014), digital two-way communications between consumers and electric power companies, the smart grid system provides the most efficient electric network operations based on the received consumer's information.

A smart grid system may consist of IT which is a discrete system of electronic information resources organized for the collection, processing, maintenance, use, sharing, dissemination or disposition of information. A smart grid system may also consist of operational technologies (OTs) or industrial control systems (ICS) like SCADA systems, distributed control systems (DCSs) and other control system configurations such as programmable logic controllers (PLCs) (Chong & Kumar, 2003; National Institute of Standards and Technology, 2014).

Industrial Internet of Things (IIoT) collects data from connected devices (i.e. smart connected devices and machines) in the field or plant and then processes these data using sophisticated software and networking tools. The entire IIoT requires a collection of hardware, software, communications and networking technologies (Electrical Technology, 2016).

Management of situational awareness in Finland

The Ministry of Finance of Finland is responsible for the steering and development of the state's information security (Ministry of Defence, 2010). The Government Situation Centre ensures that the state leaders and central government authorities are kept informed continuously in Finland. The Government Situation Centre was set up in 2007, and it has the duty to alert the government, permanent secretaries and heads of preparedness and to call them to councils, meetings and negotiations at exceptional times required by a disruption or a crisis. The ministries have the duty to submit the situational picture for their entire administrative branch to the Government Situation Centre and notify the centre of any security incidents in their field of activity. In urgent situations, the Government Situation Centre also receives incident reports of security incidents directly from the authorities. In addition, the Government Situation Centre follows public sources and receives SA information in its role as the national focal point for certain institutions of the EU and other international organizations.

Organizational changes of intelligence services in the United States

It has been seen in the United States that it is important to combine the functions of cybersecurity organizations that work separately. The Department of Homeland Security (DHS) provides support to potentially impacted entities, analyzes the potential impact across CI, investigates those responsible in conjunction with law enforcement partners and co-ordinates the national response to significant cyber incidents (Department of Homeland Security, 2018a). DHS's National Cybersecurity and Communications Integration Centre is a cyber SA, incident response and management centre that is a national connection of cyber and communications integration for the federal government, intelligence community and law enforcement. NCCIC co-locates National Communications System (NCS), National Coordinating Centre (NCC) for communications, United States Computer Emergency Readiness Team (US-CERT), Industrial Control Systems Cyber Emergency Response Team (ICS-CERT) into NCCIC watch floor 2012. The Cybersecurity Act of 2015 designates NCCIC as the central hub for cyber threat indicator sharing between government and the privacy sector. In 2017 NCCIC completes internal realignment (Department of Homeland Security, 2018b).

Cyber situational awareness at national level in Finland

The Ministry of Transport and Communications is responsible for safeguarding the functioning of electronic ICT systems. The Ministry of Finance is responsible for safeguarding the state administration's IT functions, information security and the service systems common to the central government (Secretariat of the Security Committee, 2013). The Security Committee coordinates cybersecurity preparedness, monitors the implementation of the cybersecurity strategy and issues recommendations on its further development (Secretariat of the Security Committee, 2013). The Finnish Communications Regulatory Authority (FICORA) works under steering control of the Ministry of Transport and Communications (Functions of the Finnish Transport Agency and FICORA merged to form the new Finnish Transport and Communications Agency Traficom on January 2019). The National Cyber Security Centre Finland (NCSC-FI) operates within the Finnish Communications Regulatory Authority (FICORA) and offers an increasingly diverse array of information and cybersecurity services. In its role as a statutory supervisory and steering authority with a responsibility for information security tasks, NCSC-FI gathers information. FICORA's other operations yield more information governed by legislation on events relating to incidents, deviations and disturbance situations (Finnish Communications Regulatory Authority, 2014). The information gained from nationally or internationally detected information security incidents, deviations and threats (incident response function, CERT) is combined with the information gained from inspections of information systems and telecommunications arrangements (information assurance function, NCSA) and the information received in the role as a supervisory and steering authority. The organizational responsibilities of cybersecurity are unclearly divided as Fig. 10.1 illustrated.

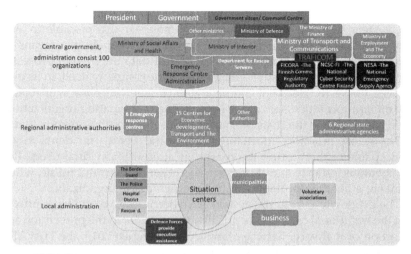

FIGURE 10.1   Organizations responsibilities of cybersecurity functions.

Cyber SA is combined; this information is used to produce NCSC-FI's combined cybersecurity situational picture, as illustrated in Fig. 10.2 (Finnish Communications Regulatory Authority, 2014).

Alert and detection system – HAVARO

HAVARO is an alert and detection system which FICORA has created in partnership with the National Emergency Supply Agency (NESA) in 2012. NESA is a public organization working under steering control of the Ministry of Employment and the Economy. NESA is responsible for planning and measures related to developing and maintaining security of supply.

For every Finnish organization, it is optional to join the HAVARO system, but joining brings many significant benefits. The information on situation awareness provided by the system increases understanding

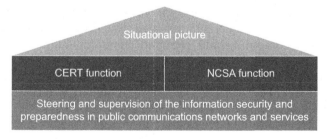

FIGURE 10.2   Producing of Finnish national cybersecurity situational picture (Finnish Communications Regulatory Authority, 2014).

about the organization's own and general state of information security. The system produces information which makes it also possible to alert other players about a detected threat and develop better means of detection. Clients can determine what sort of data the system processes and the ownership of the data remains with the company itself, in its own devices. HAVARO does not compete with commercial players or replace any other information security solutions. The participating organizations are responsible for the costs of equipment needed for their own network.

The system monitors information concerning security incidents only; it is incapable of monitoring the communication of individual users. Red observations indicate that the system has observed harmful traffic, which points to a likely information security breach in the organization.

The experiences from the system have been positive and have proved that the traditional controls are not always sufficient in the prevention and detection of malware. Between January and August 2015, the HAVARO system made a total of 1800 red observations. Red observations indicate that the system has observed harmful traffic, which points to a likely information security breach in the organization. Most observations concern utilization attempts made using mass distribution platforms, utilizing vulnerabilities in web browser add-ons (Adobe Flash in particular). A malware mass distribution platform is a program code which is run on a network server and utilized by criminals, the purpose of which is to install specific malware on the user's computer (Finnish Communications Regulatory Authority, 2014).

Cyber-physical systems

The term cyber-physical system (CPS) was coined by Helen Gill at the National Science Foundation in the United States to refer to the integration of computation with physical processes. In CPS, embedded computers and networks may monitor and control the physical processes with feedback loops where physical processes affect computations and vice versa. CPS are enabling the next generation of 'smart systems' like advanced robotics, computer-controlled processes and real-time integrated systems (Lee & Seshia, 2017).

Modern infrastructures include not only physical components but also hardware and software. These integrated systems are examples of CPS that integrate computing and communication capabilities with monitoring and control of entities in the physical world. Fig. 10.3 presents a CPS that consists of two physical layers (platform layer and human layer) and a cyber layer between them. The current trend is that the cyber layer is expanding.

Many CPS applications are safety-critical which means that their failure can cause irreparable harm to the physical system under control and to the people who depend on it. In particular, the protection of our CIs that

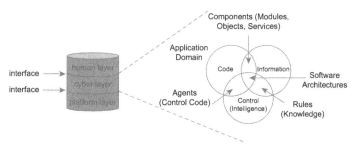

FIGURE 10.3 Layers of cyber-physical systems. *Modified from Hevner, A., Chatterjee, S., 2010. Design research in information systems: Theory and practice. Springer Science and Business. https://doi.org/10.1007/978-1-4419-5653-8.*

rely on CPS, such as the electric power transmission and distribution, ICSs, oil and natural gas systems, water and wastewater treatment plants, health-care devices and transportation networks play a fundamental and large-scale role in our society and their disruption can have a significant impact to individuals and nations at large. Increasingly many CPS are operated under automated controls and a sophisticated cyberattack can exploit weaknesses to its advantage (Hevner & Chatterjee, 2010).

Tracking in the everyday life of citizens

In the market economy, customer profiling or tracking is seen only from the point of view of data exploitation in Internet marketing. Advertisers try to focus on services and products more efficiently for the right target audience. Location-based services rely on a combination of technologies to pinpoint the location of a user with contextual data to provide more value to a mobile user. Geo-targeting or Geo-fencing with Wi-Fi, cell towers and beacons create a privacy-restricting advertisement circuit that aims to influence consumer behaviour. How can the need for CIP be understood in this context? The question is not simple because every person abandons some of their privacy by using smart devices. It does not always seem to matter whether or not a smartphone user is aware of the data 'leakage'. For example, when introducing a smartphone a user accepts many things that are required to make the smartphone work properly. If you do not give permission to provide privacy information to a third party, it is possible that the device may not work at all.

Most of the Western world carries a multifunction sensor called a smartphone. Intelligent devices are increasingly used to access the Internet rather than traditional calling. For proactive safety, data stored in a mobile phone combined with human behaviour can create new predictive ecosystems for the infrastructure. Different kinds of sensor systems are already in use. The Berlin train station has created a detection system (Huggler, 2017) with face detection technology, and for example, in Stockholm, there is an ongoing traffic safety project (Scania, 2018) which utilizes motion detector-based artificial intelligence.

From location-based services to location-based intelligence

A citizen's smart device is quite easy to locate. International Mobile Equipment Identity (IMEI) number and SIM card with international mobile subscriber identity (IMSI) helps to track a mobile. Mobile phones transmit these numbers each time a call is made and when they 'check in' to the local base stations (Pettit, 2018).

Police may use an IMSI-catcher to encrypt a call. At that point the phone call is transmitted through an IMSI-catcher. It works like a fake base station. Law enforcement teams in the United States and Europe have used this technology to locate people etc., but nowadays criminals like hackers are deploying them (Langston, 2017). According to Shaik, Borgaonkar, Asokan, Niemi, and Seifert (2016), it has been shown that the vulnerabilities in LTE access network protocols lead to new privacy and availability threats to LTE subscribers.

Customers are concerned about their privacy because location-based technologies allow mobile advertising networks to accurately send advertisements to maximize the effect of advertisement (Kini & Suomi, 2018).

Retailers of malls may use indoor or/and outdoor navigation technologies to provide location-based services, using mobile 'push' notifications to provide advertisements. With this technology it is possible to provide appropriate, personalized marketing based on the consumer's location. If customers or mobile users give permission (opt-in) to their trusted companies whose brand, products and services they like, they send them personalized advertisements when they are shopping (Yiu, Jensen, Møller, & Lu, 2011).

Technologies are currently available to not only locate the customers; they are also able to establish a history of a path taken by a typical customer during the day. Consumer-oriented organizations are concerned about how advertisement networks are able to locate and custom-deliver an advertisement to a customer with or without the customer's permission (Kini & Suomi, 2018; Metz, 2013). According to Nakashima (2018), AP investigation found that Google stored location data even though 'location history' is turned off.

New smartphone technologies combine marketers and application providers to get their strategies to a new marketing area. As Kini and Suomi (2018) write, the big data analytical tools can do the data analysis and help marketing actors produce and deliver personalized advertisements to customers' or potential customers' smart devices everywhere. There is a risk that collected data can be used for wrong purposes instead of proper use for protection of vital functions. Law enforcement may use the same tools as advertisers or marketers, but these tools are traditionally intended for marketing purposes rather than the needs of law enforcement agencies. It has been noted within PPDR authorities that the use of location-based services will become a more common tool in the field of crime prevention. As communication technology evolves, people's living environment also develops. Development of intelligent cities brings new kinds of opportunities to develop services from a safety environment perspective.

If a citizen walks to the geofenced area and receives a mobile advertisement message, the citizen might be motivated to look at and take action on the text message based on: if they permitted someone to send such a message (opted-in); if they trust such a company producing or selling a product or service (brand trust); if the product or service is relevant to the customer's current needs and wants; if the customer likes the price that is quoted on the message; if the customer is financially in a position to buy such a product or service and last, if the customer is in the right mood to buy such a product (Kini & Suomi, 2018).

If a citizen does not know the purpose of using privacy data, the situation is ethically untenable. Therefore, it is important for a citizen to be aware that he or she can be treated as a customer in marketing, but also as a potential threat to the functions of CI.

According to Sheng et al. (2006) customers' privacy concerns vary depending on their purpose or context for using the technology. Personalization has major implications in emergency situations, for example at the site of an accident where appropriate services need to be delivered to the right person and place. The effect of personalization on perceived benefits is greater in emergency than non-emergency contexts.

Research method and process

Case study of this research is carried out by the guidance of Yin (2014). Case study illustrates the attempt to produce profound and detailed information about the object under research.

The fundamental research data of this extended study are collected from earlier empirical research studies where the author has been the main researcher. Studies have been presented in international conferences and published. The research data included, for example, material of interviews and observations from four situation centres. A new type of emergency centre system was created as a result of previous research. The purpose of this study is to compare the results of the studies from a privacy perspective. Scientific literature materials and legislative publications have been used for comparison. The purpose of the comparison is to find the factors concerning privacy issues that influence the introduction of the presented hybrid emergence model.

Four regional command/situation centres have been researched in an earlier (Simola & Rajamäki, 2017) empirical study: Southwestern Finland Police department, Southwest Finland Emergency Services, Hospital District of Southwest Finland and The Finnish Border Guards in Turku. The Finnish Border Guards have their own main situation/command centre in Turku called the Maritime Rescue Coordination Centre (MRCC). The situation centre of the Southwestern Finland Police department and the MRCC are managed by the state. Southwest Finland Emergency Services and Hospital District of Southwest Finland act under the municipality. The field commanders of the situation centres were interviewed in their own work environment.

The fundamental research data of earlier studies are based on observations, interviews, scientific publications, collected articles and literary material. Participant observation makes it possible to get close to the actors. It illustrates the identities of actors' diversity (Viinamäki & Saari, 2007). Observation is made on the field and the results are recorded and saved as notes. One prominent data collecting method used was focus interviews (Brannen, 2004).

Findings

Regional situational centres use different systems and therefore the same system can be used in two situation centres without cooperation with each other. None of the regional situation centres have direct contact with the Government Situation Centre, but the connections are handled through intermediaries. For rapidly evolving situations, access to the Government Situation Centres', data connection should be arranged to the essential situation centres.

As recent major accidents have indicated, lack of human resources affects disaster recovery. PPDR actors cannot start operations if there is a human factor preventing the flow of information. Preventing domino effect after the disaster may be delayed. Recent violent acts at local and state level (from local to national level) have shown this to be a reality. The communication activities of Intermediaries have been one of the major problems in recent major accidents. In Brussels, Belgium, federal police requested to close the metro, and the main railway stations did not reach the responsible chief of the railway police because phone networks were down. A request to close the railway station was sent to the responsible authority's personal email instead of work mail. The responsible authority did not see the message until after the attacks (McLaughlin, Haddad, & Hume, 2016). The November 2015 terror attacks also did not cause a total closure of the Paris

Metro or other public arenas (Steafel et al., 2015, The Guardian, 2016). Therefore, a workable cyber environment with automated functions must be seen as a common objective of organized societies. The main issue regarding reliable decision support analysis to decision-makers is at which point in the chain reaction the human action is more harmful than useful (Endsley, 1988, 1995, 2015). There is a lot to be done to transfer essential emergency procedures into automated emergency functions.

Hybrid emergency response model does not violate privacy of the citizens more than what is required to prevent a threat because the use of technology is linked to the current law, but underdeveloped local urban infrastructure prevent utilization of intelligence collection methods including local-based intelligence solutions. The ongoing privacy legislation reform in the EU and in United States creates some barriers for the artificial intelligence developers. Protecting vital functions of society and securing continuity management PPDR authorities receive major support among the citizens. Privacy issue problems related to personal data registers can be solved by automation. The automatized method allows almost 10,000 authorities to release resources from curiosity tasks.

Emergency situations

The lack of cooperation between situation centres prevents the ability to create a common SA and picture. Starting cooperation at the scene of an accident, as Fig. 10.4 illustrates, is not enough during a major accident in a modern CPS.

The officer in charge of the situation is responsible for maintaining the situational picture and for coordinating the operations. Unless otherwise agreed, the officer in charge of the rescue operations comes from the

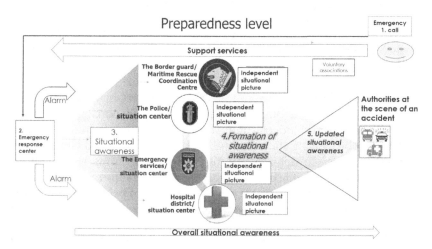

FIGURE 10.4 Formation of situational awareness.

rescue service region where the accident or dangerous situation occurred. The field commander and the officer in charge of rescue operations decide together if it is necessary to make a major accident alert. For example, the Turku University Hospital has its own command centre, which is set up in case of a major accident. The leading medical director, managing director and other managing personnel get together in their command centre depending on the type of major accident.

The differences of rescue operations illustrate the fact that it would be important to see all the resources available. However, a reliable and correct common situational picture should be created before arriving to the scene of the accident. If the scene is a modern CPS, a cyber situational picture is also needed.

As shown in picture 10.5. of the hybrid emergency response model, proactive accident/incident management begins before any physical harm has occurred. Sensor networks consist of cyber and physical elements with automated functions. The cyber environment of hybrid model works in many ways. It detects intrusions and threats in CI before any emergency call has been made. Data fusion analysis combine and produce important signals based on commands, which launch automatic processes like isolating an area under threat or robotic functions based on biometrics data such as thermal imaging or face recognition. Data fusion might also help with false alarms by fusing the information from multiple sources; also false alarms can be avoided by combining sensors. The processing device (controller) sends commands to a wireless sensor and actuator network (WSAN) which then converts them into input signals for the actuator, that acts with a physical process, thus forming a closed control loop. The field-tested DSiP solution with 4com routers (Simola & Rajamäki, 2014) enables parallel use of different network technologies in a consistent and transparent way, enabling communications services platforms to be created. In cyber-physical operations, this feature reduces network jamming. The hybrid model reduces the necessity of communication with VIRVE phones between authorities. It also eliminates errors of human activity when an accident situation is on. Automated safety measures can also bypass the problems related to the commandment of power relations. Hybrid emergency response system allows people to send pictures or video calls from the scene of an accident. Smart System allows crowdsourcing software to screen the images and videos automatically. Relevant data from the major accident will be directly shared to the field commanders and Government Situation Centres. To determinate discrepancies of limits is relevant to allocate additional reliable data. Combining pieces of information to ensure the correct and reliable information to be shared is of primary importance. The essential information is processed to the desired shape for the accident site command centre. The system is based on active operations and automated functions. Cyber defence operations are integrated and automated

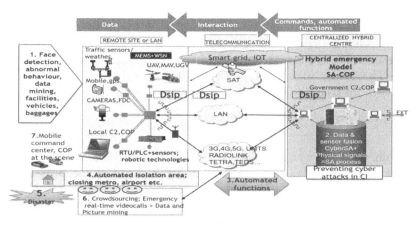

FIGURE 10.5   Hybrid emergency response model.

according to local capabilities, authorities and mission needs. In a local city area, sensor networks of a shopping mall may consist of LBS elements, for example geofencing area with automated functions like speed breakers, which automatically activate when the level of threat has risen high as Figs. 10.5 and 10.6 illustrates.

A lack of preparedness affects the cooperation within PPDR authorities in the field at a major accident. Reforms in public sector and changes in PPDR organizations with legislative amendment require changes in preparedness plans. At present, managerial personnel get together at each other's command centres depending on the type of accident.

Today, too many hierarchy levels in and between organizations exist. Therefore, deciding on new technology faces challenges. If there are too

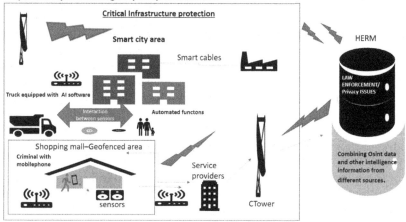

FIGURE 10.6   Location-based intelligence with OSINT as part of the HERM.

many hierarchy levels, information of a situation does not flow or, at least, it is slow (Rajamäki & Viitanen, 2014). Responsibilities for developing cybersecurity has been shared in too many factors (Finnish Communications Regulatory Authority, 2014; Kauppinen, 2015; Ministry of Defence, 2010; Ministry of the Interior, 2016; National Cooperation Network for Disaster Risk Reduction, 2012).

Discussion

Both the European and the American regulations aim at achieving cyber resilience, enhancing cooperation between public and private sectors in order to improve capacities, resources and processes to handle cyber-physical threats in CIs. But that is not enough; there is a need for common cyber ecosystem to control crossboarding threats.

In Europe there should be clearer common rules concerning which privacy issues need to be abandoned when getting around in public places and what kind of data should be considered private. Combining data from different sources can create opportunities, but also major threats at personal profiling level in the protection of CI. The collected data cannot be used if their use is unauthorized. Data must also be utilized for permitted purpose. There are also some problems in creating a monitoring system when considering political and technological aspects.

In Finland, the importance of privacy has risen to the surface of the social welfare and health care (SOTE) reform. The Finnish government's concept of human disease classification system based on patient records has raised protests. There is a clear trend for the creation of different classification systems in Europe, but the problem arises when people are classified on the basis of information and data management is given to a third party. In Finland, one of the focal points of the SOTE reform is related to the integration of patient registers and the creation of one information system.

Traditional thought within Finnish decision-makers has been that the commercial operators must be kept separate from regulatory activities. In the United Kingdom the Home Office-led Emergency Services Network (ESN) will replace the existing Airwave mobile radio system. ESN will be delivered using commercial network. The police communications network enables officers to access key databases, to take electronic fingerprints and witness statements and to stream live video while on the move (Nasir, 2016; Travis, 2015).

People have been irritated by the fact that their behaviour has been collected more widely than what has been told and for uses that are not known. Therefore, it might be important to look at the big picture of protecting the CI. What kind of elements can be included in the framework which protects the vital functions of society. When all the things we do leave some data to tracking systems, people have the right to know what information is collected and for what purpose it has been collected.

Perhaps even more important is to know who the holder (controller or processor) is of the privacy data and what is the storage time of the data. According to Waterfield (2018), the navigator manufacturer TOMTOM reported in 2011 that it has sold data stored by the navigators from citizens' movements to the Danish police. The purpose of the collected data was to show where to set up speed traps. How can a citizen be assured that a publicly commented matter and a real case mean the same if the authorities supervise themselves? However, the fact is that technological hybrid models developed for CI also need hybrid models for data collection in order to identify threats in a predetermined and error-free manner.

In a society where the limits of public and private commercial players have become obscured, the risks are also increasing. Citizens should be able to trust decision-makers, authorities and society so that they do not have to constantly think about what kind of digital footprints they have left behind in any department store control unit. As a single datum, separate information of human life is not significant, but if data are combined from different sources, the position of a citizen as a person of his or her own life and knowledge may change significantly.

Conclusions

As discussed above, digitalization and location-based technologies create opportunities but also threats to citizen's privacy life. If political power relations change in a democratic society, public power may centralize, for example on the communist regime or for a dictator. How would the privacy-related information be used in different political environments? It is essential because the world order is in a turbulent state. Different types of extremism have increased their support.

The need for a new type of standardized hybrid emergency response model reflects the following factors. It is necessary for confidence that citizens accept automatized safety functions in public places. Legislation concerning privacy issues does not cause permanent obstacles to use sensing elements in hybrid emergency response model. It is necessary to rationalize organizational responsibilities for development of cybersecurity. A human is an individual with limited observation capability, and overlapping data transmission limits the effective cooperation between PPDR authorities. Limited data transmission capacity prevents communication between the authorities. Preventive functions against cyberthreats in the emergency response model are an essential part of the overall security in situation awareness management and CIP.

It is also important for the continuity management to create a confidential base between citizens and authorities. Confidential data cannot be leaked to outsiders, for example to the press. At present, the values of those Western worlds have been contrasted with the protection of overall security and CI. Important things for us, such as the data privacy issues, can be more relieved on the grounds that the 'common good' requires it. How can we then define the common good? This issue has been controversial in Europe. Determining the public interest or limiting the need to protect society has sometimes caused difficulties. The fact that the intelligence services workers have come to the public with information acquired through the workplace has not made it any easier. The problem is related to situations where protected legal interests are incompatible.

Fighting against cyberthreats is an essential part of the overall security in continuity management. Often, urban built infrastructures represent a critical node within the intertwined networks of an urban area. A substantial part of our CPS today relies on complex systems of communication networks. There is just as much of a need to take into account the equally vulnerable built infrastructures of modern urban areas (Davis et al., 2006).

In the future a centralized hybrid emergency model with predictive emergency response functions is necessary. A shared common operational picture means that real-time communication links from local level to state level must exist. At the moment the flow of real-time data is not being transmitted to the Government Situation Centre. For example, if a cyberattack interrupted electricity transmission, telecommunication networks discontinue operating. A cyberattack becomes physical if intrusion has not been detected. Hybrid warfare needs hybrid responses. The government departments of Finland must take into consideration that cyber preparedness and privacy issues are not a separate part in the continuity management. In practice this means that there is need to integrate ERC and National Cyber Security Centre Finland emergency functions. Flow of information between intelligence authorities and data protection authorities must also be ensured. In an ideal model, privacy protection would be ensured automatically. When human weaknesses are left out of procedure, data leakage to third parties becomes more difficult. It could increase citizens' confidence in the system's activities.

The new intelligence legislation package proposed by the Finnish government would include provisions on the principles of intelligence activities. If the legislation package is approved, it is expected to enhance the ability of the PPDR authorities to respond to major national and international hybrid threats because it also allows wider use of new decision support system technologies. It requires clarification of common rules. In other words, in a public place, for example in shopping centres, privacy protection should be facilitated if citizens accept common rules which have been created in the form of legislation.

When we deal with an individual and the privacy of an individual, he or she would not immediately think it would also be connected to wider entities. What may be possible with micro-level tracking for an individual may occur at a macro level remotely by interfering with data cable connections.

The micro and macro levels will be encountered if a foreign state party intervenes to interfere with the functioning of data traffic in maritime areas. For example, there is a northeast cable project designed to connect networking activities between different continents. Nowadays the problem is that fibre optic and power supply are transmitted through the same cable. Vulnerabilities and risks have increased, though formally, the goal is to harmonize Eastern and Western data cable functionalities (Buchanan, 2018; Shackelford et al. 2017). The study shows that the most troublesome and most significant threats to national security and vital functions are related to politicians and political projects. It is difficult to anticipate the real direction of national policy in the macro level because good inter-state relations may indicate ignoring security issues. This state-level political dimension may prevent the utilization of the proposed smart hybrid emergency model.

References

Ahmed, D. T., Hossain, M. A., Shirmohammadi, S., Alghamdi, A., Pradeep, K. A., & El Saddik, A. (2012). *Utility based decision support engine for camera view selection in multimedia surveillance systems.* https://doi.org/10.1007/s11042-012-1294-7.

Ahokas, J., Guday, T., Lyytinen, T., & Rajamäki, J. (2010). Secure and reliable communications for SCADA systems. *International Journal of Computers and Communications, 6*(3), 167–174.

Aine, A., Nurmi, V., Ossa, J., Penttilä, T., Salmi, I., & Virtanen, V. (2011). *Moderni kriisilainsäädäntö.* Helsinki: WSOYpro.

Baldini, G. (2010). *Report of the workshop on "interoperable communications for safety and security" with recommendations for security research.* Publications Office of the European Union. https://doi.org/10.2788/19075.

Brannen, J. (2004). *Working qualitatively and quantitatively in qualitative research practice.* In C. Seale, G. Gobo, J. F. Gubrium, & D. Silverman (Eds.) (pp. 312–326). London: Sage Publications.

Bröring, A., Echterhoff, J., Jirka, S., Simonis, I., Everding, T., Stasch, C., et al. (2011). New generation sensor web enablement. *Sensors, 11*(3), 2652–2699.

Buchanan, E. (2018). *Sea cables in a thawing Arctic [homepage of lowy institute].* Available from https://www.lowyinstitute.org/the-interpreter/sea-cables-thawing-arctic.

Chong, C., & Kumar, S. (2003). Sensor networks: Evolution, opportunities and challenges. *Proceedings of the IEEE, 91*(8), 1247–1256. https://doi.org/10.1109/JPROC.2003.814918.

Chrisafis, A. (2016). Paris attacks inquiry finds multiple failings by French intelligence agencies. *The Guardian.* Available from https://www.theguardian.com/world/2016/jul/05/paris-attacks-inquiry-multiple-failings-french-intelligence-agencies.

Corporation, N. E. C. (2016). *Face recognition: Technologies: Biometrics: Solutions and services | NEC, homepage of NEC.* Available from http://www.nec.com/en/global/solutions/biometrics/technologies/face_recognition.html.

Davis, R., Ortiz, C., Rowe, R., Broz, J., Rigakos, G., & Collins, P. (2006). *An assessment of the preparedness of large retail malls to prevent and respond to terrorist attack. (No. 216641.* Available from https://www.ncjrs.gov/pdffiles1/nij/grants/216641.pdf.

Department of Homeland Security. (2018a). *Cyber incident response [homepage of DHS].* Available from https://www.dhs.gov/cyber-incident-response.

Department of Homeland Security. (2018b). *The national cybersecurity and communications integration center's (NCCIC).* Available from https://www.us-cert.gov/about-us.

Dos Passos, D. (2016). Big data, data science and their contributions to the development of the use of open source intelligence. *11*(4). https://doi.org/10.20985/1980-5160.2016.v11n4.1026.

Electrical Technology. (2016). *Internet of things (IOT) and its applications in electrical power industry [homepage of ET]*. Available from http://www.electricaltechnology.org/2016/07/internet-of-things-iot-and-its-applications-in-electrical-power-industry.html.

Endsley, M. R. (1988). Design and evaluation for situation awareness enhancement. In *Proceedings of the human factors society 32nd annual meeting human factors society, Santa Monica. CA* (pp. 97–101).

Endsley, M. R. (1995). Toward a theory of situation awareness. *Human Factors, 37*(1), 32–64.

Endsley, M. R. (2015). *Autonomous horizons, system autonomy in the air force - a path to the future, air force office of the chief scientist*. USA: Department of The Air Force. Available from https://www.hsdl.org/?view&did=768107.

European Commission. (2002). *Directive on privacy and electronic communications Directive 2002/58/EC, Directive* (Brussels).

European Commission. (2016a). *EU data protection directive 2016/680, directive* (Brussels).

European Commission. (2016b). *EU-U.S. privacy shield: Stronger protection for transatlantic data flows*. Brussels).

European Commission. (2016c). *General data protection regulation (EU) 2016/679, regulation* (Brussels).

European Commission. (2017). *Proposal for a regulation on privacy and electronic communications, regulation proposal* (Brussels).

Finnish Communications Regulatory Authority. (2014). *National cyber security centre: Action plan 2014-2016*. Available from https://www.viestintavirasto.fi/attachments/NCSC-FI_Action_plan_20142382112016.pdf.

Finnish Security Intelligence Service. (2015). *The year book 2015*. Helsinki: Ministry of the Interior. Available from:https://www.supo.fi/instancedata/prime_product_julkaisu/intermin/embeds/supowwwstructure/67074_2015_Supo_ ENG.pdf?cb0cc853f98ed588.

Franke, U., & Brynielsson, J. (2014). Cyber situational awareness: A systematic review of the literature. *Computers & Security,* 18-31-46 http://doi.org/10.1016/j.cose.2014.06.008.

Gervasi, O. (2010). Encryption scheme for secured communication of web based control systems. *Journal of Security Engineering, 7*(6), 12.

Glassman, M., & Kang, M. J. (2012). Intelligence in the internet age: The emergence and evolution of open source intelligence (OSINT). *Computers in Human Behavior, 28*(2), 673–682. http://10.1016/j.chb.2011.11.014.

Hanni, J. (2013). *The quality and amount of information for emergency situations management*. Oulu: Oulu University of Applied Sciences. http://www.theseus.fi/handle/10024/65618.

Hevner, A., & Chatterjee, S. (2010). *Design research in information systems: Theory and practice*. Springer Science and Business. https://doi.org/10.1007/978-1-4419-5653-8.

Huggler, J. (2017). *Facial recognition software to catch terrorists being tested at Berlin station*. Available from http://www.telegraph.co.uk/news/2017/08/02/facial-recognition-software-catch-terrorists-tested-berlin-station/.

IBP. (2014). *European Union cyber security strategy and programs handbook. Strategic information and regulations*. Washington DC, USA: International Business Publications.

Kauppinen, T. (2015). *Cyber security of supply, FIIF jam session*. National Emergency Supply Agency.

Kini, R.,B., & Suomi, R. (2018). Changing attitudes toward location-based advertising in the USA and Finland. *Journal of Computer Information Systems, 58*(1), 66–78. https://doi.org/10.1080/08874417.2016.1192519.

Langston, J. (2017). *Catching the IMSI-catchers: Sea glass brings transparency to cell phone surveillance [homepage of UW news]*. Available from https://www.washington.edu/news/2017/06/02/catching-the-imsi-catchers-seaglass-brings-transparency-to-cell-phone-surveillance/.

Lee, E., & Seshia, A. (2017). *Introduction to embedded systems, a cyber-physical systems approach* (2nd ed.). MIT Press, ISBN 978-0-262-53381-2. Available from https://ptolemy.berkeley.edu/books/leeseshia/releases/LeeSeshia_DigitalV2_2.pdf.

McLarty, T., III, & Ridge, F. T. (2014). *Securing the U.S. Electrical grid.* Washington D.C: The Center for the Study of the Presidency and Congress. https://www.thepresidency.org/sites/default/files/Final%20Grid%20Report_0.pdf.

McLaughlin, E., Haddad, M., & Hume, T. (2016). *Brussels attacks: Order to close metro sent to wrong address -.* Available from CNN.com http://edition.cnn.com/2016/05/12/europe/belgium-brussels-attacks-metro-email/.

Metz, R., (2013). Every step you take tracked automatically. Technology Review, MIT. Available from: https://www.technologyreview.com/s/510491/every-step-you-take-tracked-automatically/. (Accessed: 28.8.2018).

Ministry of Defence. (2010). *Security strategy for society, government resolution.* Helsinki: Ministry of Defence. Avalable from https://www.defmin.fi/files/1883/PDF.SecurityStrategy.pdf.

Ministry of the Interior. (2016). *National risk assessment 2015.* Helsinki: Ministry of the Interior. Available from http://urn.fi/URN:ISBN978-952-324-060-5.

Morrow, J., & Odierno, R. (2012). *Open-source intelligence, ATP 2-22.9.* Washington: Army Techniques Publication, Headquarters, Department of the U.S. Army. https://fas.org/irp/doddir/army/fmi2-22-9.pdf.

Nakashima, R. (2018). *AP exclusive: Google tracks your movements, like it or not [homepage of AP news].* Available from: https://apnews.com/828aefab64d4411bac257a07c1af0ecb.

Nasir, R. (2016). *LTE to replace TETRA network for UK emergency services - [Homepage of Networkingplus].* Available from https://www.networkingplus.co.uk/Media/Default/archive/Net1601.pdf.

National Cooperation Network for Disaster Risk Reduction. (2012). *National platform for disaster risk reduction.* Helsinki: Ministry of the Interior. Available from https://julkaisut.valtioneuvosto.fi/bitstream/handle/10024/79425/sm_142012.pdf.

National Emergency Number Association (NENA) and the Association of Public-Safety Communications Officials (APCO). (2016). *NENA/APCO next generation 9-1-1 public safety answering point requirements.* USA: NENA and APCO.

National Institute of Standards and Technology. (2014). Guidelines for smart grid cybersecurity national institute of standards and technology. In *Smart grid cybersecurity strategy, architecture, and high-level requirements* (Vol. 1). USA: U.S. Department of Commerce.

National Public Safety Telecommunications Council. (2015). *FirstNet and next generation 9-1-1 high-level overview of systems and functionality.* Available from http://www.npstc.org/download.jsp?tableId=37&column=217&id=3466&file=How_NG911_Will_Work_with_FirstNet_FINAL.pdf.

Nurmi, P. (2015). *OSINT - avointen lähteiden internet-tiedustelu.* Helsinki: Aalto yliopisto.

Pettit, H. (2018). *Are police tracking your movements using your mobile phone? Privacy watchdog to challenge five UK forces in court over their failure to deny they use 'fake cell towers' to spy on citizens [homepage of daily mail online].* Available from http://www.dailymail.co.uk/sciencetech/article-6039023/Are-police-tracking-mobile-phone-Privacy-group-challenge-UK-forces-court-IMSI-catchers.html.

Rajamäki, J., & Viitanen, J. (2014). Near border information exchange procedures for law enforcement authorities. *International Journal of Systems Applications, Engineering & Development, 8,* 2015–2020.

Rosslin, J. R., & Tai-hoon, K. (2010). Communication security for SCADA in smart grid environment. no. In *Advances in data networks, communications, computers.* Available from http://www.wseas.us/e-library/conferences/2010/Faro/DNCOCO/DNCOCO-05.pdf.

Scania. (2018). *Scanias geofencing teknik visades upp i Stockholm.* Available from https://www.scania.com/scaniasodertalje/sv/home/nyheter-event/scanias-geofencing-teknik-visades-upp-i-stockholm.html.

Secretariat of the Security Committee. (2013). *Finland's cyber security strategy - government resolution.* Ministry of Defense. https://www.defmin.fi/files/2378/Finland_s_Cyber_Security_Strategy.pdf.

Shackelford, S. J., Sulmeyer, M., Deckard, A., Graig, N., Buchanan, B., & Micic, B. (2017). From Russia with love: Understanding the Russian cyber threat to U.S. critical infrastructure and what to do about it. *Nebraska Law Review, 96*(2), 321–337. https://digitalcommons.unl.edu/nlr/vol96/iss2/5.

Shaik, A., Borgaonkar, R., Asokan, N., Niemi, V., & Seifert, J. (February, 2016). *Practical attacks against privacy and availability in 4G/LTE mobile communication systems*. USA: NDSS. https://doi.org/10.14722/ndss.2016.23236.

Sheng, H., Nah, F. F., & Siau, K. (2006). An experimental study on ubiquitous commerce adoption: Impact of personalization and privacy concerns. *Journal of the Association for Information Systems, AMCIS 2006 Proceedings, 9*(6), 80–84, 370 http://aisel.aisnet.org/amcis2006/370.

Simola, J., & Rajamäki, J. (2014). Using a real-time video to allocate public protection and disaster relief resources in rescue service process - natural diaster in Young voluntary firefigter's camp. In *5th European conference of computer science (ECCS '14)*. WSEAS Press. http://urn.fi/URN:NBN:fi:amk-201802132394.

Simola, J., & Rajamäki, J. (2016). Common cyber situational awareness: An important part of modern public protection and disaster relief. In *10th international conference on computer engineering and applications (CEA '16)* (p. 54). WSEAS press, ISBN 978-1-61804-365-8. http://urn.fi/URN.

Simola, J., & Rajamäki, J. (2017). Hybrid emergency response model: Improving cyber situational awareness. In M. Scanlon, & N. Le-Khac (Eds.), *16th European conference on cyber warfare and security* (pp. 442–451). UK: APCI, ISBN 978-1-911218-44-9. http://urn.fi/URN.

Steafel, E., Mulholland, R., Sabur, R., Malnick, E., Trotman, A., & Harley, N. (2015). *Paris terror attack: Everything we know on saturday afternoon − telegraph*. Available from http://www.telegraph.co.uk/news/worldnews/europe/france/11995246/Paris-shooting-What-we-know-so-far.html.

Travis, A. (2015). Questions over limited range of new £1bn emergency services network. *The Guardian*. https://www.theguardian.com/society/2015/dec/09/emergency-services-network-questions-limited-range-1bn.

Trottier, D. (2015). Open source intelligence, social media and law enforcement: Visions, constraints and critiques. *European Journal of Cultural Studies, 18*(4–5), 530–547. https://doi.org/10.1177/1367549415577396.

Vetter, M. (2015). *Open source intelligence techniques and the Dark Web*. Available from www.itproportal.com/2015/10/30/open-source-intelligence-techniques-and-the-dark-web/.

Viinamäki, L., & Saari, E. (2007). *Polkuja soveltavaan yhteiskuntatieteelliseen tutkimukseen*. Helsinki: Tammi.

Waterfield, B. (2018). *Tom Tom sold driver's GPS details to be used by police for speed traps - Telegraph*. Available from https://www.telegraph.co.uk/technology/news/8480702/Tom-Tom-sold-drivers-GPS-details-to-be-used-by-police-for-speed-traps.html.

Wood, M., & Graham. (2016). Social media intelligence, the wayward child of open source intelligence. *Responsible Data Forum*. https://responsibledata.io/social-media-intelligence-the-wayward-child-of-open-source-intelligence/.

Yin, R. K. (2014). *Case study research, design and methods* (5th ed.). Thousand Oaks: Sage Publications.

Yiu, M.,L., Jensen, C. S., Møller, J., & Lu, H. (2011). Design and analysis of a ranking approach to private location-based services. *ACM Transactions on Database Systems, 36*(2), 10:1–10:42. https://doi.org/10.1145/1966385.1966388.

Index

Printed in the United States
By Bookmasters